collective remarks

collective remarks

a journey through the american dressage evolution:
where it's been, where we are, and where we need to be

anne gribbons

illustrations by karen rohlf   foreword by george williams

TRAFALGAR SQUARE
North Pomfret, Vermont

First published in 2014 by
Trafalgar Square Books
North Pomfret, Vermont 05053

The text in this book first appeared in *The Chronicle of the Horse*. It appears here with additions and annotations.

Trafalgar Square Books encourages the use of approved safety helmets in all equestrian sports and activities.

Library of Congress Cataloging-in-Publication Data
Gribbons, Anne.
Collective remarks : a journey through the American dressage evolution : where it's been, where we are, and where we need to be / Anne Gribbons.
    pages cm
  Includes index.
  ISBN 978-1-57076-683-1
  1. Dressage. 2. Horsemanship. I. Title. II. Title: American dressage evolution.
  SF309.5.G75 2014
  798.2′3--dc23
                              2013047191

Book design by DOQ
Cover design by RM Didier
Typefaces: Palatino LT Std and Scala Sans Pro

Printed in the United States of America

10 9 8 7 6 5 4 3 2 1

contents

Foreword ix

Preface.. xiii

I: riding wisdom.. 1

1 stepping up 3
2 art revisited 7
3 a forum for dressage philosophy 9
4 a lot of attitude..15
5 many of us horse people share an affliction called "jack russells" 20
6 the value of a solid foundation 26
7 the ageless sport 31
8 fitness and dressage 35
9 the relationship between amateurs and professionals 39
10 dare to let go 44
11 a case for the head..48
12 practice makes perfect 53
13 dressage as therapy...58

II: coaching and being coached 63

14 the magic triangle..65
15 giving and receiving instruction...................................70
16 herbert rehbein 75
17 the amateur—the backbone of every sport 79
18 the first teacher 84
19 dressage and fly fishing..88

III: finding "the one" 93

20 looking for your dressage horse: the process............................95
21 the cast of characters..102
22 ode to the ancient 107
23 a question of soundness 112
24 putting age, size and soundness in perspective 117
25 fashions in dressage horses and myths about gaits 122
26 who wants to be a grand prix horse? 128
27 in sickness and in health: the unexpected trials 134
28 the relativity of soundness..140

IV: training and competing 145

29 on the road to grand prix..147
30 the competitor..151
31 no, it is not always about winning.....................................156
32 the other side of sponsorship 160
33 to be an owner 164
34 hello, young (horse) trainers..169
35 trouble at the grass roots...174
36 where did the extended trot go? 179
37 the battle of the frame..184
38 dedicated to members of the stuc(k) society:
    on the subject of collection...188
39 the elusive half-halt..193
40 winning the warm-up..197
41 advice from the coach..202
42 riding to music: a short history 207

V: judging and being judged 211

43 deciding in a blink of an eye..213
44 the american brand of judges..217

45 judicial temperament...222

46 judging on a jury 227

47 the scribes, our unsung heroes................................231

48 a return to tradition at the spanish riding school.............236

49 the joy of judging 241

50 suggestions about judging the freestyle 246

51 it's "all about" the young horses...............................252

52 new zealand from a dressage point of view...............257

53 the perfect show through a judge's eyes 264

54 we must trust our judges 269

VI: the state and future of the sport.................. 275

55 who's next?...277

56 a recipe for improvement.......................................281

57 our lost generations 285

58 the media and dressage..289

59 dressage for dummies 293

60 riding schools and ponies: two missing links in our program.........297

61 a wish list..303

62 are our horses on drugs?..309

63 is the dressage horse an unhappy athlete?...............315

64 about past and (perhaps no) future olympic games 320

65 looking beyond the olympics..................................325

66 2012 olympic games: in perspective........................330

67 forward bound after a last look back 335

68 what makes dressage grow, and could we do more? 341

69 new concepts and stimulating prospects for american dressage.......346

Afterword...355

Index 361

foreword

by George Williams

"A delightful collection of gems" is the best way to describe this wonderful book by my good friend, Anne Gribbons. Over the years her vast experiences with horses have given her a keen eye and an entertaining wit. These pieces prove she is as talented with words as she is with horses.

I have a photo of myself from the mid-seventies while competing a beautiful blood bay stallion at the Knoll Farm dressage show on Long Island, New York. We had trailered down from New Hampshire, and I first became aware of Anne at that show. Little did I know then what a major influence she would become in US dressage. She and her husband David developed Knoll Farm into a hotbed of activity: from putting on competitions, to breeding horses, to running a boarding stable and riding school.

Anne never stands still. She has been a member of the US Pan American Games Team; competed and trained many horses through Grand Prix; judged at many top competitions, including two Fédération Equestre Internationale (FEI) World Cups and the European Championships; was Technical Advisor/Coach for the US Dressage Team at the 2010 World Equestrian Games (WEG), 2010 Pan American Games, and the 2012 Olympics; and has been a member of the FEI Dressage Committee, numerous United States Equestrian Federation (USEF) and United States Dressage Federation (USDF) committees, as well as a former board member of the American Horse Shows Association (the AHSA before it became US Equestrian, and eventually USEF). She can write knowledgably about everything from "Fashions in Dressage Horses and Myths about Gaits" to "Looking Beyond the Olympics" to "The Elusive Half-Halt." Anne has done it all.

Twice now I have had the wonderful opportunity of working closely with Anne: Once in the nineties when we were co-chairs of the AHSA Dressage Committee, and more recently when I was chair of the USEF Dressage High Performance Committee when she was the USEF Technical Advisor/ National Coach for dressage. During these years we shared conversations about the need to develop depth of horses and riders in the United States; the importance of training our own international Grand Prix horses; and the necessity of establishing good basics in our riders. These are all themes that are reflected throughout her writings, perhaps no more so than in "The Value of a Solid Education" and "Dare to Let Go."

As her column entitled "Who's Next?" clearly shows, Anne is a visionary and a "doer." She is committed to the sport and wants to see America position itself strongly on the international scene, both today and in the future. With that goal in mind, Anne was the driving force behind the original Junior National Championships. Later on, while Technical Advisor, she put the building blocks in place for development of the long discussed "pipeline." Her piece entitled "Looking Beyond the Olympics" covers the need for a steady flow of good up-and-coming horses and riders brilliantly.

Anne's skill and knowledge of dressage comes to life in these fabulously written pieces. Whether she is being brutally honest, reflective, humorous, or instructional her passion for the sport and the horses always comes through. In the end I have to say I think one of my all-time favorite pieces is "Where Did the Extended Trot Go?" And one of the beauties of this book is you don't have to start from the beginning. You may want to begin by reading "A Way to Dip Your Toes In."

Wherever you start, I hope you will enjoy these gems as much as I do. Over the years Anne has offered a valuable commentary on the state of dressage. Her insights are as important today as when she wrote them. In my opinion, this thought-provoking book is a must-read for all dressage enthusiasts.

George Williams
President, United States Dressage Federation (USDF)

preface

When I received a letter in 1995 (back in the days we still communicated by mail) from John Strassburger (editor of the respected multidisciplinary equestrian weekly *The Chronicle of the Horse* for twenty years), I read the headline several times to make sure it was truly addressed to me. John, whom I only knew from the few times he had interviewed me at dressage shows, asked if I would consider becoming the dressage contributor for "Between Rounds," the monthly feature column in his popular magazine. I was surprised, flattered, and terrified at the same time, immediately worrying about whether I could keep up with deadlines and if I would have enough ideas and subjects to write about. In addition, the company I was being asked to join—other contributors at that time included George Morris and Denny Emerson—was pretty daunting. But in the end nothing could have stopped me from jumping at a chance to do what I actually had long wished to do and what had been a goal for many years: write!

Much encouraged by my husband David and other good friends, I accepted John's invitation. As I got into the rhythm of writing on a regular basis, the deadlines became more routine, the subject matters seemed to present themselves, and I loved being able to put into practice the education I had in journalism before my life was absorbed by horses. As my articles began to appear in print, encouraging comments from readers gave me the confidence to continue, and after a while it felt as if I was engaged in a spirited and ongoing dialogue with the dressage community through my monthly columns.

When I took on the job as Technical Advisor/Dressage Team Coach for the United States Equestrian Federation (USEF) in 2009, it became impossible to produce a column every month. Since then I have shared the Between Rounds dressage columns with (mainly) George Williams, current president of the United States Dressage Federation (USDF), whose input is always interesting and up to date.

Since horse magazines are always filled to the brim with training advice, over the years I avoided training-type content in my columns and instead tried to cover current events, comment on "the state of the art," and present my personal philosophy on various subjects related to dressage in particular and horses in general. A selection of these columns that seem to remain as relevant today as they were upon first appearing in print have been collected in the pages of this book. I hope the regular readers of *The Chronicle* who have followed my columns over the years will enjoy a look back and find morsels of advice and reflection that still resonate, and I hope new readers may find the contents to provide an interesting walk through a recent history of dressage—namely, the last two decades.

The columns that appear here are dated to show when they were originally published in order to explain why some comments may seem odd as obviously, times have changed since they were written. I chose to keep some of the "outmoded" pieces in because they help show the development in the art and sport of dressage since the mid-1990s. As you now read about things that we as an industry perhaps wished for or feared might happen, the development (or lack thereof) over the years becomes apparent. It is almost like time travel.

Trafalgar Square Books, the leading publisher of equestrian books and DVDs, approached me a while ago and asked me to write a book—but before starting a new writing venture, I proposed they publish some of my *Chronicle* columns in book form. Caroline Robbins, Martha Cook, and Rebecca Didier thought it over and decided to let me have this "fling." They helped me select the right columns and put them in an order that makes sense without being too rigid about the chronology. This way, as I intended, readers can revisit select columns and smile at some memories that are not so time-sensitive as to appear obsolete.

I am grateful to Trafalgar Square for agreeing to work with me on this project, and I also want to thank *The Chronicle of the Horse* for graciously allowing me to reuse the columns that originally appeared within its pages.

Actually, the original idea to publish the "Between Rounds" columns in book form came from John Strassburger, the editor who gave me my first shot at being a rider-writer. And because he was a superb editor and the brainchild of my original columns, I would like to dedicate this collection of essays to him. Thank you, John, for choosing me...for patiently correcting my spelling and other gaffes over many years, and for giving me a chance to pursue my passion for writing.

Anne Gribbons
Chuluota, Florida

I   riding wisdom

— 1 —

stepping up

*When I was asked to take over the "Between Rounds"
column in* The Chronicle of the Horse *for a while,
I was at first excited, because I enjoy writing as an
alternative to riding in circles. Before long panic set
in, since I cannot get half the daily things that are
on my list done before sunset. "Deadline" is not a
word that evokes pleasure, and I decided I did not
need it in my life.*

Then I thought of Hilda Gurney (Fédération Equestre Internationale—
FEI—judge, Olympic bronze medal winner, and my predecessor at *The
Chronicle*), and I was ashamed. There is nobody in the world busier than
Hilda, and I bet she never missed a column deadline.

Boundless Energy

Hilda and I both judged the Region Eight United States Dressage Federation
(USDF) Championships in August of 1995. Incredibly chipper, she arrived
at midnight and planned to leave on the "red-eye." I also know something about Hilda's schedule at home since my husband once visited her

in California and got the tour of her farm. Not a lazy guy himself, he said that after a couple of hours "in" her life, he was ready for a nap. Hilda was everywhere: teaching, training, supervising the breeding program—and yet she still found time to give David an excellent tour of the facility.

Hilda's energy and enthusiasm is abundant. When it comes to sharing her knowledge and ideas, even her horses, Hilda is uncommonly generous. I know this from firsthand experience. Light-years ago, there was a United States Equestrian Team Foundation (USET) benefit put on by Mrs. William Steinkraus,* which featured eight Grand Prix horses from all over the country, performing a musical ride. The day before the "big night," my horse went lame. Hilda had brought a second FEI horse with her. When she found out about my dilemma, without a moment's hesitation, she said, "Take 'Good Evening,' he can do it." Not many riders will hand their horse to a virtual stranger for the good of the whole—or for any reason. Hilda did, and I have never forgotten.

Because of her partnership with Keen (the 17.2-hand Thoroughbred she trained and who dominated US dressage in the mid-1970s), Hilda has become an embodiment of the American Dream—come true. When Hilda speaks, people listen. She is a hard act to follow.

"Not Really an Art..."

Although I will undoubtedly cover some serious subjects in the columns to follow, I cannot honestly promise that I will be completely solemn all the time. As much as I am devoted to and involved in dressage, I have to confess that it is not a discipline that excels in humor. At times we get so

---

* *Helen Steinkraus, wife of Olympic show jumper William Steinkraus, was a dressage rider and judge, and played an important role in the development of the sport in America.*

wrapped up in being "classical" and correct and pompous that we lose sight of the fact that this is a sport and a form of recreation.

Dressage is not really an *art*, although we like to call it that. The few times when this *sport* is truly elevated to an art form is when you watch a performance so inspiring it makes your hair stand on end and brings tears to your eyes. Not a daily occurrence, for sure. Dressage also approaches art when the horse under you *offers* to do something you have had to beg for (or force out of him) before. Then the violins start in your head, your heart soars, and riding becomes an artistic endeavor for about fifteen seconds. At most other times, dressage is discipline, sweat, repetition, and sometimes a pain-in-the-you-know-exactly-where. Getting on our dressage horses and taking ourselves too seriously does not endear us to those in other equestrian disciplines—or to each other.

An event rider attending a large dressage show as a spectator mentioned to me that she thought dressage riders tended to look unhappy and at times almost antagonistic toward their horses during warm-up. "I thought the whole point was harmony," she said. Immediately on the defense, I protested vigorously. Together we proceeded to the schooling area and observed the goings-on. I must admit she was not entirely wrong, and it was a strange sensation to watch dressage from "the outside." You do see a lot of tension, long faces, and a feeling of "we can't stand each other" projected from horses and riders alike. I am *not* speaking of appropriate corrections and momentary disagreements but an overall atmosphere.

"Uptight" Riders?

We all know that there is nothing to humble us like a horse, and every time you take that horse out in public and put him and yourself "on stage," you take a risk. I think the fear of being less than perfect, in combination with being at the mercy of subjective judging, makes the dressage rider the most uptight of all riders. One thing I have learned from many years of competing, however, is that the least judgmental of the people who will potentially notice your mistakes are your co-competitors. In one of my darkest moments, these words from Bruce Davidson helped me put things in perspective: "You know," he said, "It only happens on a horse."

Your fellow riders know and understand the problems and pitfalls, and they also know that "pride goeth before a fall." The most severe critics are the people who are seldom (if ever) seen mounted in public. They can afford to criticize without having to prove anything, and therefore, their opinion is secondary. If the dressage community as a whole had a less fragile ego, I think we would have an even better time together. After all, would the absurd outrage over Dressage Queen jokes occur if there wasn't a little "D.Q." afraid to be ridiculed hiding in all of us?

Lighten up, guys!

1995

— 2 —

art revisited

When I mentioned the word "art" in my first article in
The Chronicle (see p. 4), I knew I was in the danger
zone. Dressage as an art form versus dressage as a
competitive sport is as useless a topic to argue over as
the subject of religion. It does not yield a conclusion,
and in the end everyone is offended and upset.

It is true that dressage in its original form was not a competitive enterprise and that dressage is imperfect as a sport. The judging alone is almost mission impossible since the human factor gets in the way. Perhaps
five computers could get it right—but only if we could survive the
bloodbath caused by the disagreements sure to arise during program-
ming. And then, of course, a computer cannot evaluate the "art factor,"
which requires an ability to react emotionally in ways we have yet to see
produced by a machine.

Harmony ≠ Art

Harmony, however, is not always synonymous with *art*. Of course all
of us who ride multiple horses every day must experience peace and

harmony during the majority of our riding time, or we could not stand what we are doing. Harmony is only *one component* in art, and it is quite possible to have harmony without any art whatsoever. Picture a horse and rider lumbering about, relaxed, happy, and with no impulsion. This kind of riding is (not incorrectly) referred to by some as "watching paint dry" or "grass grow." It can put spectators and judges alike into a deep coma, and yet it is *harmonious*. A mechanical and dull performance without any power, brilliance, or chemistry can be harmonious but is hardly artistic. To arrive at *art*, everybody—human and equine—has to make efforts that go beyond attaining comfort and peace. There is a certain amount of suffering and conflict involved when a ballet dancer, an opera singer, or a painter strive to elevate their work to that of *art*—and it is the same for the dressage horse and rider.

Nuno Oliveira was an artist on horseback who, to the best of my knowledge, never was involved in competition. That does not mean that he could not have a disagreement with a horse, and although he did not compete, he had plenty of ego to go around. I used to watch him ride and teach at Potomac Horse Center in Maryland, and there was never a doubt as to who was in charge in his arena. As in all our work with horses, harmony is one of the end products desired, but the journey to get there would sometimes include a bit of stormy weather. Horses have no ambition of their own to become "trained," so the motivation in its various forms of corrections and rewards must come from the rider.

1996

– 3 –

a forum for dressage
philosophy

The idea for this column came to me when I read
Ridsport, *a Swedish equine publication. An issue*
included a short report about a sold-out lecture given
by Elisabeth Lundholm, a prominent instructor and
organizer and [at time of writing] the Director of
Dressage at the Swedish Federation. The title of her
presentation was "The Philosophy of Dressage," and
on that subject she entertained a captivated audience
for ninety minutes.

There were many "gems" to consider in the buildup of her presentation, and I will try to elaborate on some of them. Ms. Lundholm started by pointing out that it is vital to have a burning interest in the entire domain of horsemanship and the relationship with the horse before even thinking of competition. The focus on competing should never come before the consideration of the "whole horse experience," including understanding of bloodlines, physiology, equine health, and mental welfare.

Ms. Lundholm cited seven critical points of importance in our relationship with horses. The article did not divulge the details of what was said, but I am using her seven key words (which, by the way, all start with the letter "K" in Swedish) to spin on for my own interpretation.

Love

First on her list was *love*. There is a lot of love devoted to horses, probably because they are so noble and gentle and, to all of us fanatics, the most beautiful animals on earth. Love that is poured out on horses comes from different sources. The horse is sometimes, but certainly not always, a substitute for people, such as husbands, wives, children, or friends. A horse does not lie, he does not cheat on you, and he rarely hurts you deliberately. In addition, he provides you with the thrills of learning to ride, while trying to carry out your wishes. A dog can fulfill many of the emotional "needs" of a person even better than a horse, but a dog rarely offers the excitement of sport, power, and beauty that is synonymous with a horse. (And no dog can compete with that heavenly aroma!)

Knowledge

Knowledge was the second point in the lecture, and it is a sore spot in many a horse owner's life, especially the dressage rider. Not that the dressage rider is slower to learn or less interested in gaining knowledge than horse owners involved in other disciplines, but there is so much to learn and so little time. Regardless of our horse sport of choice, the horse is entirely dependent on our decisions about his health and welfare, and therefore we, as horse owners, can become very dangerous to him if we act out of ignorance. I don't know how many times I have looked back at some action I took because I thought it was the proper one, and said to myself: "If only I had known..." The horse's health is dependent on who we chose to care for him, who we pick as a veterinarian, farrier, shipper, and trainer. Only lots of personal experience or the extreme luck of having honest and knowledgeable advice can save the horse person from making mistakes that are costly, time consuming, and sometimes detrimental—or even fatal.

Communication

Communication is the next key word. Some horses, I have found, are easier to "converse" with than others, just like people. The ones that are outgoing and demonstrative are usually easy to read, while the serious and introverted types are harder to reach.

I have a horse that is very focused, very intense, and probably very worried about his performance. He is also a wimpy type who obsesses about his physique and complains through excessive body language about every little discomfort. For years I have ridden "powerhouse" horses that didn't have physical issues, could care less about footing, weather, or little aches, and were quite cocky about their ability to perform. Therefore I experience difficulties dealing with this "mimosa," and I never know if I should ignore some of his many issues or listen and worry about every one.

Another of my horses is just the opposite: He is totally tuned in to the environment, sometimes to the point where he is unaware there is a rider aboard, and only raw talent makes him get by. He is a practical joker and has entirely too many "good ideas" every day. However, he is young and very happy in his skin and as he gets older, I feel he will be able to concentrate even in the show ring. In spite of the frustrations related to his leaping and playing, I find this horse easier to understand and deal with than the solemn and fretting kind.

Consistency

Consistency is next on the agenda. The lack of consistency in work with the dressage horse is often a real problem, for the horse even more than the rider. Slowly but surely we are coming to understand this in the

United States, but we are still light-years behind the Europeans. When I was in Germany for my first "tour" of training, the legendary trainer and German Olympian Mr. Harry Boldt was amazed to see me arrive at the barn ready to ride every morning. He expected to train the horse and call me in on occasion to show me his progress. At the time I had to explain to him that I had no intention of twiddling my thumbs in Germany while he rode my horse. However, I see the point as far as ensuring consistency for the horse, and I was the only horse owner in his barn at the time who came to ride daily.

When a rider is experienced, she or he will understand the importance of the logical and steadfast program the horse has to follow to have a chance to become fully trained to the best of his ability. Many less experienced riders and owners in America are on a sure course to failure with their wonderful new youngsters by not having a proven trainer at their side. Not because their intentions are not good, but because they need to ruin at least one horse (and possibly break a bone or two) before they understand the value of following a consistent system of training.

Body Control

Body control is an all-important subject. If they sold it in bottles I would buy the stock. Do you ever have a day when you absolutely cannot make your body obey the orders of your brain? In case I am not instantly aware that I am having a "bad body day," my horses are likely to point it out in short order. It is a rare occasion when horse after horse is not "going well," so obviously there is a pilot error.

When I teach, I try to stay alert to what the rider is doing with his or her body, legs, and hands as I concentrate on the entire picture, because it is almost always true that whatever fails has its source in the riding: mainly the rider's position and balance as well as his or her natural instincts while giving the aids. Nobody thrills at the prospect of longe line lessons, but they are the answer to many body control problems.

Dressage = Life

Of all sports, I think dressage most resembles life. The seasons are long; defeat is familiar. Repetition eventually, but sometimes painfully slowly, makes you and your horse perform better. It's not necessarily fun or safe all the time. And just as things start to gel, the preparation feels right, and the goal is in sight, the horse comes up lame.

Life as a professional rider and trainer can be a rollercoaster ride, since we're dependent on the health and progress of our ever-changing equines. And still, as frustrating as it can be, it's all worth it when that flying change that was so difficult is suddenly easy and clean, the piaffe truly feels like a trot in place, and the connection is reliable.

Concentration

Concentration is the sixth key word. I guess I have been lucky working with students who were largely quite focused, whatever their level of talent. However, the few riders I have met who had problems setting their minds on course simply cannot keep the "phone line" to their horses alive. As soon as the horse feels the rider go mentally out for lunch, so does he—and not to the same place.

"Talkers" are the most difficult kind of students to deal with. They ask questions in the middle of a half-pass and provide a running commentary on their own performance. This, of course, irritates the instructor beyond belief (and makes the horse smile internally, since he knows that he is really in charge of the program).

At shows, the inability to concentrate truly comes back to bite you, and few horses will be kind enough to carry you through the test if you are worried about everything but the task at hand.

Feel

Feel is the last item on the agenda, and the most difficult to define. We often say a rider is "elegant" or "has a good seat," and therefore he or she is assumed to have arrived at the pinnacle of riding skills. I remember early in my dressage career a co-competitor who everybody admired for her lovely posture and grace. I was forever told that "Karin never moves." One day, as I watched her test, it dawned on me: neither did her horse. It is not that difficult to look serene while something does not happen.

What I mean by "feel" is the intuitive adjustments that some riders make to communicate with the horse. Sometimes, but not always, these "conversations" are invisible. However, when they produce the desired results, you have to assume that even when the aids were somewhat visible, they were correct.

Feel cannot be taught, only further developed and polished. It is the gift that separates those of us who "ride well" from the few who make riding an art.

2000

– 4 –

a lot of attitude

At a Florida dressage show, I was discussing the "dressage scene" with a woman who follows the circuit as part of the "service team"—the vendors, video recording companies, photographers, farriers, and so on. In the course of our conversation, she told me she felt that as a group, we needed to take a moment to examine ourselves and our dressage community, and to try to see things from her angle.

Her point of view is of interest, since she is in constant communication with dressage riders, judges, and officials without actually engaging in any of the same activities.

All the Talk

The woman said that often the "talk" surrounding her at dressage events is of an unpleasant nature, such as nasty gossip, untrue statements, or just negative input about another rider, a judge, or a manager. One of her rider friends was so upset with all the talk that she vowed to "give up gossip for Lent" in an effort to start cleaning up her own act first.

Especially discouraging were the kinds of things apparently being said in the judges' box about competitors, which were often overheard by the nearby video camera person and the scribe. First of all, it is inappropriate for a judge to comment on anything other than the performance of a horse and rider. Any other subject matter, such as looks, brains, or personality of the equipage, is forbidden territory. Any judge arrogant enough to assume that the people around him or her are deaf and dumb and will not assimilate and repeat the information needs to watch out. Scribes, especially the efficient and experienced ones who are a judge's delight, see and hear a lot, and they may choose not to pass it on—but there is a limit even to *their* tolerance if the person riding is a friend or family member.

The "Free Lunch" Myth

Another popular topic of discussion is the attitude of a rider who has been sponsored and then loses his or her horse. This could be due to a decision by the owner to withdraw the horse from competition, change riders, or sell the horse. As I point out later in this book (p. 160), being sponsored has its hardships, and of course we all mourn the loss of a successful Olympic combination. However, we as riders need to protect owners from our own sentimental reactions, which may be grossly unfair to them. When you are the one taking all the financial responsibility for a venture as high-risk as a shot at a team position for a horse and a rider, you deserve the right to make all the budget decisions. Sponsors can promise a lot of things, and truly mean them when they say them, but life changes, and the stock market is unreliable. The reality is that if a rider wants total protection against the possibility of losing a horse in training, he or she needs to own part of the horse and have a contract that clearly states the rules. In other words, the rider has to take a risk along with the owner by offering money or time as part of the deal.

You got it, no free lunch here either...

The Fallacy of Perfection

To continue with attitudes we seem to harbor, there is a strange syndrome going on with people looking to enrich their lives by adding an equine to the fold. For forty years or more I have been involved with finding, training, and selling horses, and the *modus operandi* of prospective horse owners is changing.

One reason is the availability of sales videos, which certainly is a mixed blessing. It cuts down on necessary travel, but many times watching videos does not give a good horse a fair chance because the poor quality of the video is misrepresenting the animal. Besides, the never-ending movie-watching leads to confusion and eventually apathy in the amateur who does not have endless stamina. Once a likely prospect has been sighted and selected, the travel starts, and with a good portion of luck, trainer and hopeful owner hit the jackpot. Now the real fun begins: the vet check. In the remote possibility that the veterinarian finds the horse in good order and has the guts to say so in clear language, that should seal the deal. Hardly. This horse has to be perfect, not a flaw allowed. Even things unrelated to the performance and unimportant to the job description have to be researched and questioned and fussed about *ad infinitum*. Reliable advice from an instructor of long-standing does little to calm the seas.

Why is all this happening? Since when are there any guarantees on health, life, or even on the sun rising tomorrow? Besides, I would like to know the kind of inspection a horse would perform before accepting a new owner, had he that option. The perfect owner is even more of a utopian fantasy than the perfect horse. Ask any horse.

The Horse as the One Thing, Not One of Many Things

Both George Morris and Denny Emerson wrote excellent columns in *The Chronicle of the Horse* ("The Evolution of Teaching," January 5, 2001; and

"We Need More Cowboy in Our Riders," January 12, 2001) in which they deplore the lack of basic knowledge, experience, and depth of horsemanship in our sport of today. I can easily jump on that bandwagon, and not because I think we ancients know everything better, but because I see the effects on the sport and the results of the "modern" point of view.

I took my first riding lessons from my grandfather, who was an officer in the Swedish cavalry. My horses were four-year-old remounts, brought up from the pastures, and it was months before I was given a saddle. The involuntary dismounts were frequent and some were spectacular. Later on, I went to a riding school where I spent years slowly climbing up the levels of proficiency under the guidance of military men with no mercy for pain and no tolerance for wimps. They definitely lacked in sensitivity and were not politically correct, but they loved and lived for horses, and they were passionate about creating new generations of riders. Having run a riding academy in this country for over thirty years, I can assure you none of my childhood teachers, although they produced competent riders, would have survived one week as instructors on our staff.

What many of today's parents want from the sport is instant success in competition yesterday. Children who cannot post in rhythm and barely can steer a pony around the ring are being encouraged to jump. But naturally the pony has to be 100-percent foolproof and is required to keep his back under the seat of that kid in every situation. If the instructor indicates that it would be prudent to extend the sessions on the flat until the progeny has a clue, we find another teacher. When the child hits the dust we make scenes, and if there is a scratch on the little darling, we stop by the lawyer's office on the way to the doctor.

On the whole, adult students are no better. School horses are expected to be carousel horses, rocking along in a zero-risk atmosphere. Any challenge has to be avoided, and learning to ride a green or difficult horse (the kind that really teach you something!) is out of the question. The attitude is that the horse ought to do all the work and be a "packer" (a word I detest!) even in dressage. Ideally the "schoolmaster" is on remote control, performing all the tricks as the teacher calls for them. No effort is to be required from the rider, who wishes to be fed the information without breaking a sweat and without utilizing legs, seat, or mind.

Alternate training methods are quite the rage. Instead of going through the tiresome everyday "do it again" of learning to ride a horse, we snap lead shanks, click clickers, wave wands, squat in pastures, and whisper to horses. In twenty-three minutes, previously untouched colts are tacked and backed in front of amazed audiences. I can't help wondering what the same horse does on the second day. When all else fails, call the horse psychic and solve the problem in the comfort of your home.

This attitude about riding is, of course, completely bizarre. The horse is not a vehicle for our glorification; he is not an exercise bike or a simulator for us to "try out" the Grand Prix movements. Horses are alive and each is an individual, and that is the charm and fascination of the riding game. Horses become a lifestyle, not one of the many things we pack into our day. The time spent living and breathing horses that is required to ever become truly proficient as a competitor, trainer, teacher, or groom cannot be replaced by the quick fix, never mind how good the guru, how splendid the surroundings, or how opulent the finances.

In spite of all this outpouring of attitude, I still think we have a great sport and a captivating lifestyle compared to most people who are not wrapped up in the mystique of the horse. As long as we can stay healthy and stay on, all other things seem to sort themselves out eventually. And to speed up our attitude adjustment, there is always Happy Hour.

2001

– 5 –

many of us horse people share an affliction called "jack russells"

Early on, our family always had dogs of "proper" size (at least knee-high) that displayed "normal" dog behavior. The Jack Russell terror in our house started with a phone call from friends who were at a terrier trial and saw these "adorable puppies" just desperate for a good home. At the time, neither my husband nor I had a clue about terrier trials or the fact that a Jack Russell is never desperate for anything.

With a lot of encouragement from people who were really just looking for partners in crime, we agreed to look at the puppy. It was a female, about fist-size. She looked harmless enough, and like all puppies, was irresistible. She moved in and immediately took over operations.

Sweet Revenge

We named her Digger, and that stopped her from ever digging anything. Instead, she concentrated on climbing trees. Her great passion in life was squirrels, and in pursuit of her prey she would hurl herself into the trees and tear up the branches in complete oblivion to the fact that this was not a dog thing to do.

If she ever downed a squirrel, I'm sure it was from a heart attack, since the creatures certainly never expected the dog to follow them up the tree.

We were forever approached by visitors who would hesitantly ask us if we thought that there was a dog in the tree out front. We would once again drag out the ladder and get Digger down while the people sighed in relief (relief that they weren't crazy).

As sweet as Digger was, she was heavily into revenge. She hated being left home alone, and she gnawed a plum-sized hole in the center of the linoleum kitchen floor the first time we abandoned her for an hour. I didn't mind the hole as much as the location. The whole floor had to be replaced.

A while later, when we thought she was grown up and could be trusted to be alone in the house, I arrived home to find a puddle in the middle of the dining table. While checking for a leak on the ceiling and finding none, it suddenly dawned on me what had happened. She would have paid dearly, except I could not find her anywhere until I had stopped laughing at her nerve.

Scary Jack

Don't think for a minute that a Jack doesn't know exactly what it is doing and why. They are truly scary.

One weekend, my mother informed me that she "had a surprise for me." Strange things happen when Mother visits, and I sure was surprised when she showed up with another Jack Russell puppy. It was a present from my groom, who got a puppy *from us* for Christmas two years earlier. Payback is a bitch, but in this case it was a dog, and we named him Chipper.

Chipper had eyes just like Lady in *Lady and the Tramp*—big, brown and sparkling—and Digger tolerated him, although she found his fascination with fetching balls, sticks, and anything people would throw a bit much. When we lost Digger to sudden heart failure, I thought a breather from the Jacks would be nice, but then our borrowed live-in kid wanted a puppy, and the circus was on again.

At a show in Tampa, Florida, I found Scooter. He was the opposite of the ugly duckling: As a puppy he was adorable, and every day he matured to become more splay-footed, cross-eyed, and long-backed. His final shape is odd, to say the least, but Mother Nature tries to keep things in balance, and Scooter is one of the smartest dogs I have ever met.

He is a hunter to the core. Left to his own devices, he will use the dawn's early light to pile up half a dozen rats, who find themselves dead before they even wake up in the morning. He never barks, just strikes and kills without a sound—and goes on to the next victim.

Chipper loved to torture Scooter when he was a puppy. He would keep Scooter at bay by growling and snapping and generally demonstrating who was in charge at every opportunity. One day Scooter, now much heavier and certainly twice the length of Chipper, decided he'd had enough. He promptly bit Chipper's ear off. As my husband dove for the half ear to rescue it, Scooter looked him squarely in the eye and swallowed hard. All gone!

After repeated fights, both dogs were neutered, a feature that only slightly tempered their urge to kill each other but in no way got rid of their basic aggressiveness. Both of them will stand up to a dog any size at the drop of a hat. I think the breed is missing the gene that helps evaluate size because it's hard to imagine that every Jack Russell was born with a Napoleonic complex.

The Trials

Recently, we hosted a regional championship Jack Russell trials, complete with agility, go-to-ground, races, conformation, and some other classes. A glaring omission in the prize list was a class for obedience— what a surprise! The Jacks are the nightmare of every dog school instructor, and perhaps the accepted fact that they "don't train well" is one of the reasons for the popularity that they enjoy with horse people.

After all, when you spend all day schooling horses, you have little energy left to train the dog. If the dog is known to be virtually untrainable, you can shrug, sigh, and apologize for his unruly behavior while feeling confident that everyone understands that things are beyond your control.

One positive feature is the "easy handling," which allows you to carry, transport, wash, and hide in hotel rooms this little dog, which will wake up the whole hotel with his sharp barking if the spirit moves him.

The Jacks always stray where they aren't supposed to be at horse shows, but they rarely get in trouble (although *you* do). They have a sixth sense

about horses and appear to know from birth how to avoid being flattened by their hooves, even while in hot pursuit of game.

A good hunting Jack—which is 99 percent of them—is far better than a cat as a deterrent for rats, since they waste no time playing games. They just carry on like little killing machines, displaying the most ardent bloodthirst and pure joy in hunting. They may look sweet and innocent curled up on the couch, but you can see your little pooch get up, stretch, yawn and say to himself, "Well, I think I'll go kill something."

Everything but Boring

A few years ago, I ran into a man at Dressage at Devon in Pennsylvania who was posted next to a cage with four Jack Russell puppies. All our relatives and friends had at least one by then, so I wasn't interested, but

I had a German girl with me who went all aflame and ran to call her parents about the possibilities of becoming owned by a Jack Russell.

While she was away, the man with the puppies asked me, "Don't you want a puppy?"

"Absolutely not," I said, "I can't stand them."

The man hesitated, then leaned closer to me and whispered, "Neither can I. These belong to my wife."

We then commiserated about the horrors of the breed until we ran out of breath. "So," he asked when we were finally through, "how many Jacks do you have?"

I reluctantly admitted to two. He also had two, in addition to the puppies. We each confessed we probably would always have at least one around. "Why is that?" I asked.

"Because," said the man, "all other dogs bore me."

1998

– 6 –

the value of a solid foundation

Watching a new generation of dressage riders come along, I cannot help but notice that in spite of all our efforts to mainstream, educate, help out, and sponsor our up-and-coming riders, the final results are almost entirely dependent on what lives in the "bottom" of their riding life.

Having a firm base to build on is vital, since a house without a foundation is unlikely to withstand the trials of nature. This image has been used a lot in sermons, but it applies to success in sports as well as to a healthy spiritual life. Looking back on my own education, I was lucky to have been firmly in the grip of my cavalry officer grandfather and a riding school that left no stone unturned to torture the uninitiated. Of course, I did not appreciate the strong discipline back then. One thing that frustrated me was the obsession with what we in this country call "flatwork," which revolved around establishing the correct seat for the rider and "on the aids" training for the horse. Riders were not allowed to start jumping before all the longe lessons; all the walk, trot, and canter plus transitions; and the basic lateral work was officially approved. It seemed to take forever before the much longed for jump equipment was brought out and we could get on with life!

The "Human Mirror"

After years in Sweden and some on Long Island competing in eventing and jumping, I met USET coach Colonel Bengt Ljungquist at Potomac Horse Center in Maryland. From there on I was on a solid dressage track, with the most consistent, honest, and all-forgiving teacher one could be blessed with. After eight years of helping and caring and guiding me and many other riders, Bengt died, and little did I realize how much I had taken him for granted. When we lost Bengt, I thought in my youthful insolence that I could go it alone, but in reality, I was lost in space. Eventually it became obvious to me that the more advanced your horse becomes, the more you need an instructor. Without that "human mirror" to correct or prevent your mistakes, you will never get the instant input you need to improve and develop your riding.

Since I started looking for help, I have enjoyed a lot of wonderful assistance from major players and big names, but none of all that can wipe out what Bengt and the old cavalry guys put in at a time when it was crucial to my future development. For many years, I have been able to build, add, improve, and even change a few things, but I never felt as if any of the new information would rip the ground out from under me and cause confusion or meltdown.

This article is directed mostly to the young people who are lucky enough to have a dedicated, established, and loyal instructor to help them in their riding on a regular basis, and those who are searching for help. Can you think of any international rider you admire who does not have a coach standing by? Of course not, and sometimes that trainer is the same one who started the rider from the very beginning. Even when the teachers have changed over time, the "first impressions" are likely to be permanent, and you need to find that basis to later build on and make yourself available to learn. If you are not one of the lucky kids whose parents are willing to support your horse activities, or you don't have a sponsor paying your way, it means you have to go and find the right situation.

Sometimes that opportunity is right next door at the local riding stable; sometimes it means going far away, perhaps even abroad. Never mind how we try to structure the horse industry: To date there is no education better and more thorough than the hands-on experience of being a working student. It may take you a couple of tries to find the situation that will work for you, but there is no way you will see, learn, live, and absorb horses and training as well as in the stable. In the barn, life is a never-ending scenario of mucking, turnouts, grooming, and waiting for the vet, and all that can get really old. Nevertheless, it is true that as long as you get to ride regularly, and you feel there is someone correcting you and taking a genuine interest in your progress, it is time well spent. While working with the mundane tasks around the barn, I guarantee you that you will learn something every day, and you won't even notice it. You will get to know every horse, and you will instantly detect when things are not right with each one. Every visit from the veterinarian or the farrier will teach you something new. You will find out how to prepare and present horses for sale, how to break a colt, and perhaps, how to manage a breeding stallion and foal out mares. In the end, you will have seen more in practice than any book can cover, and along with enhancing your own ability to ride, you will become a *horseman*. And that, ultimately, is more valuable than all the glory of the show ring. There's nothing wrong with winning, mind you, but knowing what goes on behind the scenes will last you a lot longer and get you farther than a fading ribbon.

Sticking with It

Sticking with it is a key feature, both for a working student and in a student-teacher relationship. Every day is not going to be glorious, or even tolerable; every lesson is not going to create revelations. Consistency, persistence, and a view of the big picture are essential. I spent a couple of days with US dressage rider and Olympian Lisa Wilcox when judging a show in Hamburg, Germany, at a time when she had just been invited to join the stud farm Gestüt Vorverk. She had already paid her dues working and taking her *Bereiter* exams in Germany, but of course she was hesitant to take this giant leap. At the time the German Olympic rider Nicole Uphoff was already working for the stud farm, and that was a bit intimidating. Well, Lisa took on the challenge, and it led to an eventual place on the US dressage team. With enough resolve and appreciation for the help offered, and a little bit of luck, you can get there, too.

Well, you say, but what about talent? Am I talented enough? It has been said before, but I will say it again: Talent without passion and determination is a complete waste of time. However, even mediocre aptitude can be developed to unimaginable heights with the right combination of student, horse, and teacher. I have had all kinds of students, and the most frustrating kind is not the one who struggles with the requirements, but the student that has it all and cannot be bothered to put in the work. Talent alone, although it helps, will never bring you to the top.

After you have found your niche, the one that works for you, don't become impatient and start running in all directions. Remember that all good things take time, and that everything you learn is yours to keep. Nobody can rob you of your knowledge. Stay loyal to yourself and to the people who honestly want to support you. Live with the setbacks and don't blame your trainer or your horse for your own shortcomings. And one day when you reach your star, don't forget to thank the people who believed in you, spent their time on you, and gave you a leg up when you knew nothing.

When I was in my mid-twenties, I knew everything. Since then, I have come to understand, as the great late great horseman and champion hunter-jumper rider Jimmy Williams liked to say, "It's what you learn after you know it all that's important."

2005

– 7 –

the ageless sport

*How we age is a personal and genetic affair, in
both people and horses, but both dressage horses
and dressage riders appear to have an advantage
in the later end of the game.*

A racehorse is usually retired at age three or four, and the horse that is
over five and still running is the exception. Jumpers in their late teens
have been very successful, but they are not the norm, and the hunters
and equitation horses over ten years old are considered "aged." A dressage horse, however, only just comes into his own as a fully trained
horse in his early teens, and many of our international stars bloom
around the age of fifteen. That is when they really know their job, have
all the confidence they need to perform in the show ring, and have a
body strong enough to deliver the goods.

Unfortunately, the peaking years are short, and, usually around seventeen or eighteen, Father Time moves in and ends the glory. However,
many of the past show stars continue as masters of the game for an incredible number of years in the service of young and not-so-young students of dressage who are lucky enough to learn from these maestros.

My horses have taught me never to attempt to retire a sound show campaigner, because the times I tried were total fiascos. You will never meet a horse more insulted, aggravated, and destructive than a true dressage prima donna put on the back burner. Gone is the daily detailed attention, the people admiring the various movements, the fussing before and after the show, and the spotlight. Instead there are pastures and flies, and ponies to keep you company who know zip about piaffe. I found that the retiree often tries to self-destruct in his desire to stay in the mainstream. So, back to work as a master of the game!

Even horses who in their youth were wild and woolly, and certainly had zero patience with incompetent riders, will sign up for teaching as long as it earns them attention. I spent a delightful time during one Florida season with Zander, a twenty-two-year-old Grand Prix horse belonging to a long-time student, Lisa Lipari. When she wanted to bring him to Florida, I was a bit hesitant, but I underestimated his zeal and spirit. This old gent was such a dream to work with and sit on. He truly aged like a good wine, although I have been told he was no peach as a youngster...

Age Is Just a Number

Horses, just like people, mature at their own individual speed, and therefore it is unfair to expect a certain level of performance from a horse at a certain age. I have lived with all kinds, from the child prodigy, to the one who appeared learning disabled until he suddenly caught on and caught up. At the 1984 Los Angeles Olympics, I rode a horse that was competing at age six,* and that was a strange experience, since there just had to be some holes in that creation. This horse had managed to learn all the tricks without much opportunity to develop self-carriage. Being large and powerful, he was quite the opposite of a "lady's mount," and it was all I could

---

* *In order to compete in the Olympics, a horse now has to be a minimum of eight years old.*

do to stop him from pulling my arms out of their sockets. But imagine the generous brain of the horse that let it all happen and played along!

On the other end of the stick is the very slow maturing horse. I must admit the Swedish Warmbloods, as much as I favor them in some ways, do tend to take their time. Once when Finnish dressage rider and Olympian Kyra Kyrklund was still working at Flyinge Stallion Station in southern Sweden, I watched her school a horse that just could not focus on the task but kept concentrating on everything except what was being requested of him. Finally, Kyra stopped to chat, and I asked her, "So, how old is the horse you are on?" Kyra replied, in her wonderful deadpan way, "It is a very young Swedish horse. He is nine." In defense of Swedish horses, I hasten to add that if you wait them out, you tend to get paid back on the other end; they usually live long lives and stay sound, perhaps because they "protect" themselves as youngsters.

Most aging dressage riders are as tenacious as their horses. Because our game lends itself to a longer period of being effective, even in the show ring, we forge on. I judged the Swedish Championships in Falsterbo in 2002, and one of the riders was Ulla Hakansson, many times Olympic rider and a star in Swedish dressage for as long as I can remember. One of her horses, Ajax, competed in his last Olympics at age nineteen. At the Championships, the riders who were "new and hot" for some reason could not get it together, and in the Grand Prix even the champion of the country had a bad hair day. Ulla, who was not as well mounted as some of the younger riders, proceeded to give them all a riding lesson. Every corner was utilized to the inch; each transition was clear, smooth, and placed exactly where prescribed; and her polished riding repeatedly overcame the shortcomings of her horse. The audience went crazy after her test, and exiting the ring, Ulla wore a smile that clearly said, "And you thought I was not still in the game?" At age seventy-four, Ulla was still competing and running the horse in the vet check herself.

Go with Your Boots On

Riders who may decide not to show any more, but who continue to ride and perhaps even train horses, appear to me to remain healthier, stronger, and happier than most other aging people. Barring accidents, which are always a possibility around horses, the body thrives on a daily exercise that it is accustomed to, the mind is always refreshed by communicating with the animals we love, and our passion stays alive.

There used to be training sessions at Gladstone for long-listed dressage riders, and Bert de Némethy—our longtime US event coach—kept a couple of horses in the barn. Every day he would work them on the flat, quietly, patiently, and softly, with no fanfare whatsoever. Those horses were so supple when he finished you could spread them on toast, and all he did was transitions, bending exercises, and rein-backs. Although Bert seemed to be absorbed in his own world while on horseback, he would watch the dressage training out of the corner of his eye, and he would sometimes comment on our weak and strong points, and always hit it bull's-eye!

One of my very first instructors in Sweden was a cavalry officer whose two grand passions in life were horses and women. He rode out into the forest every day, often in the company of one female or another who was boarding her horse at the riding school. Many years after I left Sweden, I heard that Major Nilsson had died, which was not surprising since he was ninety-something. The story of how he met his maker warmed my heart: He and some lady were out riding in a winter wonderland when the woman's horse slipped and the rider fell off, breaking her ankle. Major Nilsson whirled his horse around and valiantly galloped off through the snow for help. He was struck by a heart attack and literally died with his boots on, while on a mission to rescue a damsel in distress. What a way to go!

2003

– 8 –

fitness and dressage

This is not a subject I approach with any enthusiasm. I find organized exercise revolting. It is only afterward, when all the endorphins are cavorting in their released stage, that you think that maybe you had a good time.

Before Argentina and the 1995 Pan American Games loomed large, I just snorted when people mentioned "aerobics," "stretching," and "upper body strength." My standard retort was: "I ride on the average six horses a day. Getting plenty of exercise, thank you very much!" Friends had been hinting about the virtue of some other kind of exercise, and finally one of them took me, the "fit" rider, for a jog. When he was still warming up, I was cooked. We did pushups, and on the fifth one I almost broke my jaw slamming into the floor. I got the picture and finally had to admit that very few parts of me were in working order, never mind in shape!

The Awful Truth About Keeping Fit

Sometime in January I opened a horse magazine, and there she was, Betsy Steiner. She has always been one of my favorite riders and people, but she

really pushed me to the limits with her articles on fitness for dressage riders: Here's Betsy in living color contorted in an impossible position with a look of bliss on her face. She is lifting weights with "contoured" arms and practically levitating solely by the help of her abdominals. All the while smiling and saying awful things like, "Riding is not enough to keep you fit for riding." And don't think you'll get support from other prominent riders! I once asked Robert Dover, "Do you work out *every* day?"

I hate to tell you, the answer was, "Yes."

As reluctant as I was at first, and still am, to actually have an "exercise program," there's no denying that the advocates of fitness and strength training are correct. Ten months into a very modest program, with lots of cheating and excuses, I can still feel a difference in both coordination and power when I ride. I also notice when I have *not* kept up the work. Since weight is not my problem, I thought I could get away with less, but that is a fallacy. To really make an impression on those sturdy Warmbloods without having to exaggerate your aids, you need the ability to use the center of your body—the thighs, seat bones, and stomach—as well as the lower leg, with authority.

Finding (Making?) Time

The biggest problem in staying on course with an exercise program is *time*. Around horses you need to devote time to grooming, tacking up, warming up, cooling down, and cleaning up. When you're talking exercise, this translates into changing clothes, warming up, working out, cooling down, stretching, and cleaning up. Women who do not have a crew cut can count on their hair to turn into soggy Wonder® Bread. It will need help. From soup to nuts this takes around ninety minutes and it is difficult to fit into a daily schedule. If one little thing goes wrong, the allotted exercise time goes out the window.

So why should we put ourselves through all this? Well, from the horse's point of view it sure helps his work if his rider is balanced, coordinated, and strong enough to communicate his or her aids clearly. A "soggy" rider slides around in the saddle and gives contradictory signals, which are difficult, if not impossible, for the horse to interpret. Although we are all asymmetrical, we demand symmetry from our horses, and when we sit crooked and hang on the horse's teeth for balance, his performance will reflect our lack of body control. Since the horse is dependent on *our ability* to enable him to express *his ability*, we simply owe it to him to be at our personal best.

Seen from the judge's box, a rider who appears fit and athletic always enhances the picture of horse and rider together. I certainly don't recommend a starved look, since a large and big-boned, even bulky, rider on a horse of complementary size looks just fine. As a matter of fact, a bit of weight in the saddle sure can improve on the amount of respect you'll receive when you half-halt, and I have often wished I had more authority in that region.

The "Tipping" Point

There's a point, though, when "heavy" becomes "obese," and it is not only unattractive to behold, it shows a lack of respect for the horse and the sport. I have judged many tests where a horse has struggled under a rider who was much too heavy and therefore uncoordinated. At the end of the test the horse is usually exhausted from the effort of carrying and trying to balance the load. The rider is close to suffocating and sweating profusely from lack of conditioning. This phenomenon I have never personally observed at horse shows in any other discipline, and it should not happen in ours.

Involvement in dressage does not exempt the rider from the requirement of being an athlete. If you are not already a miracle of fitness, try making a resolution to be at least as fit and supple as your horse. Ask your spouse to contribute by building you a heated lap pool—covered, of course—and watch him/her applaud your most rudimentary efforts at exercising.

1996

– 9 –

the relationship between amateurs and professionals

In the mid-eighties, I spent several months training with Harry Boldt, who was then, and still is, one of my equestrian heroes. At the time, Mr. Boldt kept his horses at Iserlohn, near Dortmund, Germany. He had perhaps fifteen horses in training at the time, and when I arrived with my Swedish Warmblood "Stockholm," I discovered I was the only foreigner in the barn.

I got a warm welcome when I walked off the van with the horse, but Mr. Boldt kept looking behind me as if he expected another person to appear. And, indeed, he did. "Where is your husband?" he inquired. "In America," I said. He was apparently amazed that I had traveled without a guardian. When I arrived the second morning for my lesson, Mr. Boldt looked a bit confused. On the third day, he exclaimed: "You are back!?" I assured him that I had not come all that way with the horse to miss a single opportunity to ride in front of him, and he seemed to accept that fact with some hesitation.

By Invitation Only

A couple of days later, I started to get the picture. A lady I had not seen before arrived to ride her horse, and after the lesson, she asked Mr. Boldt when she should come back to ride again. His reply was, "When I call you!" She got back in her Mercedes, departed, and was not seen for at least two weeks. This was the way it worked with all the horses in the barn: You came to ride your horse by invitation only. I remember thinking to myself that such a system would go over in the United States like a lead balloon. When I had to return home, I left my horse with Mr. Boldt, and after a while I received pictures and a list of results from a show in which his working student had ridden my horse. I do not recall that they ever asked if they could show him. However, whenever I arrived to visit, the horse was in excellent shape, up to his elbows in clean straw, and shining with good health. Although not even Harry's expert riding could remedy the horse's canter, which was very earthbound, he was in all other ways making progress and obviously being trained according to a regular schedule.

Like the amateur rider sometimes has to, I learned to give up control of my horse and place my trust in someone I really admired, and it all worked out well because I chose the right person. However, I cannot say it was easy, and now when the shoe is on the other foot, I understand how an owner can worry about his or her horse when it is out of his or her hands. Of course, I grew up knowing how the system works in Europe, but giving up control is not the American way, and it has taken a long time for us to get a working relationship going between trainers and owners that is beneficial to both parties and also to the horse.

Mixed Greens

One year when I judged the best four-, five-, and six-year-olds in Scandinavia at the Flyinge Stallion Station in the south of Sweden, of the forty-five four-year-olds that qualified, only about five were ridden by their owners, which is completely normal by European standards, and also the best way to get your horse started right. Young horses and inexperienced riders are a dangerous mix, but this is something it took Americans a long time to admit to, and although it looks like the message is getting through, there is still a lot of "mixing of greens" out there, and it is bound to clash!

For the amateur rider who is busy with work, children, and other agendas and only has a limited time to spend with a horse, a professional trainer is a must if the horse is not to stagnate and lose his edge. It can be difficult to find a capable trainer in the immediate area, and the search for one can be as complicated as choosing a college for your child. Once you have made a selection, though, it is time to let go and allow yourself to be taught and the horse to be trained. This presupposes that you already own a horse. If not, the trainer of your choice should be in on the process of locating and selecting the horse. There is nothing less inspiring for a teacher than working with a combination of horse and rider who are totally unsuited for each other. That does not always mean that the horse and rider are not separately capable, but the partnership is not the right one. When you sense it will never work, standing there and trying to find positive energy from two negatives can wear you down. Considering how much time, effort, and money a horse with a difficult agenda consumes, it is vital to start with a rider and horse who have physical and mental attributes that match.

It is often very difficult for the part-time rider to "look into the future" and tell what is required for a horse to succeed and advance in his training, or how the test ride really went, even when he or she was on top of the horse. Trying horses out can in itself be an intimidating experience, and it is good to have someone to turn to when the pressure is on. It is well worth paying a reasonable commission when the horse is found (which is usually 10 percent, but sometimes more, depending on the circumstances, time, and travel) to avoid making mistakes and to have someone to turn to for advice. Most customers understand that the trainer has more than earned this money by delivering the right horse, but a few try desperately to avoid rewarding the professional for this service. The expertise and advice from a well-meaning and experienced horseman is every bit as valuable as that of a lawyer or doctor, and few would dream of not paying for *their* time! Admittedly, we need more clear guidelines to follow in the horse industry when it comes to the amount of commissions, and who has rightfully earned one, but that does not mean that customers can ignore the fact that they owe something for time spent and advice given.

Even if the amateur rider wisely chooses a horse that is more experienced than he or she is, instant bliss in the relationship is not a given. Horses, like people, are creatures of habit and they have their own view of how life should be. More often than not, you are looking at about a year of "getting to know you" before you have the feeling that the horse is truly *your* horse, responding to your aids without hesitating or resisting. Even if you fell in love at first sight, the engagement can be rocky because the horse anticipates aids and reactions from his "old" rider, which are not in the new rider's repertoire. There could also be some "baggage" brought along from both ends. As we know, horses never forget, good or bad, and a flashback from a horse's former life can cause misunderstandings and friction. Fear in the rider caused by incidents that have nothing to do with the new horse are likely to be picked up by the horse and can create tension neither horse nor rider can detect the source of. Here, again, input from your instructor is vital to move past the problem to better communication.

The Real Power Source

At this point in my life, I am in the lucky situation of being able to choose the kind of clients I wish to work with, but having started out young and naive, I know how tough it can be to earn the trust of the horse owners and end up with a loyal customer base. You do it, of course, by teaching honestly, riding the horses in a fair manner, and doing all you possibly can to deliver what you promise. One additional very important thing is to respect the amateur owner/rider for his or her contribution to the sport and for what they are able to accomplish outside of their riding life, while supporting us horse fanatics. To make a play on the title of one of Olympic eventer David O'Connor's *Chronicle* columns: We are powered by the amateurs, and we'd better be sure we run our barns as professionals should.

2005

— 10 —

dare to let go

It is not often I write about the specifics of riding in "Between Rounds." Part of the reason for that is because we are already showered by numerous descriptions in every horse publication of how to deal with every conceivable aspect of riding.

Another reason is that these "essays" are more about philosophy, observations, and news in the dressage realm than about teaching riding.

However, I saw an article in a European horse publication that made some interesting points about "contact," and I thought they could be worth sharing. Few things are as much written, discussed, and taught as the "connection" with the horse's mouth, and yet it remains a fairly nebulous concept. It is in effect a secret relationship between the rider and the horse. It can be observed and judged and commented on to a point. But in reality, only the two of you know the truth.

"No Hand Without a Seat"

This axiom never loses its validity, and the quickest way to a good seat is on the torturous longe line, riding without stirrups or riding bareback to acquire the balance and ability to remain within the center of gravity at all times. We start by concentrating on the rider's seat before expecting to improve on the hands and the connection between the horse's mouth and his hind leg. Hard, insensitive, and unsteady hands are sometimes not a conscious problem, and therefore, it can take a while to correct them. Inexperienced riders often lack the strength in their back and abdominal muscles to sit upright and have a tendency to fall forward. The tension in their shoulders and arms then transfers to the hands and makes them stiff. Often the rider is under the impression that by moving the bit back and forth in a sawing motion, he or she will put the horse "on the bit." What the horse will do instead is swing his head back and forth and avoid the contact altogether—or stiffen at the poll and lean into the bridle, becoming heavy and leaving the hind legs out behind him. Only when the horse relaxes and "lets go" in the poll, starts to carry himself with his hind legs, and becomes weightless in the hand can the novice rider get a glimpse of how it really feels when a horse is "on the aids."

There is no shortcut to a good seat. Even accomplished riders need a refresher course on occasion, and then it is back on the old longe line. Many years ago we had a training session at the USET Headquarters in Gladstone, New Jersey, with the then US National Dressage Coach. Ten riders from all over the country, most of them already experienced as USET team members, stared in disbelief at the coach as he declared that before our lesson we would each be longed by another participant. Some longe line lessons from hell took place, but they were productive, and the horses were grateful during the lessons to have more supple riders with quieter hands on board. And we have all heard of the years of longeing required at the Spanish Riding School in Vienna, Austria, before the apprentices are allowed to ride on their own. Well, those riders sure can sit a horse!

There is an additional way to produce a more educated hand: allowing the rider to experience sitting on a horse that has already developed collection and self-carriage, and can work on his own without needing the rider to bring him into balance. A helpful hint from a horse with well-developed self-carriage can open up a whole new door to better communication. Riding with a *bridged rein* (securing both the left and right reins with your right hand and vice versa) can help you stabilize the movement of your hands, but too much of that can imprison the hand motion and create a "dead" hand, which stiffens the horse's mouth, and that is not desirable.

When it comes to "good" hands, we do not mean absolutely immobile hands, since that can create a tight, dry, and hard mouth in the horse. We once had a girl from Europe working for us and riding our stallions while I went off for one of my training sessions in Germany. She had a lovely position on the horse and a very still hand. When I came back after six months, one of the stallions had a mouth like a rock, and the other one never went forward again. "Feeling" hands with supple wrists and fingers are far more important than immobile hands. That is why a flexible hand that may not be optically completely still can sometimes produce a softer, chewing, and more "alive" mouth than the hard and stagnant variety.

Another problem can be that the rider simply is afraid to let go. That is often the case with cheeky and lively horses who are so much forward that they worry the rider and make him or her ride with the emergency brake on. The rider is pulling the horse from front to back. The horse responds by pulling forward and cannot soften the grip. Neither can the rider, and they end in a deadlock. The rider has to take the initiative to be the first to test the waters by easing up on the pressure after a half-halt and seeing if the horse will stay with him or her. "Giving" does not mean "drop the ball"—just leaving room for the horse to go forward.

Speaking of half-halts, there is at least one article in every dressage magazine explaining the ins and outs of this, the most important train-ing tool we have. Yet, as a judge, I often see riders go through an entire test without ever attempting to use a single half-halt to help the horse with his balance or signal to him that he should get ready to receive an aid. Former US Dressage Team Coach and German Olympian Klaus Balkenhol had an extensive article about the half-halt in the August 2007 issue of *Dressage Today*, where the concept was explained in very clear language. He points out the importance of timing of the half-halt, which is something you learn from doing them over and over until they generate from your muscle memory and instincts, rather than your brain. And he says that he always tells his students, "The secret is in the giving." So, we are back to that.

Gone Fishing

The good rider's seat, connected through the hand, serves as a balancing bar in a ballet class. The horse tends to lightly touch the bit to push himself back into balance when he loses it. It is not a heavy feel, but rather like a searching for the bit. Once you have a "feel" of the horse's mouth, it is as if you were out fishing and a tiny fish is caught on the line pulling against it. It is not uncomfortable, just a sign that somebody is home on the other end. And it is very important that the connection is not broken. When fishing, there is a big problem when the contact is lost. Either the fish got away, or he is coming at you. In riding, the emptiness in front indicates that the horse has escaped, just like the fish, and is behind your aids. When the contact varies between heavy and nothing, it is as annoying as when your cell phone checks out. After a number of times of the rider saying, "Can you hear me now?" the horse hangs up.

Some blessed individuals have an innate feel for how the right connection can be maintained and preserved at all times, but most of us have to work on it. Things like the proper length of the reins, the amount of engagement attained by the driving aids, and how to maintain the poll as the highest point are all challenges we go out to face every day as we mount up.

2007

a case for the head

A few weeks before Courtney King Dye's horrible riding accident left her with severe head injuries,* she took part in a United States Equestrian Federation (USEF) High Performance clinic in Florida, working with Steffen Peters and me. As always when I watched Courtney ride, I admired her instinctive and extraordinary ability to bring out whatever positive features a horse may possess.

At the end of the day, Courtney showed me a video of a couple of horses for potential sponsorship, and we discussed which one of them would be the best match for her to make into a future team horse.

Fast-forward to the Palm Beach Dressage Derby in Florida the first weekend in February, when I observed trainer Lendon Gray receive a phone call ringside and heard her exclaim: "That's awful!" We all know what she found out on that call.

---

* *In 2014, Courtney had a baby girl and is busy teaching and educating riders.*

During the show, there was a moving ceremony with prayers to bring Courtney out of her coma. And, thank God, she not only woke up but also found a path to recovery.

Courtney isn't my only close experience with head injuries due to a horse that fell. I had a very experienced student in New York whose horse stumbled and fell with her at the walk. This rider is still in a coma, three years later. I wasn't present, but the description of the accident was as undramatic as any event could be, and yet the consequences are devastating. I stood at my student's bed at the hospital, fully aware that our roles could just as easily have been reversed.

Neither rider wore a protective helmet at the time of the accidents. Would their injuries have been less severe if they'd worn safety headgear? Since all research indicates that this is the case, the debate about safety helmets for dressage has intensified.

Just the Facts

The subject was put on the Fédération Equestre Internationale (FEI) Dressage Committee agenda, and the medical information that accompanied the issue presented the following facts and opinions:

- Head injuries appear to account for approximately 10 percent of horse-related injuries and are the injuries most likely to result in hospitalization or death.

- A fall from 60 centimeters (approximately 3 feet) can cause permanent brain damage, and a horse elevates the rider up to 3 meters (9 feet) above the ground.

- A human skull can be shattered by impact at as low as 7 kilometers per hour, and the most likely ages for injury to occur are 5 to 14 and 25 to 44.

- In Great Britain, hospital admission for equestrian injuries declined 46 percent after helmet design improved and they entered routine use.

- The US Pony Clubs decreased their head injury rate by 29 percent after mandatory helmet use.

Tradition Over Safety

You would think that the above information would make us all run for head cover, but that isn't necessarily the case. The problem with dressage, as Dr. Craig Ferrell pointed out to the FEI Dressage Committee, is that while helmets are considered ugly, the top hat is considered elegant and is also highly traditional. To some people, wearing a safety helmet with your shadbelly is tantamount to wearing a Speedo® to a wedding. It's simply the value of tradition over safety, especially when the risk of head injury appears remote, as it may seem in comparison to other riding disciplines.

In the wake of the debate comes, as always, the commercial aspect. Plans are afoot amongst the fashionable "hat makers to the stars." They're working to construct a product that looks like the traditional top hat but performs like a helmet. Some of us experience real problems calling this image up in our minds, but others have no problem kissing tradition goodbye. One person said: "Top hats should be used by magicians, clowns, men in formal attire, and people who need a vessel for their raffle tickets."

It may be the responsibility of the international governing body to set policy, but the opposition to rule changes messing with tradition is strong. I have to admit that the image of the FEI rider in tails and top hat is so ingrained in our brains and closely identified with dressage that we in the committee had severe withdrawal symptoms at the mere thought of giving it up forever. Let me hasten to point out, though, that people have always been and definitely still are allowed to ride at all FEI levels with safety helmets.*

Another side of the argument comes from the athletes: "I'll do as I wish. It's my right as an individual to choose whether or not to ride with a safety helmet."

Of course it is. And what you do at home cannot be easily regulated. At show grounds and public riding stables, however, rules can be put in place and enforced. In some countries, I found out, the insurance companies will not pay for your hospital bill for a head injury—even at your own barn—if it can be proven that you weren't wearing a safety helmet.

Helmet Hair

This subject has been difficult for me to write about because I must confess I've spent most of my riding life, except when competing in eventing and jumping, without protective headgear. I've had spectacular dismounts over jumps and from bucking horses and have broken various bones, but I know the falls on the flat are the most dangerous.

When you get thrown up into the air before heading to the ground, there's a split second of extra time when your body instinctively makes a move to protect the head. Perhaps your arm or shoulder pays the price, but not your brain. When the horse falls, there's no such downtime. The ground comes at you before you have any chance to react, and it comes at you hard.

---

* *The rule now in effect states that anyone mounted on a horse must wear protective headgear, except those riders age eighteen and over, while on horses that are competing only in FEI levels and tests at the Prix St. Georges level and above (including FEI Young Rider Tests, the USEF Developing Prix St. Georges Test and the USEF Brentina Cup Test).*

I know all the excuses for not wearing a helmet—it's uncomfortable, too heavy, too hot, too tight, and it kills my hair.

Then I go to the shows and see more and more dressage riders warming up with helmets. Our top Grand Prix riders, such as Guenter Seidel and Steffen Peters, are sporting snazzy designs in protective headgear. And during the Kentucky CDI, Canadian Grand Prix rider Jackie Brooks performed all of her tests at the show, including the freestyle at night in front of a sizeable audience, wearing her safety helmet right into the competition ring. I'm sure some people were startled at the first glimpse of her, but as soon as the music started and she began a nice ride, they forgot about her hat.

It will be a challenge to the dressage world to make the use of safety helmets accepted and appropriate and eventually desirable. I think perhaps we can police ourselves and not have to make rules a necessity.

For sure, I'm starting to feel self-conscious riding around in my baseball cap. As my close friend Sandy Howard said when we discussed this issue: If your head is less important than your hair, I guess there's not much in it!

2010

− 12 −

practice makes perfect

Top US riders are at a disadvantage to their European counterparts because they lack the opportunity to regularly practice in the show ring against competitors of the same caliber.

How often have you heard someone say, "She is so talented," or, "He is so talented," about a horse or rider? These days when I am closely following the progress of our elite and upcoming athletes, I hear this a lot.

Although I may fully agree, there is a little voice in the back of my head that says, "So what?" That is because I know from many years of teaching riders and training horses that talent is wasted without commitment, discipline, and practice. I've had some extreme talents come my way, but far from all of them achieved great things because they lacked the passion and energy to put in the necessary effort to hone their gift.

Talent Is Overrated

Journalist Geoff Colvin has written a book called *Talent Is Overrated* (Portfolio, 2008), and he provides a lot of very interesting information regarding assumptions we have about pure talent propelling people through life and earning them rich rewards. Many of the statements he makes are things that anyone who has spent time promoting and trying to improve a specific talent will agree with. Even if I didn't have proof that achieving above-average success in anything takes more than talent, I knew it from working with riders and horses over the years. When reading this book, my suspicions were confirmed.

Top riders are, as all competitors, driven by an almost blinding passion for that with which they are involved. Although riding is not specifically mentioned in the book, a number of other sports, professions, and arts are. The addition of another athlete—the horse—to some degree changes the picture, but the basic premise of the book covers any activity in which humans strive for perfection.

Starting with the passion for horses and riding, which is the reason almost every person gets involved with our sport, how far can it take us if we do not possess a great degree of natural talent? According to Mr. Colvin, as far as you want to go if you have the motivation and opportunity to devote to perfect practice.

Passion is a tremendous driving force. What else could motivate us to get back on a horse after a bad fall, tackle that youngster full of vim and vigor, or compete in front of an audience—all situations that can be considered beyond our comfort zone? What else can get us out in the driving rain at six in the morning on Sunday to warm up for an early class, drive hours to and from the show, and pay for it to boot?

A "fire in your belly" to succeed is enormously important, but there are great geniuses who actually didn't start out with a burning desire to excel. Instead, they had someone else at their side, often a parent, who, at an early age, motivated, pushed, encouraged and sometimes threatened his or her progeny into a program of practice that became the path to performance.

Unconventional Wisdom

Size Matters

After accompanying our elite riders around the country and the world in my role as Technical Advisor for the US Dressage Team—observing, training, criticizing, and praising them—I have a good grasp of the state of our dressage union. This country is blessed with lots of talent, has a sizable population of people passionate about dressage, and has a fair number of gifted horses. But when Americans look for international success, there are some definite obstacles that hinder us from competing against the Europeans on a level playing field.

One significant issue is the "lack of proximity," because of the size of our country, which greatly complicates our ability to work and learn together. With the notable exception of the intense four-month Florida season, we don't have sufficient numbers of shows available over the year, or country-wide, for the riders to get in the ring often enough. As a result, they don't get enough practice and think of every show as a huge event. In Europe, the strongest competitive countries are so close to each other that it's never more than a day trip to reach a competition, and there are plenty of choices as to where to show.

Nothing Comes for Free

Colvin repeatedly brings up real life stories of people universally recognized as natural talents, and he proves that they did not, in fact, get anything for free. He mentions examples such as Mozart, whose father, an accomplished musician, had his son playing the piano at age three; Tiger Woods, who was swinging a golf club when he was four; and Picasso, who worked tirelessly studying primitive and traditional art for a decade before "suddenly" appearing with his revolutionary paintings.

According to the author, there are two kinds of drive that make up our motivation: the *extrinsic drive* that is externally induced or driven and the *intrinsic drive* that stems from strong emotions creating the desire to perform. The latter is what helps us overcome the pain and humiliation of falling off, to get back on, and to practice some more. That is the kind of passion that makes us so totally involved in a task that time disappears and the work seems effortless.

So, passion is the driving force, but great motivation and talent are still not going to get you anywhere without practice, practice, practice. Colvin drives home this fact in one case history after another. From chess player Bobby Fischer to the Beatles, they practiced their craft over and over again for years and with high repetition.

Anyone who has audited a clinic given by Kyra Kyrklund will remember how she repeatedly says that you have to practice things literally millions of times to develop "muscle memory," which works like an automatic transmission between horse and rider without the rider having to engage the brain to shift gears. Really good riders do not "think" about what they are doing; they do it because it's become second nature to them.

We Need to Practice at Shows

This phenomenon becomes really evident when you closely observe our top competitive riders and the very best riders in Europe. What is the biggest difference between our finest and theirs? Lack of talent? No. Lack of horses with talent? No, but in the United States we don't have enough of them per rider. Lack of opportunity? Yes, when it comes to shows available within a reasonable distance and taking place all year long.

The cream of dressage riders in Europe can compete in a creditable event every weekend of the year if they choose, and most of them actually show on average every second or at least third week year round. They each have three to five Grand Prix horses to rotate and several small tour horses that go along. Take a moment and consider how many times those Europeans get in the ring to compete over a year! When they get to championships, it's just another horse show to them, while to us it is an enormous event!*

The lack of routine in actually riding the tests puts our US riders at a disadvantage in international competition. The intense activity on the Florida circuit is a fabulous opportunity and the only time our riders have the advantage of living close to each other and physically sharing their experience. But it is a four-month stint at best, and then everybody disperses to their home base, and the distances loom large once again. The vast separation between our riders and shows is one of our greatest stumbling blocks, but we bravely face the challenge by routinely driving and flying our horses across the United States and the world to get where we need to be.

Australia, Canada, and South America share our dilemma, and it sure slows down the progress and sometimes brings it to a halt. Since practice is the issue here, and instant genius appears to be a misconception, this is a problem we're constantly trying to work on. It's hard to achieve perfect practice without the tools available.

Luckily, this country abounds in energy, optimism, and inventiveness. Adversity has never hindered Americans from testing their ability and measuring their skills against others, and we do love to compete. I know we have the pool of talent we need, the will to work, and the ambition to win. All we need is more endless, perfect practice.

2012

---

* See p. 332 for more on this subject.

— 13 —

dressage as therapy

*It was incomprehensible. It was another disaster
spectacular with special effects beyond what we
had seen before, a concept we had not thought of,
a twist of evil we had not yet explored. Then they
played it again and again. It would not go away.*

It invaded our minds in the form of reality. It made our bodies shake,
and it injected our pores with fear, confusion, and an urge to wail, cry,
and strike. Norwegian painter and printmaker Edvard Munch captured
the perfect artistic expression of what so many of us felt in his piece
"The Scream."

When the twin towers of the World Trade Center in New York City crum-
bled as the result of satanic planning, and with the aid of such formi-
dable weapons as box cutters, we all realized how vulnerable we are.
I adore Manhattan—my husband sometimes tells people I am really a
"city girl," which is true. I would gladly give up the bees and the birds
to live in New York, but that makes it difficult to pursue a lifestyle that
involves horses. Then one Tuesday morning the city of my dreams got its
heart torn out, and all I could do was watch in horror.

Trapped

The first two days after the September 11 attack on America, we were glued to the television and radio—basically useless in any capacity. By sheer luck our family did not lose a close relative or friend, although we lived a mere forty-five minutes from Midtown. After the shock and denial, the fear set in. Like the ten million people in Manhattan, the inhabitants of Long Island are "trapped" if tunnels and bridges are cut off. While everything stood still in the city, Long Island held its breath waiting for the other shoe to drop—bombs or biological weapons.

Thursday dawned, and we were still paralyzed. Our pre-attack schedule would have had us at the New England Dressage Association (NEDA) fall show in Massachusetts already. The City turned away all offers of help—they did not need any unskilled people underfoot. The blood banks said to wait and schedule donations in the future, so the overflow did not spoil. A vehicle was found under the George Washington Bridge full of explosives. I wanted to crawl into a corner and suck my thumb. And never go over a bridge or through a tunnel again. And never fly on another airplane. This was not a good outlook for someone who basically lives in the air while traveling to give clinics, judge shows, and ship horses overseas.

In the eleventh hour, when Mayor Rudolph Giuliani urged people to try to resume their normal lives, I asked one of our clients—who was also entered at NEDA—if she wanted to go. She said it was her favorite show, it would be good for morale, and what good did sitting around do? My husband David shook his head, but in the end he got behind the wheel of the van, and we were off. To us, going to a horse show over the weekend was normal behavior, but of course, there was nothing at all normal about this particular weekend.

After we went over the Throgs Neck Bridge, I felt we had accomplished something already. Fear is a horrible thing when it renders you immobile. The bizarre reality was that crossing that bridge (as we had done hundreds of times before over the years) became a first step toward "becoming alive" again.

Flags and Candles and Spiderman

The NEDA show was surprisingly well attended, considering the circumstances. Most Canadians were missing since they could not get across the border; some riders had suffered personal tragedies; and some, I am sure, just could not imagine attending any public event and opted to stay home. For those of us who went, being involved in some kind of "normalcy" helped to sift out our emotions and provided momentary respite from the sadness and anxiety. This was one time when I was grateful that dressage is such a low-key and introverted affair: It is almost impossible for a dressage event to be offensive, boisterous, and loud, all of which would not have worked on this particular weekend. Normally I am always a bit suspicious of riders who proclaim that they "don't care " if they win or place. ("Then, why compete?" has always been my attitude.) Well, this was one show when all I cared about was to keep moving; to get six to ten minutes in the arena when I had to concentrate on where I was going and when to give half-halts; to get a break from the mental images of a panicked family in a plane, knowing they were headed for a crash, or the imagined scene in an office high up in one of the towers when several trapped individuals chose to jump to a certain death, holding hands.

Massachusetts had flags everywhere on houses, on roads, on cars, and in the windows. Candles were lit outside of each house when we returned to Plymouth in the evening. The lady who served us coffee in the morning told us her five-year-old granddaughter looked at her in all seriousness and said, "But, Grandma, why don't they call in Spiderman?" We only wish!

Many of us dressage riders are European "imports." Some even make a point of keeping their accents "polished," since this helps maintain a bit of the "dressage mystique." I have been an American citizen since the mid-seventies. This country allowed me to make a living doing something I love, it permitted me to compete, and it invited me to represent it in international competition. My feelings for the United States and what it has meant to me have never been challenged in all my years here. But I realize I took so much for granted without ever realizing it. All that ended on September 11 and the days that followed, when I shared the pain, the fear, and the fury with the people I now know are my fellow Americans.

2011

"The three in the 'Magic Triangle' must tango in step with each other for a long and sometimes complicated dance."

II coaching and being coached

– 14 –

the magic triangle

At the 2001 North American Young Rider Championship (NAYRCH)* in Illinois, the individual gold medal in dressage was won by Lesley Eden from Central Florida. The team she was on, with only three riders and no drop score, also earned the gold.

Since Region Three achieved this feat three years in a row, it was no great surprise to see Gwen Poulin, Courtney Raiser, and Lesley Eden victorious among the ten teams competing, but it was just that much sweeter because they came into the competition with a handicap.

What raised some eyebrows was the ascent to the top of a rider who was virtually unknown except in her own region, had never competed at the Championships before, did not ride a horse somebody else had trained, and did not have independent means at her disposal.

---

* The Junior level was added in 2006 and NAYRCH became the North American Juniors and Young Riders' Championships (NAJYRC).

What is Lesley's secret? I can fill you in on some of it, since I trained her almost twenty years, and I believe her story can be an inspiration to kids who think that getting into her position is beyond their grasp.

A Perfect Match

In the fall of 1996, I was introduced to Lesley by Lisa Giltner, the owner of the barn in Orlando where we wintered for many years. Lesley was a tall, lanky, laid-back, coming sixteen-year-old. Picasso was a tall, lanky, elastic, coming six-year-old. While Lesley was quiet and almost shy, Picasso's apparent calm could turn from a yawn to a twister in an instant. This and some veterinary concerns (which luckily never became an issue), were the reasons he was affordable for Lesley to buy. Lesley and her mother, Lynn, decided that the horse's talent and good gaits made it worth taking a chance on him, and once committed they never looked back!

There were some times, for sure, when we all held our breath because the boy had taken a bad step or had a bellyache, which made everyone "run and fetch." In addition to being a wimp, Picasso was at first a very suspicious actor. His eyes would roll in his head when he saw me in the middle of the ring, and he would undulate his body away from me like a large snake, absolutely refusing to let me near him. It took almost a year for Picasso to decide that he liked sugar well enough to overlook the fact that I was the one handing it to him. Today he allows me to work the piaffe with a whip up close, and he is completely casual about anything I do around him. (When I arrived at Picasso's stall at the Championships and called his name, he ripped his head out of the hay and gave me an eye which clearly said: "Well, I figured you'd show up!")

Lesley and Picasso were a perfect match already when I met them, but they knew not where they were going. Thanks to the timing when we all got together, we were able to form the team of horse, rider, and trainer which, when all parties involved do their part, works better than any other method to produce results in the end.

An "A" Student

Lesley is the kind of student that warms a teacher's heart for several reasons: She listens and she works patiently on every exercise until she and the horse understand and can easily perform it. She is intelligent and patient, asks questions that make sense, and is willing to wait for results. Even when things looked glum at times, she trusted me when I told her they would improve with time and proper input to the horse.

One example was the flying changes: Leslie had done some changes on my schooled horses and a couple of others before we started them on Picasso, but she had never actually *taught* them to a horse. Fate would have it that her gelding would be a real pickle in the beginning. His first year of changes at the canter produced some of the most comical variations on the theme I have ever seen. Picasso would slow to an almost stop, dig his front feet into the ground, elevate his rear to the heavens, and do a spectacular handstand. While hovering in this position, he would move his hind feet like a cricket, change leads behind, and then somehow return to the canter. Although I tried not to, I would sometimes just crack up laughing, and then I would look at Lesley's face and it was obvious she was not amused. Her mother would ask me—when Lesley was not listening—"Do you think he will ever grasp this concept?" I assured her it was just a stage.

As sometimes happens, the movement that a horse has a very hard time coming to grips with can become one of his fortes when "the lights go on." This was true with Picasso, whose awkward beginning turned into lovely, flowing flying changes awarded both eights and nines in many tests.

In spite of the fact that I was not in Florida during the summers but worked with Lesley and her horse only in clinics, this young lady was able to keep her horse in shape and her work on track according to our plan. She never changed the agenda or doubted the ability of her horse or the veracity of my information. The only thing she might have doubted at times was her own ability to produce what her horse needed or what I wanted to see. A couple of months before the Championships, I said to Lynn, Lesley's mom, "If we are a little lucky, I believe she can get an individual medal." Lynn said: "Don't tell Lesley. Too much pressure!" So I never did. Perhaps that is why, in the picture of the award ceremony, the individual gold medalist has an expression of utter surprise on her face.

Three to Tango

This column is not all about the isolated case of Lesley. Her story shows that even today, when the quality of the horses, the demands on the proficiency of the riders, and the price of everything has gone way up, you can still reach the top with a good plan and a bit of luck. However, it takes three to tango. No rider gets anywhere without a decent horse, and very few riders get to the top without a coach.

Look at all the international stars, in particular the ones who come back again and again to the arena and win with one horse after the other. In almost every case there is a trainer attached, who may be a pain in the neck on a daily basis, but is indispensable when it comes to keeping horse and rider developing in the right direction. A good trainer knows when to push the rider and when to soothe the nerves, when to be relentless, and what pots not to stir. He or she must be as familiar with the horse's reactions to the training as he or she is with the rider's, and must know the limitations of the combination he or she is working with—as well as the strengths. Most of all, there must be a trust on the part of the rider and the horse in the trainer, and a strong loyalty working both ways. Every show is not a success story, and the support of the coach is just as important when things are not happening according to expectations. In return, the rider cannot find the trainer guilty every time there is a bad showing. The trio is still in it together, and the problems have to be solved in a united effort.

Without a support crew to surround this "Magic Triangle," such as parents, husbands, sponsors, grooms, and friends, it can easily break apart due to lack of finances, planning, and all kinds of needs, both physical and emotional, which develop over the long time it takes to train and show a horse toward a certain goal. But at the core, the three in the Triangle must tango in step with each other for a long and sometimes complicated dance.

2001

– 15 –

giving and receiving instruction

Nobody gets to be a decent dressage rider without getting some help along the way. But good help is hard to come by, and honest good help even more difficult to find.

There are thousands of self-proclaimed "instructors" around, and in actuality, most everyone in the United States is just that, since we do not have an objective system of instructor education and certification that is acceptable to all. There aren't official schools to attend, and we do not have a tradition of apprenticeship such as exists in Europe. Here the market place prevails, and quite simply, "let the buyer beware."

Theory vs. Practice

The biggest fallacy of all is that a successful competitor automatically makes a great instructor. A while ago, there was an excellent article on this subject written by Denise Cummins, Ph.D, published in one of our national dressage magazines. In part of the article Ms. Cummins explains why the accomplished rider does not necessarily make a good teacher.

She dwells on the difference between *declarative knowledge*, which consists of facts and theories of the domain, and *procedural knowledge*, which refers to the skilled steps or movements involved in the domain. In short, she is describing the difference between *theory* and *practice*. She points out that many experts ride using a technique that doesn't require reasoning, just "feeling" and an automatic response. The person who has been riding since he or she was four years old, she says, may be the worst teacher because to him or her, the skill is "as natural as breathing."

In reality *riding* and *teaching* are two completely separate skills, and it is rather unusual that both skills are present to an equal degree in one person. I have watched a number of competent, even "famous" riders who could not teach their way out of a paper bag. And I have seen mediocre performers on horseback who nevertheless can produce wonderful results with their students because they have a good eye for what is needed, a thorough understanding of the theory of dressage, and very importantly, an ability to communicate. The power to convey knowledge to another person has little to do with riding, but is an essential ingredient to make a good teacher.

The Problem with "Teacher-Hopping"

If you manage to locate an instructor who is a wonderful rider and who also has the ability to make you understand how to accomplish your goals, you can "have your cake and eat it, too." In the case when you cannot have it all, you are definitely better off with the competent teacher than with the "big name" who cannot teach. Unless you are a person who can learn by watching and has years to spend doing it, you need someone who can explain *why* and *how* to make you and your horse perform.

Your first dressage instructor is likely to become the most profound influence on your riding because he or she will responsible for laying the foundation of your riding and creating your "basic system." The longer you spend with this teacher, the firmer your base, upon which you will later build by receiving additional help and advice from other sources. The lack of a basic system is one of the problems in American dressage, created by a tendency to enjoy a "smorgasbord education": The minute something goes wrong in training we look for another instructor, and of course we also have to ride in every clinic offered within reach. God forbid we miss any of the action!

For the novice rider, "teacher-hopping" is confusing at best and damaging at worst, and for the horse it will eventually prove detrimental. A horse cannot absorb and adjust to a different method of training every two weeks without losing his confidence and perhaps his mind, as well. It does not matter if the various clinicians the novice works with are all excellent trainers, they are still not going to teach exactly the same way, and at this stage, more is *not* better. It takes many years of training and riding before a rider can truly profit from a clinic by incorporating the useful parts into his or her program while discarding the ideas that do not work for the horse. You have to be experienced enough to know the difference. The best way to make use of clinics while you are still a novice is to attend as an auditor, then discuss the experience with your regular instructor, and perhaps try some of the ideas you are interested in during a lesson.

A Healthy Relationship

To get the most out of your relationship with an instructor it is important that there is a mutual feeling of commitment, respect, and trust. A teacher shows his or her commitment, first and foremost, by giving exclusive attention to the student who is paying for the lesson. Conversations on the side and phone calls with others should be avoided if possible. This applies also to a clinic situation, when the temptation of playing to the audience at the expense of the student may be great.

At shows the serious instructor is available to school and advise the student before each ride, and will observe the ride and comment on it afterward. For a teacher with many students at the show, this may be impossible due to conflicting ride times, but a schedule can be made up ahead that divides his or her time and gives everyone an opportunity to get some help. However the test goes, a teacher of the right kind stands by his or her student in tragedy as well as triumph, and all post-test corrections and negative criticism that may be necessary are done one on one. A respectful instructor does not harass, make fun of, or belittle a student, never mind how frustrating the lesson or situation may be. There are times when a harsh command—even screaming—is called for, because the student is not reacting fast enough, but if the rider does not understand the command, raising the volume creates nothing but tension and further confusion.

The student has responsibilities as well. The first and perhaps most important is to *shut up and ride*! A lesson is no time for dialogue, and it is incredibly irritating to have someone contradicting every order or constantly explaining why whatever you ask for cannot be done. This kind of behavior also interferes with the flow of information between the horse and the rider, since the horse senses that the rider is not tuned in to the effort. Questions and explanations should wait until a break or rest period, unless there is some emergency the instructor needs to be made aware of. Complete concentration throughout the lesson, a commitment to practicing what is being taught (even outside of the teaching sessions), and consistency in pursuing the lesson program are all virtues belonging to the "good student."

When to Move On

There may come a time after a long relationship when the student feels there is no progress being made. Before placing the blame on the teacher (always the easy out), take a long hard look at yourself and ask: "How talented, how persistent, and how hard-working am I as a student?" And, "Do I have the right 'vehicle,' or is my horse not right for the job?" If, after some soul-searching, you are absolutely certain that the problem is not of your own making, talk to your instructor. There may well be a mutual feeling of frustration and stagnation. If the problems cannot be worked out and you decide to look for help elsewhere, you owe it to your present instructor to inform him or her about your decision, *before* he or she hears it from somebody else.

Wherever you go with your riding, remember, when success comes your way, give credit to each person who contributed to your progress. Not just the famous "final polisher" of your now wonderful self, but also the people who put up with you when you and everybody else thought you were hopeless!

1997

– 16 –

herbert rehbein

It is a rare occasion for most mortals to ever have an opportunity to observe a genius at work. I have listened to a number of "chosen ones" tell me in their own words how incredibly talented they are, but one person who never would say, or even think such a thing, was five-time Champion German Professional Dressage Trainer Herbert Rehbein.

The irony of being a genius is, perhaps, the fact that the true genius is unaware of his or her unusual gift, because they don't know what life is like in the slow lane...

A Man with Presence

The first time I met Herbert Rehbein was at a clinic at Five Star Farm in Pennsylvania a number of years ago. Gifted, Carol Lavell's Olympic mount, was only four years old and "along for the ride" while Carol was "being serious" about some other horse. (That should date it.) I rode Amazonas, a Trakehner gelding who did perform all the Grand Prix movements, although the one-tempis were never straight.

Mr. Rehbein watched us go through the program, commented in his encouraging way, and only raised his eyebrows when the horse's shoulder jumped all over at the ones. He put his hand up and stopped me. With one finger he indicated that he wanted to get on the horse. I jumped off, Herbert mounted. He rode exactly one 20-meter circle at the canter, and then he proceeded down the centerline doing thirty or more one-tempi changes that were so straight you could have put a ruler to them. I have all this on video, and it was—at the same time—one of the most humbling, uplifting, and amusing experiences I have ever had. The icing on the cake was that Amazonas performed his one-tempis straight from that day on.

A couple of years later, I went to Grönwohldhof, "Herr Rehbein's" barn in Germany, in the company of a student and our two horses. The facility outside of Hamburg is in itself an amazing experience in architecture and efficiency, but Herbert Rehbein outshone the venue without even trying. His presence was felt everywhere, and life at Grönwohldhof revolved around him. People and horses arrived from all over the world in a never-ending stream to avail themselves of his knowledge and hopefully have some of the magic rub off on them. Along with hundreds, perhaps thousands, of dressage enthusiasts over the years, I spent hours on the bench in the corner of the huge indoor school, watching Mr. Rehbein transform ordinary horses into artists, if only for the time he remained in the saddle. Animals would arrive who had absolutely no intention of performing one movement or another, and within minutes of being mounted by Mr. Rehbein, they would not only willingly display whatever he asked for, but they looked as if they enjoyed and understood it. No amount of watching will completely reveal to you the secrets of communicating with a horse, but it certainly was fascinating to follow the scenario of the horse going from "No way!" to "Perhaps I will," to "Whatever you say," and "How much do you want?" as it was repeated with horse after horse.

An Intoxicating "Feel"

Because Mr. Rehbein understood that watching is not always enough, he would on occasion allow his students to get on a horse he had just worked. A couple of times I was offered this privilege, and the "feel" of the horses after he had transformed them into soft, comfortable, bendable, and attentive partners was intoxicating. Unfortunately I would sober up in short order, since it rarely took the horse very long to realize that the masterful touch was gone and that he had no reason to play Pegasus for me.

Every successful trainer and winning show rider is expected to teach others. In the case of Herbert Rehbein I always felt this to be an unreasonable request. When somebody is incredibly gifted as a rider, I don't think their time ought to be spent on the ground with the, by comparison, "horsemanship challenged," unless they love to teach. In Mr. Rehbein's case I never had the feeling that he enjoyed teaching, and I think I understand why. Herbert Rehbein had intuition and a "feel" for horses that went way beyond the norm, and he simply could not always relate to us "normal" riders with problems, which to him, were not problems. Einstein, according to history, was not a very enthusiastic teacher of mathematics because the brains he had to work with were below standard compared to his. There were times when I would hear Mr. Rehbein repeat a command to a student with something akin to desperation in his voice, and other times when he would look into the arena, full of FEI horses going through their paces, and I would see his eyes glaze over. You could just see him thinking: "I cannot believe how difficult these people are making the obvious!" I would sometimes feel sorry for him, because genius can be a gift, but it can be a burden which isolates you as well.

In no other way, however, was Mr. Rehbein isolated. He never allowed his special gifts to interfere with his relationships with people; he showed no pride, no arrogance, and he was always helpful and friendly. Because Mr. Rehbein was so confident in his ability, he was always generous in giving credit to the accomplishments of others, and he was immensely popular and respected by his peers.

In May of this year I chatted with him at the Hamburg Derby where his wife Karin had another successful show with Donnerhall. He said he felt fairly well in spite of the cancer treatments. As always, Herbert was positive and supportive. He knew I was going home to have an operation I was nervous about, and as we said goodbye, he looked at me and said, "I will think of you." And I know he did.

When I woke up from the anesthesia following my surgery, my husband told me it looked as though the tumor they had just removed was benign. The next thing he said was, "I am sorry to tell you—we lost Herbert Rehbein this morning."

1997

— 17 —

the amateur—the backbone of every sport

Every one of us started out an amateur. As a follow-up to that profound statement, I'd like to point out another obvious fact: Sport in its true sense is inherently an amateur affair. As soon as the sports activity becomes a way to make a living and a business, considerations enter the picture, which to some degree dilute the pure pleasure of engaging in it.

From time to time, I have a working student who is so passionate about horses that not even the everyday trudge of horse husbandry can knock the bloom off the enthrallment. She or (on occasion) he may come to me and ask how to go about becoming a professional and be able to spend the rest of her or his life working and living with horses. In 99 percent of cases of working students wanting to "go pro," I will try to talk them out of the dream. Not because I don't consider myself incredibly lucky to have had the lifestyle I have, or because I regret a single moment, but because there is still an amateur within me who wants to be heard. If the "candidates" have any aptitude and means to continue their education, I always encourage them to go as far as they can along that route. Knowledge is never a burden to bear. Learning to use your head in any formal capacity is always a bonus, and the time of life when you are still free from other obligations and ready to receive on all levels does not return later. "Off to college!" is my battle cry—then, we will see.

Usually education eventually leads to some kind of profession, and as I explain to the kids at my barn, the best of all worlds is to have a job you enjoy that is productive enough to allow you to keep a horse and have time to ride. "But," says the youngster, "I want to be the best I can be; I want to ride internationally; I want to spend all day on a horse and become a star." For all the people who have expressed that desire, a very small percentage ever get close. Some of the rest may enjoy being in the "horse business," but many of them live with frustration because the true joy of their lives is now also a source of income, and therefore wrapped up in the unavoidable drawbacks of business: responsibility, stress, fear of competition, jealousy, financial worries, and time restraints, to mention only some of the baggage.

The Three Kinds of Amateurs

The definition of an *amateur* according to the USA Equestrian rule is complicated to the point that not even Janine Malone (our valued "Queen of Rules," a very prominent technical delegate and committee member) could make it crystal clear, although she made a valiant effort at untangling it in a *USDF Connection* magazine article. The simple definition of the word is a person who engages in horsemanship strictly for the pleasure of the sport and the love of horses with no financial gain and no desire to "run the show." That, of course, does not mean that the amateurs could not be more skilled at riding in any discipline than any professional, and that they could not be on the top of the game—anybody's game!

Teaching riding is a service profession, and during a career you get to meet and know every kind of amateur. I have found that they come in three groups, and luckily the best group is by far in the majority. People who love to ride and like to learn are fun to teach and a joy to be around. They listen, they appreciate your advice even when you holler at them, and they act on it. They ask questions, which are intelligent and challenging, and they make progress. When the "good" amateurs are ready to own a horse, they inform the professional of their choice, tell this person what kind of a horse is desired, and let the instructor go to work on the mission. They don't swerve from wanting an FEI schoolmaster to desiring a just-backed three-year-old every twenty-four hours. They are realistic about prices, and they expect to pay a commission for the expertise, work, and time of finding a suitable horse. Included in this fee is the anticipation that the instructor will stand by the new combination and help solve whatever problems may occur after the purchase. As time goes on, and success comes their way, this kind of amateur gives credit to their teacher without reservations and even says, "Thank you," after each session.

The most fun members of this first group are the kids. They come with open minds, supple bodies, and little fear. Why worry about the consequences of a possible fall when there are parents to deal with the details? Young people learn fast and are often rewarding to be around because their egos, pride, and worries don't trip them up. Kids rarely have any hidden agendas; they just love to ride and are able to soak up the information we give them with no barriers, physical or mental, to hinder the progress. Smart parents would rather see their little girl in the barn than hanging out in the mall, and in the long run keeping a horse is a far better option than drug rehabilitation. Smart men say "yes" to the horse activity their wives desire, because it is more fun to listen to the tales of the stable in the evening than the complaints about the kids and the decorator. (And it sure keeps the lady occupied with less time for Lord and Taylor.)

There are some minority deviations on the amateur theme. My least favorite kind of amateur is the person who may be a killer in the courtroom, a savior in the operating theater, or a whiz in the stock market, but is a total pain in the stable. This kind knows everything. The most absurd ideas in riding, training, and horse care pop out of this group, and the ultimate victim is the horse. The owner hangs over the farrier directing how every nail should go in, lectures the veterinarian, and comments on everything the instructor says. She or he asks advice from everyone and listens to none of it. When a horse purchase is at hand, the prospective owner again forges ahead, making all the decisions, and usually ends up with an animal that is lame, unsafe, or both. In the end the unsuitable combination becomes the headache of some poor trainer who gets stuck trying to make it work, and gets blamed if it does not. Money is usually no object, but the emotional price tag in dealing with this group is high.

The opposite end of the scale is not much better. This group is the wannabes, the groupies. These people hang on every word their trainer utters and will repeat them *ad nauseam*. They fawn and fetch and linger, demanding attention and hand-holding. Admittedly some trainers encourage this kind of dependency because they like the control it affords them, and they need their egos stroked to believe they are wonderful. Usually, but not always, the groupie struggles to afford the sport and hopes to make up for the lack of finances by exhibiting slavish submission. That is, until the object of their devotion does or says something they interpret as insulting or negligent. In an instant the love affair turns sour, and negative comments and actions ensue. Like a flock of geese, the groupies move on to find a new "famous" rider to shower their fickle loyalty on.

Have I exaggerated? Sure, but I know many professionals will smile with recognition at some of the above.

For Richer or Poorer

Equine sports have long been perceived as an activity reserved for the well-to-do. In spite of the explosive growth of dressage in this country, that impression still lingers. Yet we are surrounded by numerous examples of people of all ages, income levels, and stages in life who manage to feed their hunger for being near horses, even if it means sacrificing something else. These are the people whose desire for information about everything that concerns horses is insatiable, and they never feel deprived, as long as they can spend their time on and around a horse.

It is true that some very wealthy individuals are drawn to horses, and I believe the reasons for that are obvious. When you are able to buy it all, including power over people, you tend to look for other challenges. Stunts in airplanes, sailing around Cape Horn, and jumping a Grand Prix course are the kind of things that make you feel alive, because the outcome is uncertain and real skill is demanded. A horse does not care what he costs, he does not give a fig where you belong in society, and he does not suck up. There is a truth to the reactions of a horse that tells you who you really are. Therein lies the fascination with horses among people who can have anything they want from humans.

In the final analysis, the United States is the only place, except for a handful of European countries with strong equestrian traditions, where a good trainer can afford to make horses his or her life's work. If you are knowledgeable and consistent in producing horses and students who excel or at least make progress, you can make a living here spending your time just the way you dreamt as a child. We can teach; we can judge; we can compete, buy, and sell horses; we can design courses, run horse shows, and never have to check what time it is, because we don't care about coffee breaks.

All this is thanks to the amateur rider and owner, without whom there would be no need for any one of us.

2001

– 18 –

the first teacher

Being a riding instructor is certainly a labor of love. Consider the working conditions: every kind of weather, from icy winds to burning sun, in dust and rain, mud and snow. Even if you have an indoor arena to work in, it can be damp and cold and dark.

Be aware of the absence of job security in most cases, the lack of insurance, the cancelled lessons, and the risk of injury. Riding is far from a risk-free enterprise, and many of the worst accidents occur on the ground, while holding, loading, or working with a horse. And yet every one of us had someone who was willing to spend the time to help us take the first steps toward becoming comfortable and familiar with a horse. Your first teacher is often like your first love: unforgettable. Other instructors may follow, but the person who initially opened the door to the future on horseback lingers in your memory for life.

Some of us started in a riding school situation, others had private instruction at home, but whatever the case, without that initial help, we never would be riding and showing and training and perhaps even helping others learn today.

Tabula Rasa

As with my horses, the students I am most proud of are not only the ones I polished and guided to glory as one of their many teachers, but especially the ones I started from "scratch." And the students that tickle me the most are those who had to struggle to overcome fear or lack of coordination and still went on to be successful as riders and trainers.

The first teacher, no doubt, has the toughest job of all. But there is a certain satisfaction in starting a student from the very beginning, as well. With a *tabula rasa*, you are working with a virgin project undestroyed by preconceptions. Whatever you produce is your responsibility, and if it is good, all the credit is yours. The opportunity to work with a bright-eyed youngster or enthusiastic adult when they are complete beginners can be most inspiring. Usually the student is incredibly motivated to learn, which is a perk for any teacher. The mutual love of horses creates a bond between student and teacher from the very get-go. The joy of igniting the first sparks of understanding and the satisfaction of creating that basic platform for the student to fall back on in all his or her riding life is a high.

In general, the first teacher is seldom the instructor who stands by the gate when the student rides in the national finals or goes into the Olympic arena. By that time, several other trainers have most probably added to the pot of knowledge. But instead of feeling left behind when their students move on, true educators feel part of that process, and they know that laying the foundation is their true mission in the chain of events.

Even so, starting over is not always fun. It really is not fun when, just as there is a breakthrough, the student has a fit of hubris, and feels it is time to seek more sophisticated help. Interestingly, these two events often dovetail, since the student, as he or she improves, is suddenly "discovered" by others and therefore instantly impressed by him- or herself. The mature and confident person who enjoys the position as the "original" teacher will realize and take pride in his or her role in

bringing recognition to the student, but also understand the student's urge to move on, which comes with the territory. The mature student who can see beyond his or her own ambition will give notice, thanks, and credit to his or her first teacher. The student who cuts out without any warning or sign of gratitude belongs in the jar on your desk labeled "Ashes of Ex-Students."

Mentor for Life

Having a competent first teacher often means having a mentor for life, if you handle the transition when you move on correctly. And as time goes by, the student may find opportunity to go back and seek advice and support from the original source. Sometimes, even when that source is gone, it will seep knowledge from the back of your mind. As you become more knowledgeable, you may discover that the old wisdom comes forth in a whole new light. Remember how stupid your parents were when you were fifteen, and how nicely they had matured when you turned thirty? It works the same on horseback. Sometimes it takes a long time for the muscle memory to take over and the brain to click in gear.

My very first teacher happened to be my grandfather. Being a cavalry man all his life, he was rather demanding. The horse material was perhaps not the most suitable for a rank beginner, since what lived in his fields were usually young remounts who were barely broke. Grandpa would lovingly pick me off the ground each time the horse delivered me to Mother Earth, make me catch the horse, and then put me back on board. Bareback, with the sweat of the horse burning my legs and that warm horse fragrance in my nose, I was in heaven. Eventually I got a proper outfit and moved on to a regular riding school, but I never will forget the pleasure and pain of those summer days in southern Sweden and the voice of my first instructor patiently repeating the basic rules of riding, which still ring true today.

If you get pointed in the right direction from the very beginning, you will forever have a solid foundation to build on, which makes your entire riding experience a journey forward. It is then safe to go on and experiment with clinics and try all kinds of horses without losing your direction or having to backtrack. Lots of interesting and expensive experiences can be bought using a MasterCard, but when you are in trouble and have a solid basic education to fall back on...priceless!

2007

– 19 –

dressage and fly fishing

Each year I give a series of clinics in Oregon, which is God's country and populated by people who appear to appreciate living in that gorgeous part of the world. Before leaving one spring, I was asked what I'd like to do on my day off. Fly fishing was one of the options, and I immediately went for it.

As a child I spent thousands of hours fishing with my father in the archipelago of Stockholm, and I thought I knew how to fish. So, I was pretty cocky when I arrived at the lovely Steamboat Inn on the North Umpqua River. Then I read up on the history of the Steamboat Inn,* realized that perhaps this was not fishing the way I knew it, and found out a little about the really famous fly fishers in the area. The star of them all was some guy named Frank Moore. In the evening I was casually told that "Frank would take me fishing," but not in my wildest dreams did I ex-

---

* *The Steamboat Inn is located in the middle of 31 miles of "fly-fishing-only water" on the North Umpqua, a river famous as home of some of the most challenging steelhead fishing in the world.*

pect it to be *THE* Frank. Well, a while later when I was informed that it was indeed *THE* Frank I could barely sleep that night. Imagine the Training Level hopeful who gets told that gold-medal-winning German Olympian Harry Boldt will be there to give a lesson in the morning! I was pretty nervous as we were driving to meet Frank and his wife at their huge log cabin, and fairly baffled by the "waders" the handsome eighty-year-old had me put on. Properly outfitted, fishing rods in hand, Frank and I proceeded to the bank of the swiftly running river, and so started my course in Fly Fishing 101.

Lessons from a Master

In spite of all my fishing experience, this was "a whole new game within the game," just as if I—the dressage rider—were handed a saddle horse and told to go exhibit all five gaits. For hours this infinitely patient hero of fly fishers explained and showed me again and again how to control the line in the backstroke, how to keep it flowing straight out behind you, and how to use the lower arm and wrist to land the line in the river where you actually aimed for it to be. It was all about balance, feel, and measured muscle power—a lot like when you first learn to put a horse on the aids. And just the same way, sometimes the magic worked, and sometimes it didn't!

Between sessions, Frank would take the rod and show me "how it should really look," showing off some of his variations on the theme, such as "rolling" the line over the water until it almost reached across to the other side of the river. It reminded me of watching Herbert Rehbein get on a horse belonging to another rider and within minutes, having the horse transform into a different animal in front of our very eyes.* I saw this happen so many times, and still it would give me goose bumps to get a

---

* *Read about my experiences with Herbert Rehbein earlier in Part II (p. 75).*

glimpse of what even a mediocre horse could do with a genius rider to guide him.

When my "technique" had advanced somewhat beyond catching bushes behind me and plunging the tip of the rod into the river, Frank decided to up the ante. "Let's go," he said, and before I had time to ask where, he had grabbed my hand and dragged me into the water. With the greatest of ease, Frank leapt like a frog from rock to rock, while I shuffled behind him with terror in my heart. He kept a firm hold of my hand as we proceeded with the whirling water sometimes as high as my waist. I was reminded of early longe lessons without stirrups or reins, when the horse would get silly and start playing and bucking. Stay within the center of gravity, and trust your instructor not to let go of that pony, and it may end well. Lose your balance and your faith, and you bite the dust! Eventually, I learned that looking for a spot to put your feet in this river was useless, since the foaming waters revealed nothing, and the current would knock them out of place anyway. You just had to feel your way with your feet like they teach you on the balance beam in gymnastics.

Finally, we stood on the edge of a rock in the middle of the river with six feet of rapidly moving water below us, some of it up to our knees, and Frank said: "Start fishing!" All I could think was, "If one of those wild salmon bites now, it will rip me off this rock, and they will find my remains downstream." It was the same feeling I had when I entered the dressage stadium in Aachen, Germany, and the doors closed behind me, and the wall-to-wall people, all with two eyeballs, seemed to engulf me. But somehow once you get to X, it is all about your horse again, and the game takes over. So I started swinging the rod, and the line seemed to float further into the river and be more supple than before. That same positive excitement that competition can give you was similar to the kick that the river supplied, and no energy makes you feel so alive.

The Big Catch

"What did you catch?" asked my husband when I finally stopped gushing over my adventures at the river. Not until then did it occur to me that I never landed a fish, just had a few "bites," one by a good fighter salmon, which cut the line on a rock and split. So, I didn't get a ribbon, but it did not matter. I had forgotten about catching anything; it was all about surviving and learning and being so involved, you had no sense of time passing.

It was a lot like riding a good horse and trying to find that feeling of effortless flow you know lives some place, but keeps evading you. Except for a precious moment here and there, when you can sit quite still and just melt into your horse while he carries you forward like a cloud moving in the breeze.

2003

III finding "the one"

– 20 –

looking for your dressage horse: the process

How to buy the right horse must be one of the most talked- and written-about subjects in the horse field, and yet a disaster purchase occurs every minute. Even after watching people buy horses over many years, I still marvel over the multiple mistakes and wonder why horse buying remains such a mystery to otherwise perfectly sensible and capable people. Let's go over some of the basic premises and pitfalls again.

The Job Description

Before you set the wheels in motion, sit yourself down and ask yourself these questions: "What do I really want to accomplish with the animal, and how much can I realistically produce as a rider? Am I capable of locating and selecting the horse myself, or should I work with a professional who can advise me and at least help me to avoid a serious mistake?"

If you intend to take instruction on your prospective horse, it makes all the sense in the world to involve your teacher in the selection. A horse that is inspiring to the instructor is obviously going to make lessons more productive for everyone. Even if you do not have a regular teacher, and unless you have a lot of experience, it is prudent to get advice from someone who knows more than you do. Whatever you spend on a commission or fee paid to your advisor will be nothing compared to the cost of ending up with the wrong horse.

In your search, keep in mind what your objectives are and try not to stray from your original plan. If you need and want to learn yourself, no four-year-old in the world will do the job for you. It does not matter how fabulous the young horse is, you will need an experienced trainer to school him, or you will lose your investment and ruin a promising horse in the end. The older horse, and I am talking mid-teens into twenties, that is serviceably sound and well-schooled is the ticket to quick and safe learning. You cannot go wrong by buying or leasing an old campaigner, even if he only has a few years left of working life, because not a moment will be wasted on "young horse nonsense." Instead, you can concentrate one hundred percent on your riding education, since all the physical and mental problems involved with training young horses are bypassed. It is not likely that you will be able to "steal" such a horse since people are becoming aware of their value, but naturally the horse will be priced according to his age, training, and degree of usefulness. With good care and a bit of luck the old schoolmaster can be rideable into his thirties, and you may find yourself teaching somebody else on him. The "American Way" for a long time has been to attempt to "learn along with your young horse," but as every instructor knows, this scenario is a disaster waiting to happen, and even if it succeeds once in a while, it takes forever! Things go much more smoothly if one of you knows what you are doing...

Viewing and Trying

Once you have decided what the job description of your horse is, the legwork of finding the right one starts. After the initial contacts have been made, usually over the phone, it is "movie time." Videos are the way of the world today, but I am no convert. Yes, it is very convenient to sit in your easy chair at home and view horses from all over the world. No travel, no hassles, and you can see what the horse is capable of doing. Period. Videos somehow distort the movement of horses in a way that equalizes them. Extravagant movers tend to appear ordinary, while the common movers get a bit of help from the two-dimensional image to seem more promising than they are. Precious little of the animal's personality or presence shows through, and of course you cannot ride him. Too many choices with too many videos tend to confuse the average viewer; everybody in the neighborhood puts their two cents in, nobody can agree on anything, and in the end nothing gets done. If you see a horse on a video that appeals to you, stop picking him apart, climb out of your chair, and go see him in person! After a few minutes on his back, you will know if he is an option. The view from the saddle is the one that ought to be your absolute priority.

If you don't buy horses on a regular basis, you may be apprehensive about trying them in front of people you don't know and perhaps a bit worried about what a strange horse may do. Always ask to see the horse ridden by someone else before you get on, so you can decide if the horse is too much for you to handle. As long as safety is not an issue, you ought to sit on every horse that is at all interesting when viewed from the ground. Many times a horse "feels" a great deal different than you expected, and that works both ways. I have ended up buying horses that did not drive me wild with desire when I watched them go but were so pleasant to ride, I could not resist. I have also drooled over animals from the ground that I could not wait to get off once I tried them. There has to be a certain "chemistry" between horse and rider, and to give that a chance to develop, you have to try to forget the situation and ride as you would at home. If your instructor is there with you, ask for help in trying to produce a movement you have already observed that the horse does well (in person or on video) but that you may have problems getting from him on your own. If you are alone, ask the horse's regular rider to help you request the movement, but watch out! You don't want to end up in a whirlwind sales lesson that makes it difficult to concentrate on the horse instead of the other rider's commands.

When it comes to trying out schooled dressage horses, you may find that the first ride is not the dream come true you had envisioned when watching the horse go through his paces with his regular rider. Often the educated horse is less tolerant of a new rider than the green horse that "does not know better." The horse with knowledge comes with expectations of certain aids given in a certain way, and a brand new set of directions may not work all that well the first time around. Remember that the reason you are looking for a schooled horse is so *you* can learn from *him*, which means you will have to figure out what he expects from you, and that takes time. Be especially careful not to dabble with endless attempts at tempi changes, which are likely to drive the sensitive horse to desperation when he does not feel comfortable with your aids. (Never mind what the horse's trainer will have to say about you for the next week or two...)

Rules to Buy (and Not Buy) By

A few pointers to keep in mind:

- If you are short, avoid horses that are too tall and big-barreled, because chances are you will run out of gas or lose control if the horse has the total physical advantage. Huge horses have been very fashionable from time to time, but it takes a strong and clever rider to bring out the best in the giants of the world. On average, the oversized horses are not the most athletic movers, and they also tend to be difficult to keep sound.

- Don't get hung up on breed. The beauty of dressage is that *any* breed can play; it is the individual that counts. By limiting yourself in this area, you cut down on your chances of finding the right horse, and the good ones are hard enough to locate! Remember that all Warmbloods are basically the same, and that it is the area where they stem from that gives them their names and brands. Also keep in mind that the best athletes in the horse world are Thoroughbreds, and although it is difficult for us sport-horse riders to get our hands on the really good ones, never pass up a chance to go see a Thoroughbred that is recommended. I have had some of the best rides in my life on American Thoroughbreds, and I only wish I could have my first Grand Prix horse, Tappan Zee (by Royal Charger, with two huge bowed tendons from his racing days) back, so I could ride him in a way that would better do him justice.

- My least favorite color is gray, and yet two of my best horses to date were grays. When you look at horses to buy, you must become color-blind, or you may miss the very best.

- Don't buy the trot. That is the gait that can be changed and developed the most by good riding. Concentrate instead on the canter, since so much of the upper level work has to be performed at this gait, and watch out for an impure walk, which is very difficult to improve upon.

- The perfect conformation does not exist, and if you should run into it, the horse is probably crazy as a loon.

- There is no free lunch, so expect to put up with some flaws, or you will "tire-kick" forever, and the opportunities will sail by.

- If the first horse you see happens to display everything you ever wished for, it is permissible to buy him, in spite of the fact that he was the first one you saw.

- A horse is not a better ride because he came from very far away. The equine of your dreams may be standing in your neighbor's field; why not have a look? Christine Stückelberger told me she almost did not buy her international Grand Prix horse Lucky Lord because he lived next door, and therefore could not possibly be any good. We both had a good laugh over our vanities and how the grass is always greener somewhere else!

Horse-Shopping Etiquette

To end, a few tips on proper etiquette, which ought to be part of natural behavior, but unfortunately are not:

- When you cannot make it to an appointment to see a horse, *call*. A lot of time and effort goes into preparing the horses that are to be shown, and the least you can do is let the seller know that you will not be there. The same people who would not dream of ignoring a business meeting will simply "not show up" to see a horse, leaving barn staff waiting for hours with horses groomed and ready. The horse world is very small, however, and more likely than not you will run into the people you stood up at some point down the road. They will remember you, but not the way you would like to be remembered.

- Secondly, if a horse is shown to you that you know is not for you, just say no. You don't have to give any reason other than that you are not interested in that particular horse. Every seller appreciates not having his or her time wasted, but none likes to have his or her horse picked apart and criticized.

Few things in life are more satisfying to me than selecting the right horse for a particular person, and few things more frustrating than the process of finding him. However, when I know I have helped form a great combination of horse and rider, it is worth all the research, the phone calls, the travel, the video sessions, and the negotiations to get them together. It is almost like a dating service, where every agent's goal is that human and equine be happy forever after.

1997

– 21 –

the cast of characters

"What a character" in American English refers to someone who has a funny or quirky personality. In equine lingo, "character" means a horse's basic personality—the way he thinks or acts. And we sure know there are a lot of different characters out there!

As life with horses rolls along, we get to meet a variety of horse personalities, and although I doubt I have seen them all, I have a fair idea of the different groupings by now.

Starting with the premise that there is no perfect horse, or human for that matter, we still always look for the ideal match to ourselves, which we then consider the "ultimate" equine. In horses, as in people, usefulness and success depends almost entirely on how the mind works. The fastest racehorse, most talented jumper, and most extravagantly moving dressage horse are all useless if their brains do not support their performance.

The Lawn Ornaments

The largest group of horses, I believe, consists of the friendly but unmotivated ones. They may or may not have a great aptitude for something, but it hardly matters since they are only happy when they do nothing. Incredibly difficult to motivate, this group avoids being trained by passively resisting the movement of any muscles except those used to chew their feed. Begging and forcing these critters around a dressage arena is usually more painful for the rider than the horse, since the energy crisis is always lurking and "work" is a four-letter word.

Members of this group make lovable pets and pretty lawn ornaments, and they are usually easy keepers. Just pass the grain by the stall. They also sleep well at night and any time of day.

The Chili Peppers

The polar opposite are the "hot chili pepper" group. Here the excitement starts at dawn's early light, with a vigorous romp around the stall, some weaving, cribbing, and kicking to get the day started, and perhaps a blowup in the cross-ties to demonstrate readiness and lack of patience. Once the rider is up, there will be no waiting for the aids, because a horse of this type is "Triple A," and he can do all the movements from the Grand Prix simultaneously. What he really does not need is interfering input from the saddle. This dude is so into his game, he does not notice his surroundings, the temperature, the end of the arena, or any of the details in life. He just goes, and you'd better enjoy the ride!

Although all this energy is commendable, this workaholic is in many ways just like his human counterpart: He has no time to listen, learn, and wait, and he rarely enjoys the fruit of his labor, because he is too charged up to stop for a lump of sugar. Advantages: The motor is always running, never mind the weather or conditions, and the horse never pouts or gets sour—he's too wrapped up in his own fast-forward world to even know how to get in touch with his inner self.

The Prisoner of Instinct

The worriers are the next group. Here the environment is all-important, and it is the enemy! I realize that horses are animals of flight, but a horse of this type carries the instinct to the extreme. He is on high alert twenty-four-seven, and revels in his own paranoia. Just to keep things interesting, trains, fire engines, and helicopters can go by unnoticed, while a rustling leaf or a sunspot in the arena will cause hysterics. There is always tension present to ruin the Training Scale* and hinder learning. This horse never really allows you to ride him, since he is so challenged by life. A fair degree of talent and energy is not unusual in the mix, but unfortunately most of it is spent jumping sideways and going in all the wrong directions. Only the very patient and somewhat masochistic professional can tolerate this kind of animal, since he can be unpredictable and unsafe to ride and tends to let you down at shows by going into vigilant mode at the expense of concentration.

Note: I know of several horses in this category that went on to international glory with the right rider. But only then does it work.

The Hypochondriac

The horse that is "imaginary sick" is another difficult animal to live with. He is never really fit to ride because he has a slight physical "hiccup," which is seldom the same two days in a row. He is a tiny bit stiff behind, a tad sore in front, has a slight cough or a swollen eye, all in succession. As soon as there is an important event coming up, he is unfortunately

---

* *The Training Scale in order of requirements consists of: Rhythm, Suppleness, Contact, Impulsion, Straightness, and Collection.*

indisposed. Just the mention of a horse show makes him hold his breath until he pops a splint. The most irritating thing about this character is that he can be very sound and useful at times when nothing is at stake. I call this type the "excuse horse," and in its extreme form, he becomes suicidal, cutting himself on objects nobody can find, getting repeatedly cast in the same corner, sliding into the gate and pulling all suspensories.

Of all the types of horses, this one is the real heartbreaker, because he always keeps you hoping he'll be fine once you patch him up again.

The Playboy

And then, of course, there are the breeding stallions. Over the years, I have ridden about a dozen of them in competition. They all thought the world of themselves, were rarely more than 75 percent tuned in to the present, and required constant massaging of their egos. In return, they provided power and presence and sometimes brilliance, and a considerable amount of attitude.

Most horses, like us people, have a strong need to feel secure, and stallions are no exception. An insecure stallion can easily turn into a real turkey in an instant, and then he is a lot more horse to handle than a mare or a gelding. No group of horses can be more awe-inspiring, and yet, as international competitor Lisa Wilcox* said in her excellent article on riding stallions in *Dressage Today*, there is always "behavior" to be expected when you ride a stallion. I will admit that when you manage to bond with a stallion, it is a very special feeling, and although it has only happened to me a couple of times, I am working on developing a more balanced view on the subject.

---

* *Lisa appeared earlier in Part I (see p. 29).*

The Ideal

Even the ideal horse will have some of the characteristics I've mentioned here, but none of them will dominate the picture.

He will be energetic, but not tense; careful with his own body and with yours; focused on his rider and willing to learn. He will enjoy showing himself off and never abandon you in a test. If you manage to find and keep but *one* of these in a lifetime, count yourself among a very lucky few!

2004

— 22 —

ode to the ancient

Age is relative, in horses as in people. Dressage horses, like their riders, stay in the game longer than most of their peers in other disciplines. In fact I think few sportsmen, with the possible exception of the archers, can compete with our distinction as the "oldest athletes in activity."*

A Slow Ripening

The dressage horse destined for work at the FEI levels normally does not even learn all his lessons until he is at least nine years old. There are some who are able to march along more quickly, and a few horses show at Grand Prix by their eighth year. In skilled hands a mentally and physically strong talent can handle such a lifestyle and perhaps even stay sound, but it is not for every horse.

The norm for a horse that was started as a four-year-old is to be able to perform all the Grand Prix movements by the time he reaches ten years

---

* I examine this subject closely in "The Ageless Sport" in Part I (p. 31).

of age. After he is familiar and comfortable with all the requirements, there is usually a two-year period I call "ripening," during which the horse comes to the realization that he does not have to learn anything new, and consequently, he relaxes into the cool frame of mind of someone who has truly mastered his subject. His body also builds to the peak of its strength during this period, making the movements seem less complicated and the tests easier to perform. Somewhere between eleven and fifteen years of age comes the very best time of a dressage horse's performance life.

An additional feature that often appears a year or so after a horse has learned his last Grand Prix movement is a show of increased pride. Many horses who were not previously great personalities suddenly take on a showman attitude of, "Watch me blow your socks off!" Even the shy and silly ones suddenly gain confidence and want to strut their stuff. It is a great feeling when a horse wants to perform to please himself and starts sparkling on his own.

A Gentle Fading

Signs of advancing age usually make their appearance sometime after age fifteen, although in many horses, not until they reach their twenties. The horse takes longer to warm up, develops a hitch in the "getalong," and eventually shows that he has to struggle to keep his work up to par. If the animal is basically sound and wants to work, let him! If he needs a little medication to keep him comfortable, let him have it.

The educated horse that is used to regular work does not fare well physically or mentally by suddenly being retired, any more than people who are forced into retirement. With a good maintenance program and a work schedule suited to his needs your old-timer can last and function happily into his late twenties, and we have had several horses prove that to us. Trenzado was one shining example: He was a Chilean Thoroughbred who had several careers. He started life as a racehorse, then competed in jumping and eventing and went on to be a successful FEI dressage mount, shown in this country by his owner, Grand Prix rider Linda Oliver. At age seventeen, Trenzado developed wind problems, and Linda's veterinarian recommended a change of climate, preferably close to the ocean. Linda asked if we wanted to "adopt" him, and we were delighted to bring him to Long Island. For close to ten years he was our honorable "Professor of Dressage," generously sharing his knowledge with dozens of riders. He was the perfect teacher, because he gave nothing away for free but would basically ignore the rider until he or she got their act together. Then he would do whatever was asked without fussing, and he did not mind repeating the movement until the rider became confident. Trenzado enjoyed a great deal of respect around the barn, and students had to earn the right to sit on him.

Twice we tried to retire Trenzado. The first time, when he was about twenty-three, we turned him out in the stallion paddock, which had five feet of solid oak fencing around it. After two hours he had enough, sailed over the gate, and came looking for company. A pony was turned out with him for company, and he tried to kill it. He was hand-walked, and after two days of no work he stopped eating. He hated the flies, refused to romp in the pasture, and demanded we pay attention to him. Back to work he went, and all was well. Our second attempt a few years later proved a similar fiasco, and it was now clear that this was a horse that wanted no part of retirement. If he was not allowed to do what he was proud of, he would rather self-destruct.

Finally the solution arrived in the shape of a lovely couple from Massachusetts. They were not young and ambitious but they wanted to practice some dressage, promised to ride and fuss with Trenzado every day, and had a beautiful barn on their property with plenty of trails. When we watched the three of them heading for the trailer, we knew things would work out. Trenzado lived with his new friends past his thirtieth birthday, and every Christmas we received a long letter from "him" telling us all about his life and continued happy work.

Billy Joe Freckles, a 15-hand Appaloosa stallion trained to Grand Prix by Roemer Foundation/USDF Hall of Fame Inductee Chuck Grant* and quite a competitor in his day, was another horse that worked well into his twenties and had a great deal of influence on the education of a number of riders. I bought him over the phone when he was about twelve or thirteen, and I never regretted it. In addition to his Grand Prix knowledge, Freckles performed a variety of tricks, including bowing, counting, sitting, and "playing dead."

Once when I tried to entertain a visitor with Freckles' abilities, I got him flat on the ground. When I asked him to get up, however, he just remained motionless on the arena floor, watching me with a look of glee in his bull eye. I probed and pleaded and pulled to no avail. After a while it stopped being funny, and I got worried about him being down for so long. I ran into the office and called Chuck Grant, explained the problem, and asked Chuck what the proper "aids" were to get him up. He told me what to do—and suggested I buy his book! Luckily, as we were on the phone, Freckles got bored and sat up. (I did buy the book, figuring that if we had another breakdown in communications it would be handy to have the manual.)

When Freckles was close to eighteen, he went through surgery for an inguinal hernia and after recovery, including a bout with salmonella, he was even better than before. Although crabby at times when he got into the "twenty-something" era, he functioned well and was always ex-

---

* *Chuck Grant trained seventeen competitive dressage horses, and was a noted instructor and author of books on riding and training. He is credited with introducing dressage to the Midwest in the United States, and is known for insisting dressage was for every horse, regardless of breed.*

tremely proud of his knowledge. The list could go on, and I am sure most of you could add to it one or several horses you know of who bloomed after ten, improved in their teens, and held their own for much longer than expected.

True Value

When a horse hits the "magic twelve" the insurance goes up, the price starts declining in other than very exceptional performers, and the horse is considered "aged." I could never quite understand why insurance companies perceive the teenage horse as a greater risk, since in my opinion the mature horse that is all business and has lived through "childhood" diseases and accidents is less of a liability. Unlike those of us people who would like to pretend that life starts at forty, the best years of a dressage horse are truly his mature ones. Never think of a horse as finished because he has reached a certain birthday, and avoid looking for problems that are not there. This can be especially tempting for dressage judges who have seen a horse for years and tend to jump to the conclusion that every false step the horse takes is a sign of impending doom. Evaluate the individual and keep in mind all the people who reached the pinnacle of their careers late in life. The true value of a well-trained dressage horse stays the same as long as he can perform.

1996

– 23 –

a question of soundness

"Serviceably sound" is not an expression applica-
ble to the competitive dressage horse. Perhaps you
could use it in reference to the schoolmaster that
stays at home, but in the competition ring, there
is no such thing. Because any hint of irregularity
in the normal gait of a horse is severely penalized,
"sound" in the dressage competition horse means
one hundred percent.

Consequently, affirming and preserving the soundness of your dressage
horse becomes even more of an issue for the dressage horse owner than
for most other disciplines. An exception is the eventing world—when
your life depends on the soundness of your horse, you tend to focus on
that issue!

The Pre-Purchase Crystal Ball

After much effort and a long search, you have finally found your new
equine dressage partner, and you breathe a sigh of relief. Well, you are

relaxing before your time. One of the greatest obstacles to your union, the pre-purchase exam, still remains.

In my opinion, this feature of horse buying and selling, although important, has taken on proportions that go beyond the call of duty. While I perfectly agree that one ought to find out as much as possible about the status of health of the horse one considers buying, there is an aspect of the procedure that I do not favor; I call it the psychic phenomenon.

If you went to your doctor and said, "Doc, I'd like for you to take X-rays of my skeleton and once you have studied them, tell me if I'll be doing the tango five years from now," you would be gently escorted to the psychiatric ward. Nevertheless, this is in essence what we say to our veterinarians in regards to the X-rays included in most pre-purchase exams. From pictures of hooves, hocks, stifles, and joints we expect the vet to read into the future of a horse, as if he or she had a crystal ball. And if he or she proves to be wrong after we buy the horse, there could well be a lawyer waiting in the wings... No wonder some DVMs refuse to perform pre-purchase exams!

A More Reasonable Process

A sane approach to a pre-purchase exam would be to follow these steps:

1. Inform your veterinarian of the job description of your future horse— that is, is he going to be campaigned as a show horse, used as a learning tool, working with more than one rider, and so on. In short, what are your expectations of his soundness?

2. Be present for the clinical exam, which is, in reality, the most important part of the procedure. Make sure the veterinarian sees the horse perform under saddle, or longed if the horse is too young to be ridden, and listen to his or her comments as he or she watches the horse in motion. Observe the flexion tests, the work with the hoof tester,

Unconventional Wisdom

*Un*supplementation

One day a while ago I walked into our feed room and reeled back from the chemical odor. I looked at my assistant Anna and said, "What *is* that smell?" Anna turned her shark look (cool, calculating, and in control) on me and said, "All those supplements."

I sat down and went through our list of "extras" and it was somewhat frightening. Anna watched, arms folded. In the end, she had but one pragmatic comment: "And none of them are simple vitamins and minerals!" True, it was everything else, in exact measured quantities and at great expense, relentlessly going in the feed every day. But what really made me think was the smell. One of our older horses is "high maintenance," and suddenly he would not eat at all, because his food was loaded with supplements, medications, and strange potions, and it stunk. As his fat melted away, we tried to tempt him with molasses and other "cover-ups," to no avail. Finally we removed the majority of his supplements and all but the most necessary medications. He was served clean oats and a pellet mixture, and instantly his appetite revived. Miraculously, he stayed sound, sane, and allergy-free with a minimum of additives.

He also did not starve to death.

---

the eye and heart and lung exam. If any of them are not performed, ask for them to be. Discuss the results.

3. Ask if there is anything the doctor sees that indicates X-rays need to be taken. Routine X-rays are fairly expensive, and your decision may have to be measured against the price of the horse, as well as the advice of your veterinarian.

4. If the horse has passed the physical, wait for the X-rays to be developed,* and then listen to the results without panicking about veterinary terms, which may sound horrid but have no meaning for the future of the horse. Remember that you have hired a DVM to give you all the information available about the physical state of a certain horse at a certain time. When the information has been made available, it becomes your responsibility to sort out the details and to make the decision whether to purchase the animal or go on with your search. The area where you need to be particularly careful about making any rash decisions concerns the X-rays. The pictures have severe limitations in that they show primarily bone problems, revealing little about tendons, ligaments, muscles, joint capsules, or cartilage. They can tell you if there is an abnormal area, but not if it is causing the horse pain currently or if it ever will. X-rays can be invaluable as a diagnostic tool when the horse is lame and you are looking for specific answers, but they can also get between you and that "perfect" horse and break you up for no reason at all.

The "Clean Picture" Fallacy

I have X-rayed horses before buying them for almost thirty years, and the only wisdom I have gained is that they aren't security against future lameness, and sometimes they even lie. Anybody who has spent time around horses knows that "clean pictures" mean nothing when the animal they belong to is always "a little off," and that there are scores of horses out there working and winning with X-rays that indicate they ought to be cripples.

My favorite diagnosis is navicular syndrome, the good old standby when we cannot figure out what really ails the horse. Some years ago it was

---

* *Now this happens in minutes, with new technology.*

so fashionable that a horse could hardly stumble once without evoking the "N" word, which made all owners tremble in their shoes. Any indication of "mushrooms" or even little nobs on the navicular bones in the pre-purchase X-rays would be cause for rejection and a perfect excuse to turn a horse down.

During the "Navicular Era," I bought a colt at the Trakehner auction in Germany that looked sensational during the sale but limped off the plane in New York. At that time, X-rays were not part of the action routine, so the colt had his first set done after arrival. His front navicular bones looked like an atomic war, and we were advised to put him down, since he was not even broken yet, and would never be of any use with those pictures! Doom and gloom set in, until I asked our very experienced farrier to take a look. After some probing—which sent the colt through the roof—the man said he thought the colt had a heel infection. This is a very deep-rooted kind of thrush, which the horse could have contracted from being turned out in wet marshy land for long periods. Three weeks of aggressive treatment with udder ointment and presto, no more navicular!

That horse's name was Amazonas, and he went on to many years of showing through Grand Prix, was USET long listed, and was sold twice, horrid X-rays notwithstanding.

1998

– 24 –

putting age, size and soundness in perspective

The other day I was talking with an experienced profes-
sional about a Grand Prix horse that was for sale. When
I mentioned that the horse would soon turn twelve, the
knee-jerk reaction of this person was, "Oh, then he will
drop in price, because twelve is the magic number."

Says who? Well, the insurance companies, for one, since they tend to
make the premiums steeper after age twelve.* Perhaps that is why our
minds make a mental slash at this age, although, especially in our game,
that is completely absurd. In real life, twelve is indeed the magic age, but
in a totally positive way.

Good Things Take Time

As we all know, there are dressage horses that have been able to produce
all the movements in Grand Prix at age seven or eight, but they are a

---

* See further discussion of the "magic number" on p. 111.

product of unusual talent, and mental as well as physical strength. And they are ridden by experienced and competent riders who have traveled the route many times before. A handful of them go on to glory on the international scene, but many simply disappear as quickly as they appeared and are never heard from again. To me, the exceptions prove the rule that "good things take time," and more often than not a horse that reaches his first public performance in Grand Prix sometime between ages ten and twelve will bloom in his mid-teens, and stay sound and going close to his twenties. Sometimes a horse like this will even continue into his thirties as a schoolmaster and revered teacher.

Following the proper and fair progress of training, and figuring in the "hiccups" on the way, it takes, or ought to take, at least four years to teach even a very talented horse the whole Grand Prix program. That means he will appear in his first year green Grand Prix test at the earliest at age nine. Usually, the test at that point will show green mistakes and a lack of strength and stamina for all the requirements. To achieve the appearance of ease and casualness we look for in the finished horse, you can count on two years of polishing. The horse will now be at least ten years old, and normally he is closer to twelve.

Here he is, the finished product that has just arrived at the pinnacle of the sport, and now he is worth *less*? At least for dressage horses, there is something wrong with that thinking, and we need to stop buying into the insurance companies' view of horse age and look at the truth in the sport. Check out the ages of the horses competing in the Olympics and the World Games, for a start. Then look at the ages of the winners and high-placing horses. Not too many under ten there! The ones who make history and remain in our memory from Games past are the horses who kept coming back to new Games late into their teens, only getting better as they aged.

Although most of us are aware of the downside of younger horses, we become captivated by the dream, which often remains just a dream with many disappointments on the way. We forgo the horse that already offers the whole Grand Prix for the "hopeful" younger horse, which very possibly never arrives at the destination. Of our team riders in the last World Equestrian Games (WEG 2006), Steffen Peters was the most successful on the oldest of our horses,* and Olympic competitor Kennedy was far from a spring chicken when Jane Forbes Clark purchased him for Robert Dover. At the 2007 World Cup Finals, three horses over sixteen (Briar, Floriano, and Idocus) were in the top six placings, and many past Olympic medal horses were closer to twenty than fifteen when they earned their greatest honors.

Smart people see the whole picture, and do not fall into the age trap, which especially for dressage horses, is relative to the level of the performance and the overall health of the individual animal. When it comes to purchasing a teenage horse, even the pre-purchase exam is less torturous. Instead of guessing how the horse will stand up to the workload of the job description, you get to examine his show record, and you can find out if he has had long absences from the show scene for reasons of health. If the horse has performed consistently for at least a decade, chances are he will continue on track until his last breath. Whatever shows up on X-rays he is either unaware of or has learnt to live with, and you can expect no surprises, only some "maintenance" down the road—of the kind that many of the younger show horses receive, as well. No crystal ball necessary, since what you see is really what you get!

All Horses Great and Small

The size of a horse is another topic that has been misunderstood, but here there has been some major improvement over the years. There was

---

* *Floriano was sixteen years old when he helped the US Team win bronze at the 2006 WEG.*

a time, in the days of Christine Stückelberger's champion Granat, when no horse could be tall enough. Every call about horses for sale would start with "How big is he?" You would believe this country was populated by giants, since the demand for horses over 17 hands was impossible to satisfy. Then the prospective customer would show up, all five foot of her or him, and "the look" was not a thing of beauty. The fact that there was no harmony in the picture of horse and rider never seemed to matter, and often the complete lack of communication between man and beast, due to the incompatible weight and strength of the horse, made no impression. The horse had to be big!

Since I had to train some of these oversize models, and at 5 feet, 8 inches had some problems communicating with all that volume, I could never understand this fad. As I mentioned, the tendency to favor oversize horses has luckily diminished over the years, but there is still not a great call for the smaller, better horse. The truly athletic 16-hand or under animal can easily carry most people who are 5 feet, 6 inches or shorter—and some even taller, if they are reasonably slim.

There are a number of advantages to the smaller horse. First and foremost, they are usually easier to motivate with lesser aids, which makes riding less work and more fun! Secondly, the mobility and easy "fit" in the dressage arena gives you an advantage in riding the test. There is a larger margin for error and more time to prepare your next movement. Particularly in riding freestyles, I much prefer being on a smaller model horse; if you make a mistake, you can get back on track more quickly and smoothen the picture. My best freestyle horses were Amazonas, who won the Grand Prix freestyle at Devon, and Genius, who won several World Cup qualifiers. Amazonas was barely 16.1 hands, and Genius stood a proud 15.2. Because his movement was so expansive, he was always thought of as a bigger horse, and boy was he handy in the arena! Some of my larger horses were just a bit too "filling" in the ring, and since they were not as easy to maneuver, their mistakes were obvious.

Another real advantage of keeping size moderate is the soundness issue. I have found, along with many other people, that the bigger the horse, the more fragile he tends to be. The modern sports horse we strive to produce today stands tall and "leggy," and often measures way over 17 hands. All that height without a solid foundation takes a beating while we make a ballet dancer out of an animal that was designed to do nothing but graze and wander about in a leisurely fashion. I am well familiar with the patching and pampering that goes on in every barn at the big international events, and it is not because these horses are ill, but because their job description is not really "natural" and the taller they are, the more they appear to be at risk. Ponies, as you know, hold up a lot better to the demands of being trained and ridden, and they usually live forever.

When the size of the rider and the size of the horse are in harmony, the horse is the right size. And remember that a lot of good things come in small packages!

2007

– 25 –

fashions in dressage horses and myths about gaits

Looking back on the various types of horses who have gained fame as international stars in the dressage arena, you will discern a trend which resembles the hemline fashions over the years. Let's start with Pepel, ridden by Elena Petushkova of Russia—the small black Russian ballet dancer, a picture of lightness and refinement—soon to be replaced by Granat with Christine Stückelberger of Switzerland on board—the giant who made the earth shake and the judges' boxes rattle. When the "Granat fad" died out and many riders owned an 18-hand dinosaur they could not move out of the spot, Marzog ridden by Anne Grethe Jensen of Denmark entered the arena to lighten up the picture. With the arrival of Gifted (with Carol Lavell) it was fire and brimstone again, while Rembrandt and Nicole Uphoff balanced the scale, and Bonfire and Anky van Grunsven were waiting in the wings with a whole new concept in gaits.

Duckling to Swan

This all goes to show us that good things come in all kinds of packages, and although we profess to look for a certain kind of horse for dressage, there is no true set standard for how a dressage horse should look, what size he ought to be, or even exactly how he should move. If you take a stroll through the barns at Aachen, the Olympic Games, or any large show where the cream of the dressage crop is assembled, you will be amazed by how these horses appear when they are not under saddle. At the 1984 Games in Los Angeles, I went around with a friend, looking at the conformations of the various horses while they were resting in the barns or led about in a halter. We were searching for the perfect athlete designed for dressage, a noble statue of a horse that sloped downward from his poll to his croup, sported a well set-on neck crowned by a gorgeous head, and had a great shoulder angle, a back that practically sucked the saddle into place, and hocks that looked engaged even before they were put in gear. We saw little of the above, and never all of it on the same horse. Instead we were treated to every kind of unorthodox build and shape. Many of these Olympic dressage horses would not have made you look at them twice in a sales barn. Some even had faults that would make you bet they could never function at the FEI levels. Then we followed them to the schooling area and watched miracles happen as the ugly ducklings turned into dancing swans under their riders. In the time that has passed since the Los Angeles Games there has been a certain streamlining in the breeding of dressage horses, which has produced more animals custom-made for the job. As the fashions change, the breeding follows suit.

A "10"?

Interesting things happen to judges involved with dressage breeding classes. The perfect "10" walks in, stands in front of you in all his glory, and you can't wait to see him move. When he does, you are sorry you asked. It is hard to understand why such a lovely looking animal does not have the mechanics to produce locomotion that blinds you. Another case in point is the overbuilt, long-backed, splay-footed youngster who looks like a horse put together by a committee. Standing still, he is so abundant in faults that your secretary gets writer's cramp. As soon as he moves, your mouth falls open, and when it functions again, only high scores come out. I have been confronted with this phenomenon often

enough that I have become convinced that what we cannot see—namely, the way the bones fit together underneath the skin, fat, and muscle—is what really determines the way a horse can use himself. Another factor, which is impossible to measure until you have lived with the horse for a while, is what goes on in his head, and that part is often far more important than how he is built. The horse with a terrific work ethic will overcome a multitude of conformation defects, and even pain, in his anxiousness to do a good job, while the animal that is under the impression he is on a permanent vacation refuses to even try, although he may have all the physical attributes needed to become a star.

Whenever we admire a great dressage horse at work, it is important to remember that he is unique and that our attempts at duplication are likely to lead to disappointment. Fads nevertheless appear, and today's must in movement is "having a great hind leg." How the horse functions behind is of course of the utmost importance to the dressage performance, but it is not the only saving grace. During a recent trip to Europe I saw horses who were so "good behind" that their front legs could not keep up with all this glorious action. The end result was that they trotted like hackneys and cantered like potato pickers. Terrific hind ends so overpowered the front ends that the horses became desperate to get out of their own way, and any resemblance to classically correct gaits was purely coincidental. When we get overly focused on one particular attribute in the makeup of a horse, the overall picture tends to suffer in the final analysis.

While promoting and breeding for gaits that accentuate the lifting action of the piaffe and passage, we need to keep an eye on how these exaggerations affect the entire picture of the horse. The high knee action so much in vogue often brings with it a lower leg function that paddles and rotates to the point of making you dizzy when watching the horse from the front or rear. Although some of these action-packed movers can indeed piaffe and passage for a nine, the rest of their performance may have features that are less desirable. Medium and extended trots and canters tend to lack elasticity and reach, which is replaced by speed and hectic flinging of feet, and rarely does the frame lengthen a single inch. The softness that is part of suppleness is hard to come by when the horse's legs go in all directions, the tempo is high, and the back is flat. This scenario is, of course, worst case, but there is today a tendency toward favoring and breeding to produce this kind of horse while overlooking some severe shortcomings in the overall performance because of a special talent in the highly collected work.

To Die For?

I attended a judges' forum where Mr. Eric Lette, the chairman of the FEI dressage committee, lamented the fact that the riders of today tend to over-practice the piaffe and passage to the detriment of basics and suppleness. My reaction to this was that if the FEI wants to promote more work on the foundation of the training, it can be done with the stroke of a pen. In the present tests, over 30 percent of the Grand Prix test score is earned at the piaffe and passage. Change the ratio, and the focus of the competitors will instantly go where the points are to be collected. You may object that basics ought to be everyone's first priority, whatever their ultimate goals. Yes, they are, but competitive riders are very aware of the mathematics of the test, and they are not going to spend all their energy on features that will not be appreciated in the arena simply in order to be purists.

Just think of the much revered and talked-about *walk*. We are constantly being lectured as riders and judges about the enormous importance of the purity of the walk. All of us know how easy it is to ruin the walk through "faulty training" and how hard it is to create a good walk when the horse is not a "natural." Every competitor is painfully aware of how long a diagonal on a horse with a poor walk can feel, and every judge has sat around the dinner table with his or her colleagues clucking in dismay over how many *bad* walks they saw in the FEI tests. Yet I well remember Olympic winners with the very worst walks possible. Piaff, for example, walked like a centipede, and at the Olympics in Korea, Rembrandt displayed a non-walk: He scrambled and shuffled across the ring and somehow got where he was going, but he never walked. He won anyway. How was that possible, since we all know that the walk is all-important? Well, when the piaffe and passage are *to die for*, a horse can be forgiven a lot.

As most trainers know, the trot in its raw state is the least important gait, which does not hinder the horses with the most spectacular *aktionstrab* (commonly seen at auctions) from bringing the highest prices at the auctions in Europe. A flashy trot warms the heart of any horseman, but what fills the eye that regards the young horse is not what will score points in Grand Prix. As the horse progresses through the levels, the trot takes more of a backseat position. It holds its importance through the Prix St. George and the Intermediaire I, then fades in prominence with the introduction of piaffe and passage, as well the increased amount of canter work. The trot is also the gait that can be influenced and improved upon the most with proper training. In many cases the young horse has his trot completely "remodeled" somewhere between ages four and ten with the improved balance, strength, and rhythm that good riding brings.

The horse with a poor canter is, to me, the one to stay away from. A canter that rattles along in a stilted fashion and tends to be lateral will become even more problematic as the horse moves up the levels. The tests at the FEI levels demand a lot of intricate work at the canter, and if this gait is in itself cumbersome for the horse, it tends to hinder his progress. Nevertheless, many of the fashionable horses on today's international scene display a canter with a very high rotating front leg and a locomotion so labored that just getting from here to there appears an incredible effort. If, as Mr. Lette suggested, the real purpose of a dressage horse is to provide "comfortable transportation," is this what we should strive for?

Not to worry, when it comes to fashion, there is one sure prediction: Things will change and change back again. Some old ideas and ideals will resurface and appear brand new to many people. Except, of course, to those wise old birds who have seen it all before.

2007

– 26 –

who wants to be a grand prix horse?

If it were up to the riders and owners, the answer is as many as people who want to be a millionaire. Yet only a minuscule percentage of all the wonderful "dressage prospects" ever reach Grand Prix, and of those that do, only a fraction become good Grand Prix horses. I guess that's why they call it Grand Prix. And of course the ambition of every serious rider and owner is to see that horse of theirs in the Grand Prix ring. Breeders breed for it, owners search for it, and riders dream of it.

When we write inspirational introductions to dressage there is almost always some reference to how "natural" all the movements required in the tests are to the horse. Well, you can take that with a grain of salt, if not a handful. Certainly even your most arthritic school pony, turned out on a brisk winter day, will raise his tail in the air and passage loftily in the snow. And on occasion a horse stuck by the gate and anxious to escape will piaffe a step or two. Flying changes are quite common to see when a horse changes direction, but fifteen one-tempi changes in a row? And when did you ever see even the best trained horse bend on a turn while he gallops around the field? In reality, many of the Grand Prix movements are quite a mental and physical challenge for any horse.

High Expectations

When the FEI initiated a new division for five- and six-year-old horses in order to encourage the breeders, showcase exceptional young horses, and supervise the proper training of talented equines, I attended the judges' forum in Warendorf, Germany, and saw the tests introduced to the judges and the trainers. After watching the select German six-year-olds struggle with the requirements of the test, one of the judges cautiously asked if the trainers did not find this test a bit too demanding. "Absolutely not," replied German trainer Johann Hinneman. "If a six-year-old horse cannot deal with the requirements of this test, he is not a good candidate for the Grand Prix ring." I believe most of us judges were a bit taken aback by this statement, especially since Klaus Balkenhol* appeared to feel exactly the same way.

Since then I have judged a fair number of the Young Horse classes, and although I have no objection to the five-year-old test, I still feel that the six-year-old test is on the cutting edge of what that age horse should be asked to deal with. Because the test asks for half-passes, flying changes, and several fairly sophisticated transitions, the actual quality of the horse at times succumbs to the demands of the test. So, here is the ques-

---

* *Klaus Balkenhol won two Olympic gold medals and a bronze as a rider for Germany, and he was Chef d'Equipe of the US Dressage Team from 2000 to 2008, leading us to a number of team medals during his tenure.*

tion: What is the true purpose of these tests? Is it to promote the future Grand Prix horse, or is it to show off lovely young horses who still may not have a prayer to reach beyond the national levels? The more of these performances I judge, the more evident it becomes that the judges do not have a clear "mission statement" when it comes to deciding what we want to accomplish with the Young Horse tests.

Let me give you example of the dilemma: We were three judges sitting at our separate letters at a show, judging a class of seven lovely young horses in the six-year-old division. When the class was over, we were all touchingly in agreement about which horse won that particular class. Unfortunately, we also completely coincided in our prediction that the winning horse had less than a fighting chance ever to make it to the top of the Training Scale. The horse that won was a huge mover and very elastic with natural cadence to spare. He literally "floated" around the ring, as the ads like to boast. In addition, he was obedient and supple, and by far the most accurate performer in the class. So, what was the problem? At the present time, there is no problem, but to us judges, who all had trained horses through the FEI school of knocks, it was clear that it might become extraordinary difficult to guide this animal to Grand Prix. The task of creating a quick and weight-carrying hind leg out of his slow and pushing action, not to speak of containing and compacting all that long and buoyant motion, was daunting. All of us had at some time been charmed by the "expensive trots," lofty canters that never return to the earth, and ground-devouring walks. Be careful with what you wish for, because all those features can easily turn on you sometime between Third Level and Intermediaire II.

The Path to the Top

For all the love of big, elastic gaits and great cadence, we know from experience that this is not necessarily the path to the top. I have had several heartbreaks with those kind of horses, as in the case of Escorial. He was a homebred Trakehner with luxurious gaits, USDF Horse of the Year at Training Level, and practically unbeatable through Second Level. And that's when the honeymoon was over. This horse would absolutely, positively not deal with collection. When we pushed the envelope, he developed some ugly features you never could have imagined he harbored, knowing him as a sweet-natured horse since he was a foal. Today he is a happy amateur-owner jumper, which is good for him but was a great disappointment to us.

On the other end of the scale is the story of Cyrus. I found him in Sweden as an unbroken three-year-old. Although I did see him perform some pretty interesting maneuvers while turned out in the mud, he was not a mind-blowing mover. What he had to offer was a decent hind leg, a strong back, and good natural balance. Once he was civilized under saddle (at first a very good bronc), Cyrus moved up the levels, ridden by his owner, Linda Smith. He won plenty due to accurate riding and careful campaigning, but his walk was limited, his canter flat, and his trot ordinary. The gaits were "clean" but they rarely earned more than a six. Cyrus went through all the levels from Training to Intermediaire I, winning but never really making an impression. When he hit the show ring at Grand Prix level, he was instantly put on the map. This was not really a surprise to his rider or me, since we knew the horse's secret weapon was the piaffe and the passage, both of which he could display for an eight any day and nines on a good day, and transitions were a breeze. Suddenly the mediocre gaits were forgiven, and the scores soared. And Cyrus, at least, had three pure gaits, which is more than several of history's most famous dressage horses can boast.

Naturally, the best of all worlds is to find a Rusty or a Corlandus,* a horse that combines the ability to reach and expand the gaits with the

---

* *Ridden to fame by Germany's Ulla Salzgeber and France's Margit Otto-Crépin, respectively.*

knack for carrying and lifting the body and articulating the joints. That's a rare animal.

Precious and Few

I just returned from Germany where I visited a show in Munich. Both Anky van Grunsven and Isabell Werth were there on new horses, since their champions Bonfire and Gigolo were retired after the 2000 Olympics in Sydney, Australia. Watching these two sensational riders guiding their inexperienced Grand Prix mounts around the test was a reminder of how precious and few the very good Grand Prix horses are. Slim Anky looked out of place on her new wide-bodied Gestion Idool, who had the audacity to shuffle in the piaffe, and Isabell had her hands full with Agnelli FRH, who so far lacks a clear view of some of the requirements of the test.

And then, as time goes by, the green horse of yesterday becomes the mature performer of today. Years ago, I judged Gracioso in one of his first tests when Klaus Balkenhol was still riding him. Although skillfully guided through the test and obviously talented in piaffe and passage, he was unsure in the canter work and some of it was hit-or-miss. A year later, I judged him again with Nadine Capellmann in the saddle when he was into a spooky phase where his tests would go from feast to famine in a blink of an eye (or a movement from a spectator). It appears his time has now come to display maturity and confidence, which he did in Munich by winning both the Grand Prix and the Special.

A large crowd had gathered around the ring to watch the Grand Prix. With intense concentration and knowledgeable comments, the spectators followed every one of the thirty-plus movements. There was no talk there of watching grass grow or paint dry. In Germany, Grand Prix dressage is appreciated for what it is; an incredibly difficult athletic feat for the horse and the result of many years of gymnastics, repetitions, delays, hopes, disappointments, and perseverance. Even when it is not a very good day for a horse and rider, there is a certain respect in the air for their effort—a respect I hope we will one day emulate here in the United States. As a competitor said when she came out of the arena after her first attempt at the ultimate test, "The step from Prix St. Georges to Grand Prix makes it look like a whole new sport!"

2001

– 27 –

in sickness and in health:
the unexpected trials

*It is possible that the dressage rider is the most
persevering of all horse owners when it comes to
tenacity in a situation where good sense dictates
that a horse has come to the end of his rope.*

I have seen many examples of riders, owners, and trainers of dressage
horses who should have given up long ago on a problem, but simply
could not. A dressage horse is not a throwaway item, not only for the
simple reason that every horse owner has to love and maintain his or
her horse, but also because the time invested in training before the horse
reaches his potential is immense compared to any other discipline. When
you have spent that many hours of your life focusing on another living
creature, you become close to obsessed.

Jane and Woody

One example of a rider sticking with a horse through thick and thin is
especially interesting, because the rider is one of high profile with goals

beyond the national scene—in short, the kind of person who is least likely to hang on to a horse unable to live up to the expectations.

In 1992, after being "one horse away" from the Olympic team, Jane Savoie found a replacement for her almost-team horse, Zapatero, who had been sold. Eastwood ("Woody") was a red-headed dancer, and when I watched him in his early schooling sessions, he showed every sign of being a worthy Crown Prince to King Zapatero. After a promising start competing at Third Level during the 1993 season, Woody developed a urine "leak" during a working session in January of the following year. A blockage was found in the urethra, and the horse's bladder proved to be extended to the size of a basketball. The culprit was discovered to be a kidney stone, and a nasty one at that, since eight hours of efforts to get rid of it yielded no results. Even after surgery was performed and a stone the size and shape of a person's pinky was removed, the kidney continued to malfunction. An E. coli infection showed up in a urine test, and ultrasound unveiled the fact that the kidney was not only enlarged way beyond normal limits, but also full of grit and debris. Over the next three to four months a number of antibiotics were taken for a test run, but none of them did the trick until Amikacin, at a rate of $400 per day, entered the battle. The good news was that this antibiotic knocked out the E. coli. The bad news was that it also threatened to wipe out the horse's kidney.

In the end the decision was made to remove the kidney. Although the surgery went smoothly, and Woody did not much miss his defunct kidney, a facial paralysis hindered the "legging up" process and the horse was so weak it took almost six months to bring him back to full condition.

In March of 1995, Woody returned to the show ring and was a star at Fourth Level. Although during the year and a half of Woody's battle many friends and other trainers told Jane to throw in the towel, she could not walk away from a horse that showed so much courage and fortitude during every stage of his ordeal. But there was more than that to this story.

Unconventional Wisdom
_____

Nature's Best

Although we have found many clever ways to both deal with and prevent disease in our horses, as well as some miracle cures and procedures such as colic surgery, we need to stay on the sensible side of management. Too much of even a "good" thing can harm a horse, and new fads ought to be viewed with at least a healthy dose of skepticism and common sense.

Every new product is not going to create or maintain the perfect horse, and some "sports medicine" needs to be practiced with caution and an eye on the laws of the universe. If you stray too far from those boundaries, don't be surprised when nature strikes back.

_____

Jane and Eastwood had already been through difficulties of other natures, such as overcoming shying and bolting, and learning to negotiate flying changes, which were a major stumbling block for the horse. The daily problem-solving that the dressage rider and horse go through together tends to cement their relationship to the point that there is no way you can break them apart, and even the difficult times you have together become a bond that is remarkably strong.

Lisa and Calumet

Another story along the same lines is that of Calumet. I knew this horse well; as a matter of fact, I knew her before she was born. Her mother, a Swedish Warmblood, was almost mine, until she became the top three-year-old in Sweden, showing in hand. Her breeder asked me to "unbuy" the mare and promised me the first-born filly out of her instead. This filly turned out to be a 17-hand moose with a head like a suitcase. She had a lot of suspension in her gaits, however, and I knew she had the genes to be a wonderful broodmare.

In America most imported mares do double duty, so Calumet went on to a dressage career, was sold, and ended up in Florida. As things turned out she became the mount of rider and trainer Lisa Giltner, who is also the owner of a lovely dressage facility. At the end of the 1995 show season, Calumet and Lisa had earned their USDF bronze medal and the only fly in the ointment was that every so often they would have to forgo a show due to lameness and "ouchy" front feet. It was suggested to Lisa that injecting the coffin joint in the right front foot, which was the more sensitive one, would make Calumet more comfortable. The veterinarian was called in, and after injecting the right foot with Adequan®, he asked if he should not do the left one as well, while they were at it. Said and done.

A few days later, Calumet had a joint flare in the left foot, which was dramatic. She went from acting as if she had an abscess to having her body jerked in seizures as the pain sent her into shock. With the help of painkillers, the mare was transported to an equine hospital in Ocala, where several vets worked through the night flushing the joint and administering large doses of antibiotics. For a while it looked as if the danger was past, but weeks later, still at the clinic, the mare was diagnosed with a pastern joint infection. How the infection traveled from the coffin joint to the pastern is a mystery that was never solved. What followed was a nightmare of drugs flowing through a catheter while the horse was down on her side fifty percent of the time or hobbling around as if she had a broken leg. A serious bout of colic looked like it would put a natural end to the mare's suffering, but she rallied and survived, though she remained practically immobile. Finally two vets, the insurance company, and even Lisa agreed that it was time. The grave was scheduled to be dug on Monday, and Sunday evening Lisa groomed her mare for the last time, beginning her grieving and goodbyes.

Monday morning was a beautiful, crisp, and sunny day, and as Calumet hobbled out to her pasture she suddenly looked a little better! She even put a minuscule bit of weight on her left toe...and that was all it took to call off the "hole-digger" and the vet and give her another chance. A very creative farrier invented a special glue-on wedged shoe, which enabled Calumet to better distribute her weight on her bad foot, and she started back from zero. Slowly but surely the mare returned to full health, and in 1998 she had a lovely filly, which made her forget all about her handicap when she had to follow her newborn romping across the fields. Eventually she was even rideable, and when turned out and feeling good, there was a remnant of that big spectacular trot she used to dazzle the spectators with.*

Anne (as in "Me") and Amazonas

Yet another case in point is my horse Amazonas. Halfway through his career, after a rocky start as a three-year-old when he was diagnosed with navicular disease, which proved to be a heel infection,[†] this Trakehner gelding was in trouble again. He showed signs of losing his balance and his face became progressively more paralyzed until the right side of his mouth could no longer chew and his ear hung like a wilted flower. Soon he could not walk a straight line, and swallowing became a problem.

This was my horse, and of course we had every test run and every possible diagnosis explored. Finally, when he had to tilt his head sideways to make the food go down the throat, and his right eye started to cloud over, I had enough, and was ready to put an end to Amazonas' struggle. My husband disagreed, and with never ending optimism, he rigged up a

---

Calumet lived to be thirty-one and was put down on a beautiful, crisp, and sunny day in January 2014.

[†] *I tell the story of Amazonas and his "navicular ordeal" on p. 116.*

sling in the trailer, placed the chestnut in the sling, and drove nine hours to Cornell Veterinary School. There they were met by Dr. Alexander de Lahunta, a pioneer in veterinary neurology, who took one look at the horse swaying down the barn aisle and said, "I have a hunch!" He put Amazonas under anesthesia and examined him to confirm that his suspicions of a deep-seated ear infection were correct. Six weeks and mega-doses of antibiotics later, Amazonas arrived back home.

The word was that he would never be rideable again, except perhaps as a trail horse. This was of course a disappointment, since he already had good results competing through Prix St. Georges, but at least he was still alive and comfortable. About four months later, I was working another horse next to Amazonas' pasture and suddenly I saw him galloping around, slide-stopping into the gate, and rearing up, all in seemingly perfect balance. I remember the eyes of my groom growing big when I asked her to bring him in and tack him up. To make a long story short, Amazonas went on to win the Grand Prix freestyle at Devon, competed at the 1984 Olympic Selection Trials, and went on to more than ten years of competition at the FEI levels. He died from colic at age twenty-two, and his owner in California sent me a lovely letter telling me what had happened and praising Amazonas for the education and mileage he had given her.

Stubborn persistence is one of the trademarks of a dressage rider, and there are times when the horses we have in our care benefit from that trait. "Against all odds" is not that scary a thought to many of us. In our slow and detailed fashion, we go out to fight windmills, and sometimes we even win!

1999

− 28 −

the relativity of soundness

In the January 30, 2009, issue of The Chronicle of
the Horse *is the fabulous story "Graf George—What
I Remember," written by Dr. Paul McClellan, the longtime treating veterinarian for all the horses belonging
to Dick and Jane Brown and ridden by Guenter Seidel.*

Having just helped Graf George, Guenter's first Olympic mount, move
from this earth to greener pastures, Dr. McClellan tells us about the long
and fascinating relationship he had with this horse. It's a beautiful and
also a realistic and fulfilling tale about taking risks, and having faith and
passion overcome real and imaginary obstacles.

Particularly interesting to me is the story of George's physical state at
the time of purchase and during his career. Graf George, or just "George"
as he's referred to in the story, had already put on considerable mileage
when he and Guenter met. He had been to one Olympic Games with
his original trainer, Michael Poulin, and then worked with another
rider in between.

Dr. McClellan described in touching terms the excitement and happy
anticipation obvious in prospective owners Dick and Jane when they

presented him with their new hopeful acquisition. The veterinarian started by examining George's feet and found them pleasing.

Unfortunately, anything above the hoof had "issues" galore, such as ringbone, enlarged suspensories, and an unusual knot on the side of his right knee. But Dr. McClellan wasn't discouraged, because he had already noticed the boldness, determination, and brilliance in the eyes of this gray gelding, and he knew the horse had the will to overcome the odds against him of going to another Olympics.

The road there was by no means easy, and maintenance was a priority. Obviously, the magic worked, because George and Guenter qualified to participate in the 1996 Olympic selection trials in Gladstone, New Jersey.

In the middle of those trials, George was shipped off to New Bolton Center in Pennsylvania with a severe case of colic. He didn't have surgery, and in the end he made the Atlanta Olympic Team, but it was a close call, and the most perfect set of legs would have been of no value if his digestive system hadn't responded to treatment.

Disappointing Results

So many times when I'm involved in a pre-purchase exam at either end of the spectrum of sellers or buyers, it becomes obvious to me how futile and sometimes frustrating those events are. We are really fooling ourselves if we think a "clean" vetting will lead to a career free of physical problems or even guarantee that the horse will live to see another day. What Dr. McClellan saw in George when he looked at him was not his weaknesses, but his potential strengths. And that aspect is often overlooked or pushed into the background when we try to protect ourselves from future problems.

Many years ago, when I first started buying horses from Europe, I would ask the seller for X-rays, and sometimes the reaction was violent. In particular, the breeders who had lived with the young horse for years and seen him every day since his birth would balk at this requirement. They took it as a personal insult, and on several occasions the issue of X-rays would put a stop to the sale.

Although I argued all the reasons for my point of view, I knew in my heart that those sellers were not wrong. For years, I found myself turning down perfectly sound horses—who remained sound for long careers—because of "bad" navicular pictures.* At that time, many American veterinarians were used to examining the images of Thoroughbred feet and were not familiar with the Warmblood "look," and therefore they were cautious. Even today, however, I find that when a potential buyer gets "cold feet" and wants to drop the ball, it's often the navicular bones that get blamed.

How many times have we gone over an ailing horse with a fine-toothed comb and not been able to find what's wrong, or found it only when it's too late to fix the problem? Quite often those are just the same horses who pass their pre-purchase exam with flying colors. After that they are no good to anybody.

For example, as I told you earlier in this section on p. 105, some horses are what I call "excuse horses" and never really fit for action because they have a new little problem every day. The best X-rays in the world will not protect you against that kind of horse, because they are allergic to effort and have "work avoidance" down to an art form.

---

* *See the example of my own Amazonas described on p. 138.*

The Heart of the Matter

It's the other kind of horse that makes the grade and wins your heart, the George kind of horse, who overcomes his physical shortcomings and belies all of our dire predictions. I have been privileged to meet several of those noble animals, and every one of them makes me grateful for the experience.

My very first Grand Prix horse was one of those special creatures. His name was Tappan Zee; he was a Thoroughbred by Royal Charger, and he had two huge bowed tendons from racing to win. Not only did he change careers, allow me to train him to Grand Prix, get to the selection trials at Gladstone, earn a USDF gold medal, and allow me to enjoy numerous wonderful events on his back, he also did it unconditionally.

At nineteen, Tappan fell in his stall during the night and broke his pelvis. We found him in the early morning, fighting to get up. His efforts had steamed up the windows, and he was soaking wet. While waiting for the veterinarian, he finally put his head in my lap and died. I was too young and inexperienced then to know what a rare, brave, and generous animal I was losing, but I know it well today.

We have had school horses with impossible conformation, legs like corkscrews, and I would hate to know what X-rays might have revealed. They made up for all of that with a never-failing work ethic and a will to succeed. For years and years they did their jobs and were never lame or cranky.

In the meantime, we had some show horses with near-perfect conformation, wonderful potential, and all the care and maintenance in the world who could never get through the day without complaints. I understand what Dr. McClellan saw in George's eyes, which overcame whatever he observed in his body. That keen "look of eagles" and the body language that spells pride and energy should mean as much to us as images of bone and conformational flaws. In the case of George, and several horses of his ilk that I've met, the spirit and will (and sometimes a high pain threshold) combine to overcome the science.

Today the technology is so advanced that every deviation from the "norm" can be detected with radiographs, ultrasound, and blood tests, and you can pick a horse apart before he even takes a step out of the barn. These tests often override the original purpose of searching for that right horse.

I have seen people walk away from the equine that would have fit right into their picture of what they wanted because of a shadow on cellophane that may have been an artifact. Taking risks is almost disallowed in our American society. Everything must be so "safe" that our instincts are rubbed out in the name of proper procedure.

Well, the fact of the matter is that life itself is a dangerous business, and chances are pretty great you will die from it. Just like people, some horses can rise above it all and beat the odds. If you think you can see that quality in a horse, and dare to bet on him, you may not end up at the Olympics, but you could be in for the ride of your life.

2009

In the third year of Grand Prix, the horse realizes he has "arrived,"
and the only mistakes he makes are when he tries to do too much.

IV training and competing

− 29 −

on the road to grand prix

*After faking my way through the very first test of the
ultimate difficulty on yet another green horse that
will not be fit to carry the label "Grand Prix horse"
for at least another year, I talked to one of the judges
who had patiently watched as my horse and I went
from the ridiculous to the sublime and back again.*

He laughed and shook his head, saying, "We always think it isn't going
to be that way *this time*, but it always is." First-year green Grand Prix
is a rollercoaster ride, and by the time I began my tenth journey in this
regard, I knew to ignore anything that happens in the first year and only
pay slight attention to what goes on in the second season.

The Whole Enchilada

As you start out on the adventure of dressage, your aim may be simply to
be able to communicate with your horse and look less than pathetic while
you do so. As time goes by, your goals may change and your ambitions
grow. I know exactly when I decided to go for the "whole enchilada."
When I first arrived in this country I was too thrilled to own a horse at all,

and way too involved with school, eventing, and figuring out the ins and outs of life the "American Way" to have time to concentrate on dressage alone. After a couple of years without a real focus, my husband decided I needed a lift, and he bought me a wonderful Thoroughbred schooled by Jordan Miller and his father Michael to Prix St. Georges. Tappan Zee was a gorgeous and capable animal, but it never occurred to me when he arrived that I would want to do anything but learn from this superb master, and perhaps one day perform the ultimate Prix St. Georges test.

Two days after the horse arrived in our barn, I received a call from a so-called professional who said, "I hear you bought Tappan Zee." I confirmed his suspicions and waited for him to say something like "Congratulations!" or "Good luck!" Instead he bluntly pronounced: "Well, he will never make Grand Prix," and hung up. At that moment Tappan Zee and I took on a whole new mission: From then on, the poor horse had to deal with expectations that may not have been beyond *his* capabilities, but certainly were not within those of his rider. Good help, luck, and a very generous horse made Grand Prix not just a reality, but a pretty decent act, and I still have a nasty phone call to thank for the inspiration.

The road to Grand Prix is long, sometimes tedious, and always demanding on time, consistency, and above all, faith. Anybody who has lived with a rider who is in the process of schooling a horse with Grand Prix in mind knows that nothing is a sure thing. The highs are tremendous and the lows are a disaster. Living with an intense dressage rider is like cohabiting with a writer or composer or painter who is so consumed with his or her creation that a bad day in the saddle can sour the atmosphere in the entire household. When the horse has a revelation of whatever nature, all is well; but the many times he has a setback, the rider easily loses confidence in the whole process.

As you get some more horses under your belt, the emotional swings become less violent, and you learn to take each day as it presents itself.

Eventually a pattern emerges, and the similarities between the different horses give you a method to follow and some security in past experiences and successes to build on. A bad day no longer makes you want to give up, because you feel pretty sure the horse will come around, given time. Time is the key to it all, in combination with a clear method and consistent work.

Hit or Miss

In almost every horse I have schooled, the same pattern has evolved as we approached the beginning of the end. The very first Grand Prix test a horse performs in competition is often surprisingly pleasant. He may make mistakes, but the overall test is forward and happy since the horse is blissfully ignorant of how hard all this really is. Then it hits him, and for the next couple of shows he is overwhelmed and confused. You never know who you are sitting on after the initial halt, a concept that is enough to drive any dressage rider to drink. Then comes Stage Three: the one where the horse wants to renegotiate his job description and insists on a lot of unwanted input, especially at the transitions between the piaffe and passage and the pirouettes on the centerline. They don't call it Grand Prix for no reason, and your horse is likely to wake up and start to protest any time after the first go.

The first season of Grand Prix is usually a hit-or-miss deal with a couple of decent trips and several disasters. After that first year, the break between seasons supplies precious time to polish the rough spots and improve the horse's physical strength as well as his confidence in his ability to pull it all off. Second-year green Grand Prix is usually the time for the truth. The act is still not a sure thing, but now you find out if it will ever be good enough. Your horse will have more clean tests, and the scores for such a performance indicate whether he is heading for the big times or is limited in scope and brilliance. This is the year when the horse shows if he is intended for the national or the international game, and depending on the ambitions of his rider and owner, this may be the year he changes home and lifestyle.

About two years after a horse has gone through his first Grand Prix test, I have found an interesting thing happening to several of my equines. It suddenly occurs to them that they have graduated. One day at about this stage in your horse's life, he will take a deep breath, exhale, and say to himself, "I have arrived!" He finally believes there are no more movements to be introduced, no additional demands. As of the day when your horse comes to the realization that he is a graduate, you will ride a different, more confident mount.

If the horse is still with you, sound and ready to roll, when he enters his third year of competition at the highest level, get ready for the payback for all those times of doubt, of sweat, of nursing, of worry, and just plain grit. You can start to enjoy knowing that your equine partner is a tower of strength, wisdom, and cool, and not only knows what to do and why, but will even cover for your inadequacies at times. He checks out the action around the ring as he trots outside the arena, eyeing the judges with amusement. When the bell rings, he puffs himself up and enters with an air that says: Here comes the main attraction, check this out! If he makes mistakes, it is because he gets carried away and tries to do too much, too soon, or you get in his way. On days when you two are in sync, there is no stopping you from getting that "winning feeling," and boy, it is sweet!

Good things take time. As a matter of fact, most everything that is worth doing takes time. When it comes to training a horse to Grand Prix, it takes even more time. But when you get there, I think you will agree it was worth every minute.

1998

– 30 –

the competitor

Of the many "hats" I wear, I like my top hat the best. Of the many things I do, nothing gives me a charge like entering the arena in a competition on a horse that knows his job and likes to show off. Naturally, I may not feel as enthusiastic by the end of the test, but that is another story.

Like many people, I started riding because I was born with an addiction to horses, and for many years just being around them was all I asked. Competition did not enter my mind as I learned that life on top of a horse did not feel anything like the way it looked in *National Velvet*. At age six or seven, just being allowed to take lessons on, help with the care of, and breathe the aroma of these magnificent animals was heaven!

As you continue to learn and develop your riding, competition tends to sneak into your life because of local stable and club events that suck you in, and because it becomes too much for your curiosity not to find out if you are up to par when compared to other riders. I started competing in junior jumpers and went on to eventing, and therefore had to practice my dressage. If the quality of our dressage work was not sufficient, we sometimes were not allowed to jump at all in our lessons, and that was a fate worse than death...

Eventing has always remained my first love, and I look back at those years as the "pure" years. They were blissfully free of the politics and subjective baggage that is part and parcel of dressage, and they were sometimes "pure" terror as well! When I went white-water rafting in Colorado that same feeling of riding cross-country came back to me as we approached another shelf in the river—there was no going back. We had to trust our guide, never mind what waited behind the drop, the same way you have to trust your horse and just go on. There is no feeling of satisfaction like that of finishing a cross-country course, knowing that the horse has jumped well and that you are both safe and sound: So much adrenaline flowing to an ebb, and so much respect and gratitude for the horse that took care of you.

The Rush of the Stage

Nobody can be a competitor for the better part of their life if they do not enjoy the "rush" of the moment and the sweet taste of victory, which make up for the abyss of defeat and the many inconveniences leading to the moment when they enter the arena. Dressage is different from any other branch of equestrian venture because of the lengthy "on stage" performance, which requires a different kind of courage than jumping in a ring or cross-country. In the latter the element of physical danger replaces stage fright to a great degree, and you frankly don't give a damn how your form is as you gallop on the course, as long as the horse goes clean and stays within the time limit allowed. Dressage riders cannot disappear into the woods and "get the job done"; they have to solve their problems imprisoned by letters and inspected every moment by judges and sometimes even spectators.

Dressage is a sport for exhibitionists. The more the competitors like the attention, the more they exude presence and flamboyance, the better they deal with show nerves. Well, not always. I have observed people with all the *élan* in the world literally shake at the door of an important event. And I have seen them mentally glue themselves together and go in anyway. That takes courage, too. Although many competitors do not mind the tension, don't assume that every "famous" rider is devoid of the jitters. They just deal with or hide it better.

A Competitor's Wish List

Like every other group of players on the show scene, competitors have certain wishes they appreciate being made priorities and some problems they like help with.

- As much as the show managers like to have their entry blanks in good order, the competitor appreciates not having to feel like he or she is filing tax returns every time he or she enters a show. Some of those forms are so cluttered and confused that it is hard to grasp what is being asked for where—and never mind why. Is it not possible to make a generic, clean-looking, and clear sheet that is good for most shows countrywide?

- Early deadlines for dressage entries, which are usually due at least a month before the show, are sometimes hard to live up to. It is understandable that a competitor has to pay for the time slots reserved, but a lot of money is wasted when you have to scratch a horse after the closing date. In Europe, and lately at some shows in California, there is a system of offering one date for declared or provisional entries when you send in part of the entry fee, followed by a later date, considerably closer to show time, for definite entries. This way the competitor who is already unhappy about missing the show can at least keep some of the money, and the show will have time to fill the empty slots with post entries.

- When you arrive at the show grounds, sometimes after long hours of travel, it is very appreciated if someone is there to show you your stall and say something encouraging like, "Welcome!" True, you sometimes arrive late, and that only makes it worse, since you cannot find your way around in tents or strange barns with dim lighting and dark surroundings. It sets the whole tone of a show when you feel like the organizers are happy to see you.

- The condition and safety of the stall where your equine partner is going to spend the better part of the show is of essence. Filthy stalls in tents that are falling down, with torn sides and doors that don't work, will bring out the worst in the Dressage Queens, guaranteed!

- The only thing that will turn on an even higher voltage of royal rage is poor footing. And we are talking schooling areas, as well as performance rings. The long haul of the show is spent by the horse in the schooling ring, and the risk of injury is greater there than in the arena.

- Times allotted are usually carefully planned, with the help of computers—which is easier than in the "old days" when a secretary's entire living room was filled up with time cards, which had to be placed correctly to avoid conflicts. But, as we all know, computers have no tact or feelings of justice, and they don't care if the same combination of horse and rider goes first in every class they entered at the show. The rider does care, however, and he or she also would love it if at a three-day show with five rings they did not have to ride in front of the same judge in five of their six classes. Gathering different points of view is one of the reasons we show, and it does not work if the management does not rotate the judges and check the computer glitches.

- Proper judging is, of course, a major concern for every competitor. What good does it do to practice diligently, seek help from the experts, and get yourself and your horse to the show if what you read on your sheets makes no sense? Luckily, it does not happen very often, because we are blessed with well-educated and enthusiastic judges in this country. And they are getting better all the time! What does happen at times is that a judge will have a bad day, get caught up in who is who, or miss noticing that you and your horse just had the performance of your life! In general, you can forgive an occasional show of human weakness, but not if it becomes repetitive and an obvious problem. Show management should keep an ear open to the comments by *all* riders in regard to the judging—not only the winners or the people who think they ought to have won, but also the frequent competitors who "sample" a lot of judging and are able to compare with some objectivity. In some areas of the country where shows are few and far between, it helps educate the competitors if the shows get together and avoid inviting the same judges in the same year.

The dressage competitor is a creature of planning, consistency, persistence, and eternal optimism. And why shouldn't we be optimistic? After all, it is extremely rare that any physical damage happens to us in the ring, and dealing with the mental aspects eventually becomes a habit. When a show does not work out to our satisfaction there are always more lessons to learn, other clinics coming up, new horses to train, and another season around the corner. Actually, it's a great sport compared to many others.

After all, if at first you don't succeed, so much for skydiving.

1999

– 31 –

no, it is not always about winning

When I read the commentary (on my piece about September 11)* by Mr. Tom Kimmel of Evansville, Indiana, in the December 14, 2011, issue of The Chronicle of the Horse, *I wondered how he could so have misunderstood what I tried to say.*

Tried is the key word, because when I read my column over, I realized Mr. Kimmel had a point and according to the way I arranged the words, his interpretation was correct. What I meant to say, and did not express at all well, was that when a person does win or place and acts as if it is all the same to them, they miss out on the euphoria of success, which is a real high when you have worked hard to obtain a goal. What I tried, and failed, to point out was that although my horses did quite well at the NEDA show, the excitement that would normally have accompanied winning was so totally overshadowed by the enormity of current events

---

* *See "Dressage as Therapy" in Part I, p. 58.*

that the whole show scene right then appeared unimportant and out of touch, just something to occupy our minds so we did not have to deal with reality.

Life to the Triumph

In spite of the fact that I am an avid show rider, my personal views on winning dovetail very nicely with those of Mr. Kimmel. Like most of my colleagues in the arena, I love to compete, and I like to win, but I certainly do not compete only for ribbons and placings. If that were the case, I would never be out there on a horse green for his level, or ride a horse in a show that is not perfectly programmed to the task and a "sure thing." We have all been around people who will never enter a competition without carefully selecting the judges, who always play a level or two below the horse's capability, and who immediately scratch the horse from the next class if he is not in the victory gallop in the first one. They carefully work their way to lengthy year-end awards dinners and get their picture in the local horse magazine, but there is no real life to their triumph, because it is contrived and achieved without risk.

I must admit, though, that it is easier to be elated with thirteenth place at an event than in a dressage or jumper class (unless you are talking Olympics). Eventing is, in my opinion, the "crown jewel" of equine sports disciplines. It is the most well-rounded training of the horse on display, and going cross-country has no equal, except for combined driving. It is perfectly possible to end up thirty-fourth at the end of the day and still drive home with a song in your heart because your horse jumped beautifully over every obstacle without pulling you around, without hesitating, and without ever feeling tired. The two of you were breathing in unison, eating up the ground, and had but one purpose: forward to the next challenge! There are enough highs there to last for days.

I am sorry I cannot say that about most dressage tests.

However, there are some very solid reasons for competing in dressage, even when there is little chance of ending up in the limelight. First and foremost, you need to compare your horse's state of training with that of others at the same level, getting the input from the judges as well as observing the "state of the art" for yourself. The observing could, of course, be done as a spectator, but without putting your horse and yourself on the line, the fact that your horse "piaffes at home" is a moot point. Second, all horses on the way up the levels need exposure to the show scene and mileage that cannot be supplied in the back yard. And showing is a way to build character, especially when you are not having a good day. The true competitor learns how to deal with all the "hiccups" and disappointments, and still return for another go. He or she gets to know how to savor a win without ever forgetting that tomorrow things may take a completely different turn. Horses teach us nothing if not humility!

Full Circle

When I was a kid and started riding, competition was the farthest thing from my mind. All I wanted was to be around horses, to breathe in their wonderful sweet smell—to me more exhilarating than any other fragrance on earth—and to touch their velvety coat, to look into their sad and all-knowing eyes. Riding them was a privilege and a joy beyond anything else I could desire. In short, I was just like any other horse-crazy kid in the world. Years later, my whole life became involved with horses, and with serious training arrived the need for competition; the fire it lit in my blood was a whole new aspect of riding. Jumping and eventing keeps you on your toes, but even dressage can be exciting when there is a good class and you have a long-term goal in mind.

Today, after many years of competing and after obtaining some of those goals, I must admit that I look at showing differently. The few minutes in the ring still makes my blood run faster (although the reasons may vary from joy to alarm), but the rest of the scene can appear as just "more of the same." The planning, packing, traveling, loading, fussing, waiting, re-packing, and traveling again is a *lot* of work, and when I think of all the weekends in my life that were absorbed by horse shows, I sometimes wonder about my sanity...

After all this time, I have almost returned to base. Although, thankfully, more experienced, I am back in the mode where I am totally satisfied staying at home with my horses. The training, which has always been the true motivation for diligently showing up at the barn every day, is the constant that never becomes monotonous, uninteresting, or exactly the same two days in a row. It would be impossible to stay inspired while training horses but for the fact that every single horse has something new to offer, which gives you reason to add to your pool of knowledge and meet the challenge of dealing with that specific individual.

My triumphs today are not measured in ribbons and scores, but in the satisfaction of having a day when a horse who had a problem suddenly catches on and performs a movement with ease, or a particular sequence of exercises feel just like you know they should: no tension, no resistance, and no effort, just horse and rider gliding together. The ultimate satisfaction is to look at a horse you have known from the time he was broken and watch him grow more beautiful every year because of the building of his muscles and strength. The finished, happy, and sound Grand Prix horse is a work of art, and all the time it took to bring him there is well worth it. Things of quality take time, and your trained horse does not have to go to the Olympics to give you an enormous amount of pride and joy in your accomplishments together.

Thank you, Mr. Kimmel, for inspiring me to try to get the words right.

2001

– 32 –

the other side of sponsorship

Any rider with great ambitions to achieve success but limited funds to realize this quest will at some time wistfully long for the "bottomless purse" of sponsorship. We read and hear about the "sunshine stories" of partnerships between riders and sponsors that lead straight to the USET and Olympic medals. Sound glorious?

Well, the reality can be very different from the image, and I have come to believe that the lasting and successful relationships are among the rare ones, while I have witnessed a number of situations that did little to advance the sport or produce the desired result for either the sponsor or the rider/trainer involved.

Soul-Selling for the Big Leagues

To begin with, it is not that easy to secure a sponsor, unless you have a great deal of confidence in yourself, an inborn marketing ability, and a healthy measure of luck. More often than not, promises are made in the heat of the moment, which never get followed up on, and the hopeful rider is made to feel like a fool. I have, on several occasions, had starry-eyed riders come to try horses in the honest belief that a "Fairy Godperson" would buy them any horse they wanted. When they did find that horse, the Fairy's funds suddenly dried up.

Sometimes the riders, in their eagerness to get their leg over those horses they could never afford to buy or keep on their own, will literally sell their souls for the prospect of playing in the big leagues. Before they know how, they are caught up in a web of social obligations and extra duties that interfere with their private lives and put a lot of pressure on them, which has nothing to do with training and showing the horses. I have watched friends become caught in a "spider web of ownership" in which total control and major paranoia have made their lives miserable, down to having their homes bugged by their sponsor and all their private phone conversations monitored! There is a lot of power in holding the purse strings, and anybody can easily understand the danger of losing your income. Only a rider, however, can appreciate the additional threat of losing the animal you have bonded with and invested time, sweat, and dreams in. The words, "I will take the horse away from you," are more frightening to the rider than, "You are fired," because often the essence of his or her life is *that horse*. Good horses are few and far between and, especially in dressage, the time you have to spend to accomplish even the smallest progress is considerable. You cannot help falling in love with the object of your daily attention, and no matter how determined you may be not to become "emotionally involved" with the horses you know are not yours, there is no escape from growing closer as you progress together.

There are people who, whether they are aware of it or not, *enjoy* emotional torture and will use the horses they own to play games with people's heads. I have seen some of them up close, and the frightening part is that this kind of person usually appears intelligent, charming, and benevolent. There is nothing they would not promise to do to make your dreams come true, and your happiness is the only reward they expect. Watch out: There is no such animal, unless it is your mother.

No doubt a generous sponsor deserves your very best effort when it comes to training, showing, and promoting the horse or horses you are lucky enough to ride without having to pay. To a rider who has just been presented with the horse of his or her dreams, plus promises of more horses, and is caught up in visions of glory, the details of everyday life under sponsorship may seem unimportant. This is where riders often go wrong by not insisting on a "prenuptial" agreement. Before going into any situation when somebody else gains the right to be an authority when it concerns your time, your image, your performance, and your results, get a contract put together that clearly states what is expected by each party involved in the relationship.

Changing riders/trainers is every horse owner's right, but there are different ways to go about it, and to make the announcement that you are removing the horse between tests at a horse show or right before the last ride in the Olympics is not considered good timing. It is just plain mean.

Not a Free Ride

So, are the sponsors always treated the way they deserve to be by their protégés? Unfortunately not. One interesting observation I have made is that quite often the sponsors, anxious to support a sport they love and be part of the action, tend to choose a rider to support who neither really deserves a "leg up" nor has the kind of personality you'd wish to promote. Lazy characters who do the minimum required, and tricky operators with all kinds of hidden agendas, are picked out for sponsorship *at least* as often as the riders who truly deserve a chance. And thus, having gone wrong at the source, the unsuspecting promoters of dressage end up with disappointments in training and show results, as well as in the behavior of their chosen rider. When the sponsor receives endless bills for frivolous clothing, expensive accommodations, and unnecessary equipment, the project ceases to be fun. Feeling used is no more pleasant to the sponsor than the sponsored. As in all relationships, the lack of trust and loss of the sense of striving together will eventually kill the partnership.

Sponsorship is not a free ride, and it should not be. The lucky person who finds a sponsor has a responsibility not only to the owner of the horses but to the entire sport. By doing his or her level best to train the sponsored horse or horses, represent the owner and the animals in a positive way, and show his or her gratitude through loyalty and respect toward the sponsor, the rider can become an ambassador for dressage. And he or she may help to encourage more people to become "owners" willing to create more horse/rider combinations through their financial support.

It can be the best of all worlds, or a living hell. But when it works, a sponsorship situation brings everyone what they want. The owners have fun and bask in their well-earned glory, the result of years of planning, dreaming, and making investments that would cause most financial planners to develop a migraine headache. And a talented and dedicated rider gets a chance to ride and show horses he would otherwise only fantasize about.

That's the best of all worlds, but it is a rare bird.

1999

– 33 –

to be an owner

*Due partially to circumstances beyond my control,
I was unhorsed and became "an owner" when I
leased Metallic* to Jane Clark for Robert Dover to
try out for the Olympics.*

After Robert took over the reins, I arrived at the first "non-show" for me
and was called to the secretaries' stand to receive an "owner's hat" as a
present from the staff of the WEF Dressage Classic in Wellington, Florida.
I was surprised, touched, and suddenly frightened. I looked at that hat
and realized I did not know the first thing about being an owner.

Learning on the Fly

I was in heavy training and while trying to learn, I developed a whole
new respect for the art of ownership. If you think it takes discipline to be
a rider, try ownership for a while. Here are a few of the things I learned:

---

* *I schooled Metallic from breaking to Grand Prix, and together we were part of the
1995 silver-medal-winning team at the Pan American Games. I was unable to ride on
the Olympic team due to a medical issue.*

- Find out where, when, who, and how yourself, because the rider is sometimes too involved to remember to clue you in.

- Be on time, dress correctly, and stay out of the way.

- Go to the schooling area to point with pride or view with alarm, whatever the occasion requires, but zip your lips even when you suspect you could be helpful. Unsolicited advice irritates the rider and upsets the routine. Talk about snags and strategy later, in private.

- Don't get in the way of the groom, especially before the class. Keep a low profile, trust the people you chose to do their job, be supportive, and keep your nerves under control.

- When you are bored, keep it to yourself.

Dress or Help

At the Olympic Trials at Gladstone I had plenty of time to watch some expert owners in action—Dick and Jane Brown,* for example. They brought two horses from California and almost immediately had to face the fact that one of them showed some lameness. The Browns decided to withdraw the horse, which is quite a tough decision to have to make after a long trip with all its inherent risks, costs, and work involved. Naturally the horse was just fine as soon as the competition was over...

On show day Jane was dressed to the nines, heels and all, carrying a bucket of something or other for the horse or busy cleaning his bridle. Dick, also in full regalia, cheerfully joined in. I decided I would either dress or help, since I don't have Jane's capability to stay clean while doing both. Metallic's groom, the very capable Katherine, had absolutely

---

* *The Browns were longtime supporters of US dressage, sponsoring rider Guenter Seidel for twenty-three years, and fulfilling roles for the USET and USET Foundation. The main arena at the USET headquarters in Gladstone, New Jersey, is named for them.*

no use for me, so I dressed. Then I joined my husband for the long wait. The longer we waited, the more I appreciated the numerous times he has "hurried up and waited" for me at endless horse shows. I never realized before how time flies when you are the rider, while it positively crawls when you are the owner.

Another great teacher to emulate is Jane Clark* who has ownership down to a fine science. I followed her around the Festival of Champions as she flowed with the greatest of ease between the dressage, jumping, and carriage venues, inquiring, encouraging, and praising her different equipages. Jane is a show rider herself, and this appeared an asset in her case, while at times the fact that I trained Metallic got in my way. While Robert rode his tests, I was there "on" the horse in every movement. Luckily, Metallic had no idea he had two riders, or that one of them was frantic on the sidelines in her dress. Of course these had to be the only Trials to date to be a cliffhanger down to the last ride! After Metallic and Robert were announced to be on the team, I felt more beat than if I had ridden every horse in the Trials myself. I drove home and slept twelve hours.

Part of my problem with ownership is that, like most dressage competitors, I am a control freak. Although I had complete confidence in Robert's ability to get every ounce out of Metallic, the knowledge that I was unable to influence the action just about drove me nuts. Although you get nervous before you ride yourself, the nervous tension turns into positive energy and becomes useful once you start warming up the horse. The passive watching made my toes curl in my shoes and was truly exhausting.

A "Show" in a Class by Itself

By the time the Atlanta Olympics rolled around, I had grown accustomed to being grounded and wearing hats, and had even grown a couple of

---

* *Jane Forbes Clark, one of the most actively involved high performance horse sport supporters in the world, owned horses that for many years took Robert Dover to the Olympics.*

quite respectable fingernails. The sunny side of ownership was starting to dawn on me. When we arrived there was lots of time to watch everyone school, chitchat with the riders and coaches, go to parties, and even spend time with family members. What a concept for a horse show! The Olympics, of course, is a "show" in a class by itself, and the tension ran high. One big worry was the Georgia weather, which contrary to reports by optimistic organizers, is normally at its most toasty in the end of July with temperatures in the high nineties. As by a miracle, we had two weeks of clouds, rain, and drab, which kept the average temperatures down to livable. One of our USET veterinarians, Midge Leitch, kept saying before departure for Atlanta that she'd be very happy to come home moldy. She almost got her way, and had some help from nature to keep our horses going. The facility at Conyers Horse Park was magnificent, seen from a horse's point of view. Safe and airy stalls, lots of warm-up rings with excellent footing, a fully equipped veterinary facility for emergencies (which also included every type of state-of-the-art therapy), lots of washstalls and even small roundpens for longeing or turnout. I heard nothing but praise for the way the barns were set up.

For the spectators, getting to and from the horse park was not a disaster in spite of the great volume of people. The parking lots were large enough to accommodate everyone, and although there was a healthy walk to the buses, golf carts were constantly on the run to pick up people with small children and the disabled. Free water was available at all stations, and yes—there were acres of Port-a-Johns! In the first parking lot, there was a jolly guy who greeted every single passenger with a cheery "Good morning!" and after a couple of days, we started looking forward to seeing him there. The lines at the buses were sometimes very long, and yet the loading and shipping went smoothly most of the time. Only once did we have a driver who had done too many hours on shift. He cut the twenty-minute run through the woods in half and treated us to an Indy 500 performance, talking and singing all the while. Perked everybody right up, it did.

The main sand arena was vast with seating around it available for 30,000. It worked great for the jumper course, but the dressage arena looked a little bit lost in this desert. In an effort to dispel that impression the organizers had added a number of 3-foot statues of women to the greenery around the ring. These received some very long looks from several of the horses in the Grand Prix who probably thought they were children ready to spring into action. The statues were a great excuse for shying, and they evaporated prior to the Grand Prix Special, supposedly as a result of a coaches' meeting, and were replaced by less frightening decorations.

The competition itself was of top quality. This was my third Olympics as a spectator, and both in Canada in 1976 and Los Angeles in 1984 there were rides that inspired you to go for a hot dog. Not so in this group. Not every single ride in the Grand Prix was awesome, but not one looked like it did not belong in the ring. Watching the reactions of the other members of a team while a ride of their nation was going on was very amusing. The Germans were intent and superior in their bearing; the Swedes aloof and stoic; the Spaniards waved flags and chatted; while the Italians piaffed in the stands to help their horse along.

After almost two weeks of watching triumph and tragedy in the Olympic arena, we had our fill, and it was nice to leave Atlanta and return to reality. Welcoming Metallic home after more than seven months was a lovely bonus. Whether you own an Olympic horse or one that competes on the local circuit, I am certain many of the experiences and concerns are the same. Hopefully my encounter with ownership will serve to make me more understanding when I deal with owners of horses I ride.

In any case, having walked a mile in the moccasins of an owner, I am quite anxious to get back in my boots.

1996

– 34 –

hello, young (horse) trainers

*On the initiative of USEF National Young Horse
Coach Scott Hassler, Maryland sport horse facility Hilltop Farm hosted a seminar for trainers of
young horses in fall of 2006.*

While we worked on the seminar as clinicians, Scott Hassler, German
sport horse breeder Ingo Pape, and I all enjoyed watching and listening to the interaction between the sixty or so trainers present, and we
certainly had some flashbacks to our personal career tragedies and triumphs. During the wrap-up session at the end of the last day, the three of
us went over some of the subjects covered again, and we agreed it would
have been so much easier if in the beginning of our own careers, we had
been able to network like trainers now can.

Relationships 101

One of the many subjects that came up during the dinner discussions
was the issue of properly dealing with the owner and client who
is our employer and source of income. Although "some of my best
friends are horse owners," the relationship between horse owner and
horse trainer/instructor can be a balancing act for both parties involved.

Sometimes the only person who feels that way is the trainer, and the horse owner is unaware of any discomfort on the "other end."

When you start out in any business, you are sort of "tiptoeing through the tulips" and trying to please everyone, because you are not really sure where the boundaries are between your expected availability and your right to privacy. The horse business is a strange venue in this respect. Horses are at your mercy all the time, and they are completely dependent on your support twenty-four-seven. This every horseman understands and respects. Problems begin when the horse owners who leave their mounts in our care come to think that the horses' all-access pass also applies to them. Some owners think nothing of calling all hours of the day and night to chat about their horse, since the trainer is a "horse lover" and consequently he or she must be available and interested at all times. If the trainer or stable owner is not at their beck and call, or if he or she is distracted, it is sometimes seen as an insult to the owner of the horse.

In the beginning of your career as a horse professional, it is very difficult to separate your private time from your time with the horses, and often it runs late into the night before subjects of discussion move off everything equine. As long as this is dictated by the horses, we rarely mind, but when our time is invaded by lonely people who think trainers are also psychologists, babysitters, and a source of free advice (about everything), it is time to put on the brakes.

During one of the dinners at the trainers' seminar, a young trainer carefully broached the subject, asking how to go about setting boundaries for her clients, since her husband was becoming quite irritated with the late evening calls and the interrupted dinners. The response was enthusiastic, and I do not believe all the trainers present realized they shared this common problem. I was amused at how lively the discussion became, and how some of the trainers said they had solved the problem.

One of them proposed setting up "office hours," just like any business. She gave her clients a couple of hours each day, during which she would be available to talk about their horses—and only then. Another trainer announced that, aside from during lessons, she is happy to talk about horses—but she charges per minute of advice, just like a lawyer. That sure cuts down on the small talk, and people get right to the point!

Room to Experiment

Another subject we touched on is how inventive we can allow ourselves to be in the training process without putting ourselves at risk legally. To state an example: You think the client's horse would benefit from some free-schooling over jumps to increase his flexibility and inspire his mind. Do you just put up the jumps, let the horse go, and have at it, or do you call the owner first and tell him or her what you are planning, because there is an additional risk involved in free-schooling? As a trainer, you are certainly expected to make decisions about what is appropriate for the horse at any given moment, but when a horse runs and jumps loose, you really do not have the same control as when you are riding. Horses in general are an accident waiting to happen, but you sure do not want to appear as if you helped the horse along in his suicide mission!

In this country, more than anywhere else in the world, we have to be very aware of the possibility of a lawsuit, often in cases when there is no real "villain" and no true wrongdoing. It behooves the trainer to think twice before following his or her instincts to have the horse enjoy a free-school-ing session (for example), and perhaps you need to put a lid on your enthusiasm and get permission in writing for anything above and beyond the run-of-the-mill workout.

Words and Dollars

I spoke privately with one trainer who said he usually had no problems with the horses in his care or their progress, but one of the owners who showed up for lessons drove him insane with constant comments during the ride. Yes, haven't we all had the "chatty ones"—the riders who feel compelled to give the instructor a running commentary on how they feel at every moment and what they think is going on?* This is the most annoying habit a student can have. Not only is it impolite and disruptive, but it immediately telegraphs to the horse that the rider is not focused, and the horse goes out to lunch. Every time the instructor makes a remark, the student comes back with, "But he's hanging on my right rein, and it feels like this or that..." Dialogue is not always a good thing, and a riding lesson is a perfect example. Effective riding is impossible for a student whose mouth is flapping, creating an excuse for not being able to concentrate and make a true effort. The reason such a student has trouble making progress is that most of the time he or she listens only when he or she is talking!

Another topic in our more private talks was on the subject of how to handle commissions. Handle them straight, I advised; let your client know that for you to be involved in the search and training of a new horse, you will expect to receive a commission once the horse is found and bought. If the client values your time and advice, he or she will agree. If you are good at your trade, the client's money will be well spent, and the owner can depend on your continued support and help.[†] Watch out for the buyers who proclaim they want to do their own thing, but then use up your time with videos of their adventures. Or the ones who have found the perfect horse but want to "pay you for the day" to check it out. That can become a catch-22. If you nix the horse, your motives are suspect, because of course they will think you'd rather approve a horse you found,

---

* *I explore riding lesson etiquette in Part II: "Giving and Receiving Instruction," p. 70.*

[†] *Revisit "Looking for Your Dressage Horse: The Process" in Part III, p. 95.*

and if you bless their choice, whatever goes on later will be your fault, although you did not pick the horse. Just say no, and wish them luck.

At the end of the seminar at Hilltop, Scott, Ingo, and I each gave a little farewell speech with some advice to the trainers. My "pearl of wisdom" was to encourage them always to own at least one horse. Nobody is immune to having a horse removed from them by the rightful owner, but as trainers we all understand the emotional toll such an event can extract. If you have one horse of your own that nobody can tell you when to show, how to campaign, or when to sell, your sanity stands a much better chance in times of stress. Training horses is a labor of love, but for the passion to survive through the years, we have to learn to conserve our free time and avoid the pitfalls of the trade.

2007

− 35 −

trouble at the grass roots

In 1998 I had contracted to judge two of the most prestigious shows on the East Coast. Both were USET qualifiers, both were oversubscribed with entries, and both shows were well run by capable and experienced people. I was looking forward to each event.

Due to the fact that I was competing in one of the USET divisions, my schedule was moved around in a way that kept me working with the AHSA* levels for between sixteen and twenty hours at each three-day show. It has been a while since I have spent that much consolidated time concentrating on mostly Training through Third Level, and I wish I could tell you it was an uplifting experience.

The American Horse Shows Association (AHSA) was the governing body intended to maintain clean competition and fair play in the show ring from 1917 to 2001, when it became USA Equestrian to better designate the member organization it had become. In 2003 USA Equestrian and the United States Equestrian Team (USET) became one cohesive group: the United States Equestrian Federation (USEF).

The Desperate State of Things

This was the scene that repeated itself *ad nauseam* at all levels: *Horse weaves into arena and slams to halt, head up, back down. While rider salutes, horse tries to leave the ring. Reluctant approach to C followed by a dive around the corner and a mad run on sort of a circle above aids with no bend. Screech to walk and fall into comatose wandering across diagonal. Lumber into trot again and then ambush horse into canter that is a parody of the gait because it is so flat, fast, and unbalanced. Jam on reins and retrieve trot, find centerline, use emergency brake, and crash to halt. Salute.*

Throughout the many hours of rides, there were rarely any transitions that looked as if the horse was in any way forewarned or prepared for the occurrence. Busy, tossing heads, often with twisted necks, were the norm, and if a horse did lower his head for a moment, he then usually became over-flexed and tight in the frame. Trots and canters lacked cadence and balance; no bend was evident in corners or on circles. The weakest level of them all appeared to be Second Level, where the requirements sharply increase and the poor basics take their toll. To my horror, I was regularly handing out scores in the forties and low fifties—something every judge hates to do, but in the name of honesty sometimes cannot avoid.

At the end of the two shows, I was so frustrated I could not get over myself. I had a chat with one of the technical delegates about the desperate state of things, and she pointed out that the "lower-level riders are our greatest financial supporters of the sport. They do it for fun and they don't really expect to advance, so chill out." Perhaps that is true, but personally I find it hard to believe that anybody who presents him- or herself on a horse in a show does not care about the image he or she projects or does not have a desire to advance. Moreover, we should not forget that dressage means training *for the horse*, not for the rider, who is supposed to know what is going on.

What upset me was not the fact that some riders had bad rides. God knows I have contributed my fair share of awful rides and bored judges to tears. But there was one big difference: I am usually aware when I have had a poor quality performance. What was scary in this scenario was that many of the riders who had bad rides appeared clueless! After five to seven minutes of exhibiting a horse that did not go forward; was crooked when he was supposed to be straight and straight when he was supposed to bend; was never on the aids; was oblivious to any signals for transitions; and displayed non-gaits due to poor balance, these riders left the ring with smiling faces and happy auras. (And they were probably shocked at my scores.)

I have no intentions of making fun of our lower level riders or discouraging them, but rather to warn them about something they may not be aware of: There are many of them out there who are not getting the right information. Somebody sold them a horse and introduced them to dressage. Somebody taught them the tests and told them how to dress and which classes to enter. Somebody probably got paid for this advice, which in practice is money down the drain. It is not the fault of the students when they follow to the letter directions that are incorrect, but the students pay for it in embarrassment as well as wasted time and money. The least anybody can ask from his or her instructor is that he or she tell the truth about the requirements of the sport, the readiness of the student to compete, and the scores he or she can expect at any given time.

One thing that occurred to me is that the problem could be even more severe: What if some of the teachers themselves are oblivious? After almost thirty years of dressage developing and growing in this country, that is a scary thought. We should not have to "start over" every single season as if we have no background or tradition in dressage. There are today scores of wonderful horses in this country, but no horse trains himself, and it is alarmingly easy to ruin a promising youngster. We have a number of American riders who have proven that they are able to repeatedly produce competitive FEI horses, and they ought to be just as able to help newcomers to the sport and young riders to get started right. So why do we have these "lost lambs" floundering around in the arena like ships without a rudder?

The Failing Link

Admittedly, my sampling is small by comparison to the thousands of shows all over the country, but my experience was not in a remote area at some local show. I arrived expecting to see the cream of the crop, but there was precious little splendor in those grass roots. I saw plenty of lovely horses and plenty of enthusiastic riders, but precious little positive influence from the failing link: the instructors. At USDF meetings, we spend endless time and effort creating ideas and programs to educate and help riders, trainers, and horses at the "grass roots level" to advance. Are we missing the boat somehow? Perhaps we need to plow up the whole bloody lawn and start an entirely new fertilizing program?

In the 1998 "Dressage Issue" of *The Chronicle of the Horse* Lilo Fore* touched on a related issue whose time may have arrived: She suggested a system of showing in which you would have to earn your way to the next level of competition before being allowed to advance. To control volume of entries, this method has been in use in Europe for a long time, and it also provides "quality control." This system might help riders gauge their own progress and would give our amateurs and juniors a way to measure their own advancement, as well as the quality of the instruction they receive.

---

* Lilo Fore is a successful rider, trainer, and coach, as well as an FEI 5* Dressage Judge, 3* Para-Equestrian Judge, and USEF "R" Sport Horse Judge. She is a founding member of the USDF Instructor Certification Program.

A Simple Recipe

In the meantime, a simple recipe for becoming a dressage rider is as follows:

- Start with months of frequent longe lessons for every rider who does not have a seat independent from the support of the reins. This is the most boring thing in the world for the rider, the instructor, and the horse, but it is the only sure way to learn how *not* to get in your horse's way.

- The next step is to rent, borrow, steal, or buy a horse that knows more than you do, and make sure that the teacher is way ahead of both of you.

- Add to that soreness and pain, perseverance, frustration, and a pinch of almost fanatic devotion to the sport.

- Bring to a boil, reduce heat, and stir methodically for three to five years.

- Remove from heat and let cool.

The proof will be in the pudding.

1998

− 36 −

where did the
extended trot go?

It is rare to see a horse in our competitions these days presented at a level where he really does not belong because he cannot fulfill the requirements asked for. This was a fairly common occurrence only a dozen years ago.

Nowadays our Grand Prix horses really do know how to piaffe and passage, and if there is a problem in the piaffe and passage "tour," the tempi changes, or the pirouette, it is more due to the form of the day and the riding. Most of the time there's a feeling that the rider is trying hard to fulfill the basic demands outlined in the FEI and USEF directives, as well as those of the Training Scale—and succeeding.

But there is one exception, as I have noticed after judging extensively, and that is the extended trot. The so-sought-after "expensive" trot, which we pay a premium for at auctions and look for in the young horse, does not routinely appear to develop into the extensions that are, after all, one of the highlights we desire in the performance of a dressage horse. I am not talking now about the young horses who have not yet achieved self-carriage or power to be able to develop and maintain a true extension, but of horses that are seasoned at Prix St. Georges and above. What judges repeatedly get treated to is a variety of trots that are "faking it" one way or another.

Seeing What's Not There

To begin with, there are no distinct transitions. Sometimes the beginning and end of the extension is so subtle that it is impossible to discern, even when the judge is awake and focusing. In reality, absolutely nothing happens, and you feel like you are a part of the tale "The Emperor's New Clothes," pretending to see what isn't there. That is the bottom of the heap. The next variety is when the horse hurries through the corner, and instead of coming onto the diagonal in balance and with his haunches "loaded" for takeoff, he is running in front-wheel drive. Arriving out of the corner in that fashion makes the transition "mission impossible." The honest horse makes a desperate effort to salvage the movement, and by the time he reaches X he is hopelessly lost in forward balance, often irregular, and struggling to reach the end of the diagonal. The less ambitious equine crawls behind the leg and does less and less to go forward, until the movement fades to a working trot before he reaches halfway. Then we have the "mad run," in which the horse develops a flat-footed scramble with a hollow back and the hindquarters trailing hopelessly. He reminds you of a bicycle flying by. The really fascinating extension is the one when the horse's frame gets shorter for each stride, his back lower, his front legs higher, and his neck tighter. That is almost as hard to accomplish all at once as it is to get an actual extension.

Naturally none of the workouts described just now have much to do with the directives for the movement.

The Ideal

So, how would an extension for a "10" look? Let's start with the transitions: They should be prompt and smooth without the slightest resistance. The horse should proceed accurately from point to point and in a straight line. There will be a clear difference between the extended trot and the medium trot when there is one called for in the test.

Going on the different aspects of the Training Scale (see p. 104), for a "10":

- The *rhythm* of the trot has to be absolutely regular in a clear two beats from beginning to end with a distinctive moment of suspension.

- No stiffness or tension can be present for a perfect score for *suppleness*. The back must swing under the rider, and the completely unconstrained steps must show superb elasticity.

- The *contact* has to be light and steady, with the nose more in front of the vertical than at a medium trot. In spite of the ultimate lengthening of the frame, the poll must remain the highest point.

- To accomplish all this, the requirements of the *impulsion* are strict: The hind legs are expected to propel the horse forward with very energetic and active steps, while the hind feet touch the ground as much as possible in front of the footprints for the front feet. Front and hind feet reach equally forward, and the front feet touch the ground on the spot toward which they are pointing.

- Naturally the horse's *straightness* is unquestionable, while the very engaged hind legs give the impression of a horse in complete balance, exhibiting freedom of the shoulder and lightness of the forehand found via *collection*.

- Under those circumstances the *submissiveness* is total, and there is no resistance whatsoever evident.

It is doubtful that many of us has experienced this state of bliss for an entire diagonal, but those are the directives if you strive for "excellent." Naturally there is a range of talent and ability that plays into the score, and there are horses that are superb at collection but have no true ability to become "airborne," never mind how they struggle. The springs for the suspension just were never installed. Interesting to observe is that all the way to the top placings in the Olympics, there are horses that lack the ability to use their back in the extended work and who possess almost no elasticity in their gaits or ability to stretch over the topline. What they do have is a tremendous knack for articulation of their joints. They can twist and turn and bend their knees and hocks like performers in *Riverdance*, and in the "Three Ps" (piaffe, passage, and pirouette) this is a real asset. Since we have shortened the Grand Prix there are only three extended trots to be displayed and no medium trot. There is no coefficient for the extended trot, so in the whole program of thirty-two movements it counts for very little. What should be one of our "crown jewels" has been put somewhat on the backburner. Anyone who trained with Colonel Bengt Ljungquist will agree that he would watch this development with a jaundiced eye. I will never forget the endless sessions he had me do on the 20-meter circle, practicing transitions in and out of trot lengthenings. Bengt would insist on the horse becoming "like a rubber band," and he was relentless about all the features I mentioned above that can lead to a "10."

So, the question is, will this trend toward rewarding collection—that is, the ability to compress—quite a bit more than elasticity, power, suspension, and volume stay in our tests? If it does, there will be even more horses bred, trained, and exhibited that actually can produce only one side of the coin, the collected movements, and will "fake" their way through the extensions at all gaits. One of the great difficulties in finding a dressage prospect has always been to get one that can "do it all." Some horses that are fabulous in the power and elasticity department can be very difficult to collect, and a challenge to train. These horses surely cannot get away with pretending to perform the movements that call for the ultimate in collection. However, it appears that the opposite type of animal, the one that falls short in the extended work, has an advantage in the numbers game.

We saw examples of both in the Athens Olympics. But we were also treated to the exceptional and "go for broke" trot extensions of horses capable of doing it all, such as Rusty (Ulla Salzgeber), Weltall (Martin Schaudt), and Bonaparte (Heike Kemmer). No holding back in those extensions! It just hit me as I was writing that all three of those horses were on the German team. Well, I guess there is a reason they are still on top.

2004

– 37 –

the battle of the frame

Over the past decades, it has been interesting to follow the controversy of the "top line" and discussions of various methods resulting in a horse that displays balance and engagement without any signs of lacking submission.

In 1996 I wrote an article in *Dressage Today* entitled "Behind the Vertical," which dealt with the issue of over-flexing the horse as a training method.* At that time, an outspoken German professor by the name of Meyer who contributed articles to the *St. Georg* equestrian magazine voiced some strong objections to the practice of bringing the horse's head behind the vertical, sometimes rolled up with his head between his knees. Mr. Meyer accused riders of keeping their horses' heads "attached" to their chests for up to an hour at a time without a break. He also strongly objected to the practice of twisting and yanking the animal's head and neck from side to side while forcing them to go forward. All this he observed in the schooling areas of various shows.

---

* This controversial technique became known as Rollkur or "deep and round."

"Rolled Up"

The rage of riding the dressage horse "rolled up" in front was, and still is, an attempt to copy the style of some of the most successful competitors in modern times, mainly the superstars Isabell Werth and Anky van Grunsven. Even before them, Nicole Uphoff used to ride her champion Rembrandt in a very deep frame, which she explained by saying that it minimized his tendency to shy.

Like many people, I have spent considerable time observing the riders mentioned here preparing their horses for tests. The horrors Mr. Meyer describes do not come into play when Isabell or Anky ride. The method is quietly and consistently used to supple and stretch the horse's top line as well as "tune in" his mind. When the warm-up is done, these accomplished ladies simply adjust the frame of the horse to position his poll as the highest point, and ride into the ring. I have observed the process enough times to know there is no undue stress or suffering involved when this technique is used by very skilled riders who have a true feel for and understanding of the purpose and limitations of the method.

Could it become cruel? Of course it can if used, as Mr. Meyer says, for hours at a time and involving "cranking" of the neck back and forth. Looking away from this extreme, should any but the elite riders attempt to use this method to supple their horses? Well, it depends on the horse's conformation and ability to focus on the rider, as well as on the sophistication and experience of the rider.

A Long-and-Low Religion

America has long been in love with the concept of "long and low," which can be very beneficial when used correctly and at the right time. I believe the same concept has also confused some horses and riders and permanently cemented many animals on the forehand. Instead of being an option for horses that need to stretch to operate through the back, and instead of being prevalent as a stage in training, it has in some cases turned into a religion, which has put an effective stop to collection.

Any trainer who has brought several horses up the levels will have found that some horses do not do well if asked to go very low in the bridle—in particular, the horse that tends to "lean" on his shoulders, is lacking withers, or has a low set-on neck. A horse with this kind of conformation cannot stay balanced behind the vertical, never has a chance to "discover" his hindquarters, and therefore operates in "front-wheel drive," to the detriment of his ability to carry himself and eventually his soundness. Other horses, who may not suffer physically from a deep-and-round frame, may become claustrophobic and tense in the body and mouth, which is rather the opposite of what riders are attempting to accomplish.

Following the discussion about the frame has been intriguing, but also sort of amusing, since I think there are many "rights," depending on the situation and the horse. When I started taking serious dressage lessons, I never remember being given a recipe to ride every horse a certain way. None of the trainers I worked with for extensive periods, such as Bengt Ljungquist, Harry Boldt, Herbert Rehbein, or Volker Moritz ever told me to keep the horse's head up or down, they just wanted the horse "on the aids." That concept may mean a slightly different thing for each horse, and that is where the trainer has to make the right call. Horses come in different shapes, temperaments, and abilities, just like people. What works for one animal does not necessarily do the trick for another. When I rode with Herbert Rehbein, he would often ask us students, "How does he feel in your hand?" Not that Herbert could not see if the horse was correct in his outline, but he also wanted to know what the rider felt, and I liked that kind of interaction between the three of us.

Since the days of the old masters, our perception of what is correct has evolved to the very high caliber of performance the top riders of today are expected to produce. Our modern competition horse displays more "body building" and more power and has higher demands on precision than the dressage horse of yesterday. Thanks to improved breeding methods he is also a better machine, built for the job. Our methods of training have taken some new roads, but in principle we all return to "forward and straight and on the bit" as our basic daily gospel.

2000

– 38 –

dedicated to members of the stuc(k) society: on the subject of collection

The inspiration for writing on this topic and a great deal of the input has been given to me by Karen Rohlf,* who has been my student for close to twenty years and my assistant trainer for over a decade.

One morning while walking our horses between work sessions, Karen told me about her "secret society" of students struggling with the concept of collection: the "STUC Society." She pointed out how the introduction of collection in the work sometimes confuses students, and makes them insecure and even angry because it can be disruptive to the harmony between horse and rider. Certainly, I can identify with her observations, as trainer, teacher, and judge. Before we picked up our reins, I asked Karen

---

* Karen is also the talented artist who provided the illustrations in this book.

to share some of her thoughts with my readers, since I know the step up to collection is difficult both for the horse and for the rider who tries to introduce it to a horse for the first time.

The Simple Becomes Complicated

The most common problem for her students, Karen says, is to grasp the concept of shortening and making the gait "smaller" without losing power in the process. "I tell them collection is *more* trot or canter in a smaller space, like in a pressure cooker, and they are not allowed to let any of the 'air' out to make it fit in the smaller space," she explains. She takes pains to address the issue of straightness, which is intimately connected with the ability of the horse to collect. Many students have problems feeling the straightness or crookedness in their horse, and this deficiency comes back to bite them later on when the horse, asked to collect, starts to "drop the ball" and fall sideways rather than taking responsibility for his own balance.

As soon as collection is introduced, things that used to be simple tend to become complicated. Karen, who is a licensed massage therapist, is convinced that body awareness is a major issue here. Yoga, massage, tai chi, and chiropractic adjustments in whatever combination needed can all help to supple and mentally tune the rider in, to facilitate "feel" as well as promote understanding of the problems the horse may experience.

On the subject of half-halts, the tool that creates balance and strength, Karen is silent until she feels the student has developed a reasonably independent seat. Otherwise any amount of explanations cannot prevent the pulling, clutching, and hanging on the reins that the mere mention of the word "half-halt" tends to produce. Instead, she prefers to wait and watch for an "instinctive" half-halt and the proper reaction from the horse to follow. Only then does she inform the student of his or her advancement in the art of horsemanship, and goes on to explain the details of the mystery of the half-halt and its benefit for promotion of collection. While waiting for this magic moment to occur, she might say things like, "Reinforce your aids," or "Push him into your hands," in the hope of detecting the first signs of communication leading to increased balance and self-carriage. By not forcing the issue of the half-halt, there will be fewer bad habits to correct later on.

Small Bites

Lack of stamina and lack of perseverance are two of the prominent features Karen has observed in her "STUC Society." Once they have taken that first step toward understanding the feel and purpose of the "pressure cooker," the students tend to think that one half-halt is going to make the day. The concept of repeated attempts at coordination and muscle effort often has to be spoon-fed to the riders. Few of them realize that the half-halt has to be constantly renewed in order to maintain the balance in the horse. Here she recommends that the student should be content with short periods of collection with "rest periods" for both horse and rider in between. At this stage it is more valuable to go back and forth between working and collected gaits for short periods, in order to avoid fatigue and cheating, when the rider holds the horse in a small frame with his hands rather than generating the power to "lift" the forehand from behind. This on-and-off approach also benefits the horse, who learns to compact and carry himself in small "bites" until he builds the strength and stamina to sustain his collection without needing to fall back into the working gaits.

In the enthusiasm of developing collection, a member of STUC may also become so enthralled with the prospect of new horizons in riding that he or she starts to over-ride. He or she adds stronger and louder aids to the pot, and eventually becomes more active than the horse. The type of horse that is not frightened or made nervous by the "shouting" of aids tends to do less and less in this scenario. Eventually the horse loses his sensitivity to the aids, leaving the lion's share of the workload to the rider. Keeping an eye on this situation is vital for the instructor, to avoid producing a horse that is difficult to motivate and becomes uninterested in his work.

Checking In

Our check points are the transitions. Collection in its true sense is supposed to make everything easier. If it does not, it is time to examine why, and the transitions will tell the story. Whatever goes wrong in the transitions was already a problem before the rider asked for a change of gait—that is, the horse was not "through," not in front of the leg, or not mentally prepared to respond. In short, he was not truly collected.

Often when this stage of training arrives, it causes trouble in what was, before collection, paradise. The student was happy, the horse was round, and the lessons flowed in harmony. Then, like the snake in the Garden of Eden, the instructor ruins it all by telling the truth about the horse's lack of self-carriage, engagement, and ability to "sit" behind.

Innocence gone, the student suddenly stays awake at night worrying about the shortcomings of a performance that used to be quite satisfactory, and the horse in his stall says to himself, "I had them convinced things were just great. What got into these people? What's all this sweating and lifting all about?"

Karen says this is the "transition period" that she does not look forward to. The time has arrived when she has to ruin the fun by insisting on things neither rider nor horse wish to dwell on. The best of all worlds, of course, is to have a well-schooled horse available to show the student the purpose of all this work, and to let him or her experience riding an animal that truly carries the rider and has the ability to rock back on his hocks, elevate his withers, and give you that feeling of balance and power under the seat bones that promises you he can do anything, go anywhere, from there. Lacking this tool for furthering understanding, the teacher has to paint a very convincing picture of the benefits of a thousand half-halts and transitions, leading to the ultimate goal of achieving collection in all its glory. It is a tough step up, but once the horse and rider capture that first sensation of collection and enjoy a few moments of perfect balance and harmony, they will be eager to return to that feeling, and that's when Karen knows she's got them hooked. Clever girl, that Karen!

Once collection has become a major feature in the everyday work, maintaining it turns into a challenge. Balance, engagement, and self-carriage are all ingredients that are part and parcel of the concept of "collection," and the whole package does not always stay together. While riding a test on a horse recently introduced to serious collection, you can rarely count on it staying in place for the entire performance. The trot goes flat just as you need that extra bounce in the half-pass. The canter dies and turns into a walk in the pirouette. It is just like the saying from the 1970 film *Little Big Man:* Sometimes the magic works, and sometimes it doesn't!

Judges rarely see any collection until Third Level, and by that time, both rider and judge appreciate it if it is somewhat consistent. As one of my very experienced scribes pointed out, there is only one place where collection can be guaranteed: in church on Sunday.

2001

— 39 —

the elusive half-halt

Among the many body signals we use to communicate with our horses, the half-halt reigns supreme. Its importance cannot be overstated, and yet a great number of equestrians pursue their riding with only a vague idea of what they are really expected to do when asked to "make a half-halt," never mind why.

Let's Start with *Why*

Imagine you are a spectator watching a Prix St. Georges test. The horse enters the diagonal at the canter, and you know that the next movement required is a half-pirouette—a 180-degree turn and return to the corner of the arena. Now, how is the horse going to know ahead of time what the big plan is? Why would he not canter on in oblivion or suddenly scoot sideways when the rider gives the aids for the pirouette?

Well, without the presence of a half-halt, he probably would! Consequently, the most important function of the half-halt is to prepare the horse for the next item on the rider menu. When the horse recognizes the half-halt as a call to attention, he focuses on the rider's aids and mentally makes himself "available" to the rider. It is as if he picks up the phone and says, "You rang?"

Secondly, the half-halt, when it "goes through," as we say in dressage lingo, will serve to balance the horse by helping him to shift more of his weight to the hindquarters. A horse without a rider normally has no problem with balance, but once a passenger comes on board, the horse tends to travel on the forehand, unless he is taught to change his method of operating. Most horses are built heavier in the shoulders and neck, and when the rider's weight is added to the already heavy forehand, the horse goes into front-wheel drive, a most undesirable feature in dressage horses. Repeated and successful half-halts will eventually "remodel," shifting his "traction" to a lowered hind end, changing his balance like a seesaw, and even lifting and lightening his shoulders.

Thirdly, the half-halt is the regulator of speed—that is, miles per hour—and it can effectively be used to set the correct pace.

To summarize the purpose of the half-halt: It serves as a line of communication in the preparation for transitions and movements; it balances and engages the horse; and it controls the tempo. As an additional bonus, it has a guaranteed positive effect on your instructor, who will thrill to the completion of every successful half-halt. No riding teacher will ever complain because you made too many half-halts!

Let's Discuss *What You Do*

So far, so good, but how do you make it happen? To simplify beyond belief: Think of the half-halt as exactly what the name says—a half of a halt—using your "seat" (meaning your lower back, stomach muscles, and seat bones) and closing your legs, pushing the horse into a closed hand (squeezing your fingers around the reins as if you had a sponge in each hand), and keeping a steady rein connection with the horse's mouth. Your driving aids will be saying *go*, but your hands will say *stop*.

This juxtaposition of aids only lasts for a moment, about as long as it takes you to breathe in and breathe out. If there is resistance in the form of pulling or head-tossing, or no reaction at all from the horse, do not persist. The charm of the half-halt is that it evaporates in efficiency if you overdo. No amount of hanging on the reins after the magic "window of opportunity" is past will help—just the opposite. It will shut down the engine and cause disagreement instead of useful dialogue.

When the right reaction occurs, the experience, or the "feel," is as if the horse's hind legs keep going, the front end slows slightly and elevates, and the back of the horse rises up under your seat bones. When the stifles and hocks push toward the momentarily restricted forehand, the horse contracts the muscles in his belly and literally lifts his back and withers upward. What a great feeling! Then it is time to get over your euphoria and ease up with your fingers and wrists before the horse becomes claustrophobic and starts to protest. (Wonderful is short-lived!) As soon as you feel a response and a tendency by the horse to think "halt," you release the restricting aid and encourage him to go forward again. Your body language says to him, "Thanks for listening, but I was only kidding!"

The correct and effective use of the half-halt is one of the secrets of good riding, along with understanding how to employ the outside rein and developing a feel for cadence and true hand-to-mouth connection. When these ingredients are in place and working to satisfaction to produce results, you have become an "insider." You are now speaking the silent, ancient, and universal body language of classical training, which will enable you to get on any well-trained horse in the world and have a fulfilling discourse with him.

2002

– 40 –

winning the warm-up

The most interesting place for spectators to stand at a dressage show is not necessarily next to the competition ring. Both competitors and trainers know that a class can be lost or won in the schooling area, and what happens in the test is sometimes just a reflection of the events in the warm-up.

A Few Extra Minutes

For the competitor, the "test" starts when you arrive in the schooling area. For each horse I have brought up the levels, the preparation for competition has been a little different, and it can take several shows on a new horse to figure out what formula works for him. In general, I have a tendency to favor long and slow warm-ups, which has driven some of my instructors to mutter and fuss. One of my reasons for this is that I try to beat Murphy's Law. Notice, if you will, how stirrup leathers break, hairnets crawl off your hair, safety pins snap in half, numbers pop off the bridle, and if all else fails, spurs crack and fall to the ground. Some of these things may happen at home, but they are a hundred times more likely to happen within half an hour of your test. A few extra minutes to set things straight is a good thing.

I also like to take time to walk the horse for a while to get him comfortable with the surroundings, "oil up" his joints, and loosen his muscles. Often we travel long distances to shows, and the footing is not likely to be identical to the one at the homestead, so some time to get used to the way it feels and get rid of the stiffness from travel helps both horse and rider. It also gives me an idea of the "traffic pattern" in the schooling ring at large, busy shows so I can avoid a lot of stop and go, which irritates the horse.

A Basic Routine

Once you change gears, it helps to know if your horse warms up better at the canter or the trot. I often start at the canter, especially with horses that tend to tighten their backs in the beginning of a ride. After a few minutes of canter in a round and fairly low frame, I'll go to trot and canter transitions to check on "throughness" and the ability of my horse to focus. If all systems are "go," I start working on achieving the engagement and frame appropriate to the level the horse is showing at. Finally, I work through the movements I feel we may need checking on. I like to have the time available for all this, plus a few minutes to take a breather before stripping bandages, crawling into the jacket, and putting the final touches on the preparations. All this takes approximately forty-five minutes from soup to nuts.

This time period works for most of my horses, but certainly not all. The chili-pepper-hot horse may need upward of an hour to settle into the "show mood," while the very laid-back variety can easily run out of steam in twenty minutes and leave all his energy in the schooling area. Some horses do better with an early dawn warm-up, and a short reminder a few minutes before the test; others need to be worked thoroughly before

Fat-and-Happy Athletes?

Fat is a big national health problem in people, but in horses it is apparently a bonus. At least half of our horse population is overweight, and many a leg and wind problem is related to over-fed, under-conditioned horses being asked to work beyond their capacity. A dressage test is only eight to ten minutes long, but the warm-up at a show can take up to an hour. The FEI tests are demanding, and by the time the horse goes into the Grand Prix ring he really needs to be fit to be able to perform this athletic feat in all sorts of weather and footing.

going in the ring. Once you know your horse and can "customize" his warm-up, you will have a good handle on things—unless life intervenes.

The Thing About the Weather...

Changing weather can easily throw a wrench in the works. Many years ago, when I rode in a Pan American Games Trial in North Carolina, the weather was unusually hot for the spring. I was on a horse named Kristall, and his warmup routine was to have a single session right before the test. Because it was so hot, I decided to ride early in the morning and then do a short warm-up right before the test. It was a disaster. When I got on to prepare for the test, there was not an ounce of gas left in Kristall's tank. Riding down the centerline into the indoor arena, where the temperature was about 100 degrees, I could feel the horse get further and further behind my leg. We dragged ourselves through a seemingly endless row of exercises, while I cursed my lack of judgment. Mentally, this horse was done for the day when his morning ride was over, and I was a fool to have split his sessions at such a critical time.

The opposite happened in Dusseldorf some years later. It was an icy winter day, the warm-up was in a tent, and my stallion, Leonardo II, was first to go. A horse was being longed in the very limited schooling ring until ten minutes before the start of the Grand Prix class. It was "get on and go," and we had less than five minutes of warm-up for a horse who needed considerably more. In spite of his desire to explode, the generous Leo kept the lid on and "winged" the whole thing with me, ending up with a decent test.

Behind the Curtain

At international shows and trials, spectators gravitate to the schooling area to try to predict the quality of the test-to-be, to learn, to admire, and to criticize. It is often more informative than watching the test. At Bromont (Canada) in 1976, I saw Harry Boldt do twenty half-passes to the right, which all looked fine to me, until he found the one that did it for him. I watched Granat bolt up the hill and take his rider back to the barn when he caught sight of his trainer, one-time Chief Rider at the Spanish Riding School in Vienna Georg Wahl, standing in the ring. Considering this was the eventual gold-medal-winning horse, that is an interesting memory. On many occasions, I have followed the schooling sessions when Anky van Grunsven and Isabell Werth have ridden their horses "rolled up" behind the vertical, only to put them up in a proper show frame a few minutes before the bell tolled for them. The first time I saw Ulla Salzgeber was when she appeared on the German team in the European Championships at Verden as a replacement for another rider. I had no idea who she was, but as soon as she entered the schooling area, she took command of the warm-up with an air of determination and zest, which put us all on notice. And we have all paid attention ever since.

In Europe, there have been recurring complaints over the last ten years about some of the techniques applied in the warm-up area, which are considered less than kind to horses. In particular, riding for long periods with the horse's chin on his chest and exceedingly long sessions of piaffe and passage have been called into question. Klaus Balkenhol spoke to me not long ago about his wish to have a system to better oversee the schooling. He suggested placing a judge in the schooling area who would watch and take notes on the last thirty minutes of each horse's warm-up. The judge would then give a score for the warm-up, and this score would be factored into the final score from that horse's performance. Although I believe this is more a problem overseas than here in the United States— since we have Technical Delegates who are proactive and see to it that issues in the schooling are usually solved fairly quickly—it is certainly an interesting concept.

The perfect warm-up is a rare animal, and curiously enough, it does not by definition lead to the perfect test. Many times we can have had "that winning feeling" while putting the hat and coat on because the horse feels so "on." And then, as you depart from X, he turns into some animal you have never known, and in the end the only thing you won was the warm-up!

So, the moral of this story is to try to deliver a customized warm-up for each horse, because it gives you both confidence and a winning edge. However, if the warm-up turns out to be less than wonderful, remember the old saying: Bad rehearsal, good show. It does at times apply to dressage, as well. When everything goes wrong in the schooling ring, pray for a miracle, go for it, and let your horse surprise you.

2004

– 41 –

advice from the coach

Sometime in the eighties, I saw the not-yet-Olympic-champion Klaus Balkenhol competing at an indoor show at Bremen, Germany. It was an important event, because it counted for team selection for whatever championships was on the agenda that year, and the stands were packed.

The Riding Policeman

Klaus was mounted on a chestnut, I believe stallion, named Aponti, and it was not just the police uniform that set him apart from the rest of the field. While the official team hopefuls were not having their best day, Klaus was clocking through the test with a casual ease, as if it was all just another day's work. When his comparatively low score was announced, the audience growled threateningly and a banana peel landed on one of the judge's boxes. I had never seen an audience react to judging with such gusto before, in particular since we were not spoiled with spectators of *any* kind in the United States. Being quite amazed and amused by the whole thing, I found the award ceremony to be another treat. For the first nine placings, there were polite applause. When Klaus Balkenhol was announced as placing tenth, the place went ballistic. People stamped and clapped and shouted and stood up on their chairs and refused to stop in spite of the pleading from the announcer. It was crystal clear that the "riding policeman" was the choice of the people.

As the years went by, he also became the choice of the dressage judges as he kept coming back with one horse after the other, proving he was no "flash in the pan," but an outstanding trainer and show rider. The rest is history, and we have been lucky to have this talented and dedicated man as our team coach.

When Klaus trains a rider on a horse, he pays a lot of attention to the details that do not necessarily have to do with the actual riding, but with the many things that surround the performance. He worries about the fit of the tack, the way the horse looks at him, the feed and supplements— all the things most trainers leave up to the rider and the grooms. In short, he is a horseman, not just a rider.

Tips from True Horsemen

In the end of September 2003, Klaus Balkenhol and Gerd Heuschmann,* a veterinarian who has competed at Grand Prix level, gave a young horse seminar at Stromsholm in Sweden. Some of the general advice they gave the participants and the audience is worth sharing here.

- Because of the delicate relationship between the neck and the back, the young horse should not be dictated into any kind of a frame during the first year of training. Contact with the hand is of great importance, but any forcing of the neck into position or pulling the head into a frame is detrimental to the future of the horse and likely

---

* *Dr. Gerd Heuschmann is the author of the international bestsellers* Tug of War: Classical versus "Modern" Dressage; Balancing Act; *and* If Horses Could Speak.

to ruin the development of the back. The two gentlemen made no secret of their opposition to the "rolling up" of the neck and riding behind the vertical favored by some very successful show riders.*

- Never walk right up to a young horse and look him straight in the eye. He may consider this a threat. Instead, approach from the side of the horse and let him initiate the contact. (Sounds like some of our "natural horsemanship" sermons, which are, at their best, just good, sound horsemanship.)

- Avoid using a foregirth. According to Dr. Heuschmann, the foregirth puts uncomfortable pressure on the horse's ribs. This I found interesting, since I know of prominent and successful trainers who swear by them and use them on every young horse, whether they need one or not! I have not had a lot of luck with them, but there are cases when saddle fitting is a nightmare and there is no other way to avoid ending up on the horse's neck. This a good reason to strive to breed horses with well-defined withers.

- When you buy a new saddle, put a thin piece of cloth under the saddle to begin with, and the saddle will form to the horse through his warmth and sweat.

- If a horse is broken to ride as a three-year-old and then turned out for a year or two, he has as great a chance, if not a better one, to reach Grand Prix as the horse that is worked continuously. Then he can grow and develop in peace. A horse is not an "adult" until he is seven or eight years old. (I agree with this, but find this statement contradictory to the development of the international test for young horses. I was present at a Warendorf, Germany, judge's forum in 1998 when the judges were first introduced to what was to become the FEI

---

* *See my discussion of this subject in "The Battle of the Frame," p. 184.*

Young Horse Championships six-year-old test.* Many of the judges, me included, considered that test too demanding for the age, while the trainers, Klaus being one of them, insisted that "any six-year-old worth his salt should be able to do that test." Well, that won't happen if he hangs out in a pasture until he is five...)

- Don't ride in a tempo too fast for the horse. He then loses his balance and becomes nervous, since he is afraid of falling, and tension sets in. So much for the "fast forward" we all run into at clinics at times, when our horses get run off their feet to demonstrate that they respond to our driving aids and are just dying to do our bidding, never mind how confused and scared they may get. Everyone gets treated to that clinic at least once! And after living with your post-clinic horse, you are much smarter about what you *don't* want to do.

- The extended trot is difficult to learn for most horses. At liberty, the horse would fall into canter, rather than lengthen his stride at the trot. The extended trot, according to Klaus Balkenhol, is a product of the highest collection, and therefore it must be ridden "in collection." It is not the collected work that puts wear and tear on the horse, but the extensions at trot and canter if the horse falls on the forehand and supports his weight on his front legs.

- Nervous youngsters need a varied program, and all young horses need lots of walk periods on a completely loose rein, but they must continue to march willingly. If the horse shies away from something, don't force him to confront it and look at whatever upsets him. Eliminate the problem, if it is removable. Reward the horse as soon as he does something positive, and always cease work before the horse is exhausted. Leave some gas in the tank for future use, and allow the horse to end on a fresh note.

---

* I talk about this subject at greater length in Part III—see p. 129.

- A young horse does not need to go to competitions more than two or three times a year, and the more time you allow for the horse to grow and develop, the better he will last and serve you in the future. The tendency to strive for six- and seven-year-old horses to go Grand Prix leads to the loss of many a fabulous talent—before they turn ten they are gone from the sport. A normal age for a horse to "know" all the Grand Prix movements and be starting competition at that level is about ten. He can then polish his act for a year or two, and still be in the limelight and on top of his game at seventeen or even older!

2003

riding to music: a short history

In February 2002 I gave a short talk on the history of the freestyle as a part of the National Judges Forum USEF and FEI 5* Judge Axel Steiner and I conducted together. It occurred to me that perhaps some of my readers would be interested in the background of our interest in riding to music.

Beginning at the Beginning

When we look into the history of classical riding, we often start by mentioning the Athenian Xenophon, one of the first equestrians to take the initiative to study other riders and put his observations into the form of a book with the intent of passing them on. Xenophon, who died in 354 BC, was a philosopher and a historian, but also a soldier. This Greek cavalryman closely studied the style of warfare exhibited by the Iberian Cavalry because of its ability to perform fast and exact maneuvers with horses. At this age, cavalry was of the utmost importance to any civilization.

From humanity's domestication of the horse to the twentieth century, the expansion of nations and the development of cultures depended on the strength and power of cavalry.

Among the ancient tribes of Europe and Asia, the cavalry performed ritual rides on religious days. These could be held by a tribe around the grave of a hero, for instance, or with mounted presentations showing off the strength of the horse-borne troops through various maneuvers. The rituals were always accompanied by music, which in those days was performed by an assortment of trumpets and drums, so called "open air music," all of which is well documented on Greek and Roman stone carvings. From these performances stem the Latin word *tornare* and the German word *turnam*, which mean "turning quickly on horseback." In the Middle Ages, this developed into the *tournament*, which always opened and closed with parades of participating knights and their horses, with music playing a major part.

With the introduction of firearms, knights in heavy armor became obsolete, and the style of riding had to change. The type of horse needed to survive was not one strong enough to carry a heavy weight, but rather a mount that was light and agile, and could dodge the enemy and go faster over long distances. The Middle Ages were followed by the Italian Renaissance, which strived for the glories of old Rome, and the various courts of Italy started to imitate the cavalry celebrations of ancient times, again including lots of music. During the ensuing Baroque period, the first form of the *carousel* appeared. The carousels usually included a parade followed by fights on horseback, but in a choreographed form that created rather harmless games (on a circle) without any real danger to the participants. In Italy, especially at the court of Medici in Florence, a form of carousel was created to celebrate the *Festa de Caballo*, the "festival of the horse," presenting a story on horseback. Normally it exhibited a theme from a saga or allegory, artfully accompanied by music.

This syndrome lead to a rash of "horse ballets," which were performed all over Europe, some of them almost becoming elevated to the status of operas on horseback. Out of this were born *quadrilles*, which were also usually based on some theme from an already-known story. The composers at the courts would write music specifically for horse performances.

The most famous and largest horse ballet took place in Vienna in 1667, and it included more than 600 horses and about 1300 people. It was performed to celebrate an imperial wedding, and the choreography, the music, and the story (which presented the Emperor of Austria as the "Master of the Elements") have been preserved to this day, partly through engravings. An entire orchestra was involved in providing the music, including clarinets and violins.

The extravaganza in Vienna rather knocked the air out of any other attempts at one-upmanship, and after 1667 very few horse ballets are mentioned. Instead, the carousels enjoyed a short revival as indoor events accompanied by a full orchestra.

The end of the nineteenth century closed the era of carousels and instead horses entered the arena of sports, when in 1912 equestrian disciplines were made part of the program at the Stockholm Olympics.

Two world wars put a stop to a lot more than horse activities and sports events, but through it all equestrian traditions have survived in their purest form at the Spanish Riding School in Vienna, Austria; the Cadre Noir in Saumur, France; the Escuela Andaluza del Arte Equestre in Jerez, Spain; and the Escola Portuguesa de Arte Equestra in Queluz, Portugal. For the most part, these institutions keep the art alive in quadrilles, and there have been some serious debates to determine whether quadrille should become part of international competitions. Having watched the freestyle explode onto the competition scene in every division, I don't doubt this is a possibility.

The Closing of the Circle

The freestyle is both loved and hated: loved by the audiences because of its entertaining nature, loved by some riders who enjoy riding to music, and hated by some riders because of all the work, and sometimes expense, involved in creating and practicing the rides.

By judges, the freestyle is often considered the most difficult test to score correctly because of the many considerations on the artistic side of the score sheet.* However, once judges are comfortable with this new addition to their duties, many of them look forward to the freestyle because horse and rider often perform to music with more *élan* and improved relaxation. That is why we decided to work on the details of judging the freestyle and emphasize this feature in our 2002 National Judges Forum.

When you watch the freestyles from the World Equestrian Games or the Olympics, you are actually seeing the closing of the circle: Riding to music has come back to stay.

2002

---

* *I speak more to the subject of judging freestyles in Part V, p. 246.*

V   judging and
    being judged

– 43 –

deciding in a blink
of an eye

*While I was at the World Cup Finals, my friend
Jim Lewis gave me a book as a present and
said, "All judges should read this." The book was
the bestseller* Blink *by Malcolm Gladwell (Little,
Brown and Company, 2005), and it makes some
powerful points about how our brains function in
decision-making.*

The premise of the book is to show the power we have to *think without
thinking*—in other words, it addresses our inherent ability to make decisions without gathering information or deliberating. How many times
have you met someone you instantly disliked at, "Hello"? You know
nothing about this person, but all your instincts tell you to stay away
even before he or she has uttered an entire sentence. If you become more
familiar with the person, does the first impression prove to be the one
that persists, or do you later change your mind? Or the opposite happens,
and there is an immediate feeling of comfort and joy in the presence of

213

a perfect stranger. If you get to know this person, it usually proves to be the lasting impression over time.

"Thin Slicing"

In a weekend of judging, a judge has to make thousands of instant decisions, and this book is about exactly that: first impressions and, as Gladwell terms it, the process of "thin slicing." What we judges pass on to our scribes is our very first impression of every movement produced in a test. Sometimes we wonder, after the test has left with the runner, if a certain movement should not have had a higher or lower score, and we wish we could change the score. As a rule, it is not a good thing to fool with a score that came up in your mind as you watched the movement. The instant instinct is mostly the correct one, and if you deliberate too long, the moment is lost and you cannot recapture the true essence of what went on. Your instincts become weaker as you analyze the movement. You go off in a different direction, and not necessarily the correct one.

Since most of our judging is instant feedback without any time to reflect or reconsider, it is comforting to read a book that supports the argument that our instinctive first impressions are the ones that prove to be true, even after close scrutinizing and research. There are a number of examples in *Blink* that show that first impressions and "thin slicing" are reliable methods for finding the truth and making the right decisions.

My favorite example is the very first one, which describes a rare find for the J. Paul Getty Museum in Los Angeles, California, of a *kouros*, a statue of a nude male youth, of which only about two hundred are known to be in existence. The statue in question and available for purchase was very well preserved, which was unusual, and although the museum moved with utmost caution, consulting with several experts, the kouros passed every scrutiny with flying colors. After months of deliberation, the museum was ready to make the purchase. Shortly after, trouble arrived in the form of doubters who were, indeed, very knowledgeable, but did not base their doubt about the authenticity of the statue on their expertise but solely on a "feeling." One said he could not help looking at the fingernails of the statue, but could not articulate exactly what was wrong with them; a second person was overwhelmed by the "freshness" of the statue when it was unveiled in front of him. A third immediately disliked the color of the stone, which he felt looked like it was dipped in a latte from Starbucks.

Well, all these people ended up being right in the end. After exhaustive research, the statue was, indeed, proven to be a fake. What is interesting is that although all the doubters were experts in the field, none of them used scientific methods or even reason to make their decision that the statue was a phony. They all just looked at it for about two seconds and felt an "intuitive repulsion." It took the research team at the Getty Museum fourteen months of research to come to the same conclusion.

Judging on Instinct

The very best dressage judges, in my opinion, are those with that really keen instinct for what is going on. They have a "feel" for the game, which is almost as if they were riding the horse along with the rider. I have sat with, worked with, and ridden in front of several judges I admire because they have that extra ingredient, which is not only about placing the class—although they are usually right on target—but rather a special "beam" they possess that absorbs and evaluates the horse's effort as it is happening and with no hesitation. My main hero among judges is one many people agree was a genius, and I am glad I got to spend time with him before he died. His name was Jaap Pot, and he was a human judging machine in that he never forgot a horse or a movement, and yet had a wonderfully positive attitude and an open mind. His judges' seminars were a treat to those of us lucky enough to attend, and he had a "feel" for judging like Herbert Rehbein had a feel for a horse.* And, just like with Herbert, most of it was pure instinct.

In the last chapter in *Blink*, the author gives us another example that hits home in a different way. In 1980, the Munich Philharmonic Orchestra needed a musician to play the first trombone. In fairness to the players, the audition was done with the players performing behind a screen. Twenty-three candidates later, the auditors were unanimous about who they wanted: Player Number 16. They were stunned when a woman, Abbie Conant, walked onto the stage. The chaos was total, because everyone "knew" that a woman was "too weak" to play the trombone properly, and furthermore, it was just against the unwritten rules of tradition to have a woman in the position of first trombone. Everyone backpedaled as fast as they could, and only after eight years and many tours through the courts did Frau Conant get reinstated in the position she had already earned behind the screen.

When we listen to music without looking at the performers, do we see it differently? It sure appears that way. So, if the judges truly were unaware of who was riding the horse, or what breed it was, would the scores come out the same as when they know the rider and are familiar with the breed? If five computers could be programmed with all the specifications for riding the perfect test (and anyone remained alive after the battle over how they should be programmed), do you think we would still see the same horses and riders on top all the time? When competitors jokingly say to each other, "We should all enter with paper bags on our heads, and no numbers," are they really only kidding?

Read Gladwell's book, and see what you come up with—in a blink.

2005

---

* Read "Herbert Rehbein" in Part II (p. 75) to find out about this "feel."

– 44 –

the american brand of judges

There are not many areas of dressage where we could say that this country is leading the way, but our system for educating and examining our judges is one sector in which we are truly the pioneers. While we admire and try to copy the education of riders and horses in Europe, we have here developed a method of producing dressage judges that is causing some other nations to take notice.

I remember a time when all anybody needed to do was to apply to the AHSA and pay the fee to be a candidate for judging. I discovered this when a person I knew to be completely incapable as a rider and horse-man proudly announced that she had applied to become a judge. The thought of her in the judge's box sent chills down my spine, and I decided to find out what her chances were to achieve this status. Well, they were quite good, it appeared. My very first encounter with the AHSA Dressage Committee was when I asked for a few minutes of their time to suggest that some requirements of demonstrated riding and training ability ought to be established before a person could apply for a judge's license.

This was many years ago, and we have come a long way since then.

Education as the Key

Our judge's education is quite extensive, and the prerequisites to get into a program are fairly rigid. Documented riding, teaching, or training knowledge at Fourth Level or above is a basic qualification for an application to be considered. In addition, the USDF "L" program has to be completed with a minimum of 70 percent score in order for a person to be eligible to apply for enrollment in the "r" program. The "r" program calls for apprentice judging in addition to classroom sessions with written and oral exams. The requirements can take a year or more to complete and will be costly in terms of application fees, travel, and most of all time spent—a valuable commodity to all of us. After living up to all conditions, the applicant will once again be reviewed and granted or refused a license according to the recommendations of the faculty and the examiners, as well as the references furnished by the applicant.

A three-year period of judging is required before a person is allowed to apply for promotion to the next step: "R" status. The process then starts all over again, with training programs and apprentice judging at the new level. The procedure is repeated for those wishing to reach the highest national status of judging, which is "S." (This stands for "senior," not "senile," as has been suggested at times.) By the time a judge has worked his or her way up the ladder to "S" promotion, the education and practical experience is solid and spread out over a period of time, which gives the official an opportunity to mature into the task.

The Cost of Knowledge and Experience

Critics of our judging programs have several valid points, which cannot be denied. One major complaint is the cost. It is true that achieving a license can become an expensive enterprise, and that this is more of a burden to some people than others. On the other hand, there is a potential for a certain amount of income from judging, which will hopefully offset the cost in due time. Few judges make a living off their work at horse shows since this is to a large extent a labor of love, but if a person does a good job I'm fairly confident the books will at least balance in the end.

The apprentice judging appears to become difficult in certain levels where the entries tend to be sparse. In particular, Second and Fourth Level tests seem to suffer from this syndrome. It becomes almost "mission: impossible" for some apprentice judges to get the required amount of a specific test experience done at this level, and yet the lack of experience with those particular tests could impair the judge's future progress because the tests include movements that are introduced for the first time. This is a problem that has been brought up, but needs to continue to be addressed.

The apprentice judging is perhaps the most important part of our judging programs, since it gives the candidate the opportunity to test his or her knowledge under "virtual reality" conditions without actually having any impact on the results of the class. When it is done well, the candidate will also have the opportunity to compare notes, discuss problems, and ask questions of the official judge he or she is working with. Here, again, there are snags to work out in the system. The apprentice program puts additional pressure on the official judge, who may have a tight schedule and a long day only to be "stuck" for hours in the evening with a candidate who needs attention, while the other judges go off to dinner and relaxation. If this does not occur too often, it is no hardship, but it sure can take some of the fun out of judging when it happens regularly. Show management is also inconvenienced by having to supply an area for the apprentice judge or judges to sit and a place to discuss the tests, and for being involved with details in organization, which in no way enhance the show. There are show organizers who flatly refuse to allow apprentice judges, and perhaps with good reason, but in the long run those who will welcome an apprentice may do themselves a favor by helping to develop a judge they can get good mileage out of in the future. Naturally management that is positive toward apprentice judges also ends up being a benefactor of the entire sport.

Fast Track

The loudest complaints about our judging program come from the competitors and trainers who are active, successful, and far too busy to get involved in the time-consuming process, leading to a license. The requests for a "fast track" for the truly qualified riders and trainers are constant, and they have validity, but there are serious reasons why no alternate route for this group has been devised. One reason has nothing to do with dressage, but is based on our legal system. In a country where litigation is a national pastime, it is incredibly difficult to devise a procedure that separates the "good" from the "mediocre" and the "bad" based on anything other than a program that is the same for all. To slip even obviously highly qualified persons through is a lawsuit waiting to happen from others, who perceive themselves equally fit for "instant judge" status. Another reason is the fact that although someone may be an excellent rider or trainer, that does not by definition mean that the same person will be an equally competent judge. Riding, teaching, and judging are not the same skills, and many riders who try to judge not only find it difficult but also excruciatingly boring. A sense of impartiality and proper judicial temperament does not necessarily go hand-in-hand with skilled riding, just as a good rider is not automatically also a good teacher.* Some outstanding trainers are unsuitable as judges, simply because they are unable to separate themselves from the training process and just judge what they see. These flaws are the things that became apparent in the judging programs.

The present structure of our program does unfortunately result in the loss of or at least retardation in incorporating some talent and experience we could have used better, and this is sometimes very frustrating.

---

* *Find further discussion on the topic of "judicial temperament" on p. 222 and on riding versus teaching in Part II, beginning on p. 63.*

The danger of jeopardizing what we have is the other side of the coin, and our program is worth protecting.

A couple of our "S" judges returned from their first international forum in Europe in 1996 and reported that, to their amazement, several of their colleagues at the forum had asked them about their background and education. The reason for the interest was that our American representatives were consistent and confident when giving their scores and offered clear and rational explanations to back them up. In short, they stood out in the crowd. These judges are a product of our judging program, which has no equal anywhere else and has been "discovered."

Committees from our governing bodies have worked hard over the years to shape the system we now have, but one individual has worked more tirelessly than any other. A major portion of the credit should go to noted judge Marianne Ludwig.* Time and again she has had to go back to the drawing board to change, improve, and extend this ever-evolving program.

I have a feeling we will never be quite "done" with this project, which is perhaps positive because it will have to change with the development of dressage in order to best serve the sport.

1997

---

* *Marianne Ludwig was inducted into the Roemer Foundation/USDF Hall of Fame in 2003 for her contributions to improving the quality of dressage judging in the United States.*

– 45 –

judicial temperament

On every application for a judge's license or promotion processed by the American Horse Show Association,* there is one question that concerns the suitability of the person applying when it comes to his or her basic character.

The term used is "proper judicial temperament," and to me this item has always been of major importance. Through years of serving on the Licensed Officials Committee, which is the committee that reviews and recommends or opposes the granting of licenses, I have become only more convinced that this issue is not just one of, but perhaps the most important ingredient that makes for a "good" dressage judge.

Quality Control

Let me start by giving you some insight into the workings of the Licensed Officials Committee (LOC). It is important to understand that without the existence of the LOC there would be no "quality control" whatsoever

---

* As noted on p. 174, the AHSA is now USEF.

when it comes to licensing or promoting the judges you face when you look up after your salute. Without such a committee the granting of a judge's license would be just a matter of a rubber stamp. Anybody who had fulfilled the general requirements could become a judge and remain one, never mind how his or her life in the judge's box took shape. I will hasten to confess that many times during my committee work I have thought that laissez-faire would be a splendid idea, as long as we did not have to sit through another painful hearing or send another disappointing letter to a hopeful candidate. Although 95 percent of the committee work is smooth and simply a matter of checking and passing, the five percent that is not can be a real headache, not least because the nature of the committee's work is a catch-22. If a person is granted a license or promotion in spite of a controversial "report card," members who oppose him or her are unhappy. If the committee turns a person down, it faces hearings, sometimes lawyers, and always a very upset and insulted candidate. You cannot win on this committee, and at times it is a truly thankless job.

An important thing to point out is that no decision is made independently by the members on the committee. Every single person up for review is seen through the eyes of the membership, and it is the opinion of the people writing in to recommend or reject an appointment that is the deciding factor in every case. Therefore, if you receive an application and have been chosen as a reference for an official to enter a program or to be promoted, it is of vital importance that you return the questionnaire and help the committee to do its work by stating your opinion for or against this individual. If an applicant does not receive enough responses in proportion to the number of forms sent, he or she could appear weak on that basis alone. If the committee does not have your input, it cannot act on it! All information is confidential, and every member is allowed to write to the LOC in regard to a candidate. Naturally, any anonymous correspondence is never presented to the committee.

A Question of Attitude

As the LOC works through scores of applicants, letters received that are opposed to the passing of a certain candidate often deal with the question of "judicial temperament." Almost anybody of normal intelligence and appropriate background and education can learn to appreciate the technical requirements of a dressage test. The technical part of judging is the focus of every judge, and potentially each experience in judging could bring improvement and growth in this area. How people use their knowledge to convey their impressions to a rider when they sit in the judge's booth is, however, very much a matter of their individual personality, and that does not change.

There is not a judge born who has never made mistakes while trying to do their best; they are human, after all. The manner in which they deal with their own shortcomings is the interesting part. Judges who get nervous because they don't feel quite certain they are up to snuff, or who worry about looking good in comparison to their colleagues, can be deadly. Because they are insecure, they tend to get defensive and become self-righteous. This causes the, "How dare you have a less-than-perfect test in front of *me*?" syndrome, which can easily be confused with the "truly pompous" syndrome, belonging to a judge who is suffering from delusions of grandeur. The latter type, on closer observation, is often one of limited background who would be lucky to be able to ride half as well as many of the people in the ring. The categories I've mentioned so far go well with the "power trippers" who are getting the very most out of being in charge for a couple of hours before going home to the regular pecking order of life. Then we have the "professional" judges, who are out there working every weekend and sometimes during the week as well. The good news is that this group is generally very proficient, has a tuned eye, and is informed about the latest in rule changes and how to implement them. If there is any bad news, it mostly appears as complaints about the judges showing obvious boredom, because it is hard to stay fresh and interested in something as detailed and "picky" as dressage without periodic breaks from the judge's box.

Riders are very sensitive to the various attitudes of the officials, and it is apparent that many judges are not aware of how clearly their ambiance is telegraphed to the exhibitors. Although there is no excuse for showing ill temper, there can be many explanations for a judge to be in a bad mood. Many horse shows are not well run; sometimes plane rides take forever; accommodations can be deplorable; and scheduling is often a disaster. When you are shaking in the rain or melting in the sun for hours without relief and still facing an endless list of Introductory Test A, it can become difficult to remember why you got involved in judging this sport to begin with. Never mind what your problems are; the trick is never to discourage anybody else from enjoying their involvement in dressage by writing acidic comments, which could make people turn away from showing.

Fair and Just

The most important aspect of good judging is good ethics. Although complaints about negative or irritable attitudes of judges are serious, none are more depressing than the complaints about deliberate unfairness. As an official, you will be put in situations when you have to judge someone you dislike as a person. This can in no way be allowed to affect the score he or she receives. The same goes for a rider who is popular, famous, or influential in the sport, or a close friend, who you can easily over-score because you see him or her through rose-colored glasses. (Just as bad would be to under-score your friend to demonstrate how unbiased you are.)

The pitfalls are many, and the hundreds of decisions that have to be made every hour by the judge are not all going to be perfect. Even the best-known and most experienced of our judges make mistakes. A judge can be excused for missing a score, having a bad day, not smiling enough, or even seeming bored on a hot afternoon, but there is never an excuse for political judging. It is interesting to note how most serious competitors instinctively know when they have been unfairly treated, and how they will accept the same score and situation more gracefully if they feel it was the result of an honest mistake.

The ultimate goal for every official should not be to become popular, but to become a judge who gains the respect of the competitors by judging the technical aspect of the test correctly, earning their trust because of a consistent demonstration of proper judicial temperament.

1996

– 46 –

judging on a jury

The first time a judge is faced with the task of judging a class together with his or her colleagues could be a time accompanied by stress and apprehension.

The demands each of us judges put on ourselves to judge accurately and fairly is usually enough to keep our adrenaline level up, so when you step into the box in symphony with two to four other judges the blood pressure is likely to rise. You cannot help wonder how your work will compare with the rest of the group, and when the announcer gets ready to reveal the scores, your mouth goes dry.

As time goes by, however, most judges grow to prefer the team variety of judging for several reasons.

Group Benefits

• First of all, it becomes a relief not to always have to be the only opinion. You get pretty tired of being so "right" all the time.

• Secondly, the opportunity to view the test from different angles makes for a more interesting show.

- Thirdly, you are not always in charge of navigation. While the judge at C is keeping track of the road map, you can concentrate fully on the performance.

- And finally, you grow to enjoy the teamwork and the comparison of the scores.

The scores from a panel of judges will, and should, differ to some degree, since a horse viewed from the front and from the sides at E and B can in certain movements look like two different animals. However, when the difference between two judges on the same jury is more than twenty points for the same horse, it is a source of irritation for the rider and should be of concern to the judges. In such a case, I like to confer with my fellow jury members and try to figure out what made us see that horse so differently. More than thirty points of disagreement on a ride is a bit of a disaster, and then it is *really* time to talk!

Common Traps

It is dangerous to assume that it is always the judge who is farthest from the norm who is incorrect. On many occasions, I have watched classes from the sidelines when I did not have a student or friend riding and could be objective, and have found that I agreed with the judge who was the "odd man out." Sometimes it takes a great deal of courage and conviction to call even a "famous" spade a spade, and at other times an unknown and therefore unexpected horse and rider combination could have the go of a lifetime. When this occurs, you have to be ready to jump in and acknowledge what really happened, and on occasion only one or two of the judges in a jury are on the ball. It is human to transform expectation into reality, but this is a real trap for judges. Another trap is when you start the first horse in the class off on too high or too low of a scale. When this happens, and it does to all judges on occasion, you have to be careful not to try to "compensate"—for example, being on the lower end with one horse, and then giving the next horse too high of a mark. It takes a lot of self-discipline to stay on the low end and look like the sour judge, but by doing so, you can make sure the placings come out right in the end.

One odd thing about the scores is that although the announcements may sound as if all the judges are pretty much in agreement, the placings can be very mixed. This occurs especially when it is a close field of riders with few outstanding performances. When only one or two points separate the horses, the individual placings can be all over the map, and as a competitor I know how the riders feel about that. It also makes the judges cringe, so nobody is really happy! One mathematical phenomenon is the situation that sometimes presents itself when a horse wins a class, although none of the five judges has placed it first! That's when the whole jury stands around and helplessly shrugs.

In the final analysis, you may not have all your ducks in a row on the sheet of placings, but usually the top four to six horses are the best placed on every judge's list. Even if you felt (along with every one of your colleagues) that you had your horses in the correct order, you can normally live with the final results, even if your champion did not finish first. What happens is a "melting" of opinions, which more often than not puts things in their proper perspective in the end.

Geography and Loyalty

Most judges have a favorite position to judge from. Mine is to see the test from E or B, since you have a much clearer view of most movements from there. Some people love to be the head of the ground jury at C, worrying about where riders are going, deciding on errors and eliminations, and generally presiding over operations. Not me. I much prefer to hang on every motion and muscle movement of that horse and to have no rules or other distractions to interfere with the picture. Nobody I know likes to judge from M. We call it the "blind man's seat," because in a majority of tests the only thing you see is the rear end of the horse. An educated guess about what is going on in the front end is sometimes unavoidable, which is not ideal from any point of view.

Adding to the attraction of working on a panel is the socializing it affords, which is a welcome feature after a day's work. Interesting to note is that off the show grounds, judges rarely discuss the rides or even talk about dressage at all. And even on the rare occasion that there is a strong disagreement on a score, the differences normally do not get in the way of the loyalty within the group. What is really fun is when you are working on a jury that really "clicks" and is able to sort out even a difficult and unpredictable class by getting the final order of placings right. That's a true feeling of satisfaction that the judges can share with the competitors.

The advantages to a competitor of riding in front of a jury, rather than a single judge, are obvious. The opinion of three or five people gives the comfort of a somewhat level playing field, even in a sport as subjectively judged as ours. And at least you know chances are good that someone will stay awake until the end of your ride...

2003

– 47 –

the scribes, our
unsung heroes

*Every experienced dressage judge realizes how
important the person next to you in the judge's
box is, but not many competitors understand
the value of a competent scribe. Except, of course,
when they cannot read his or her writing.*

There are so many ways a scribe can make or break you as a judge. The
longer I officiate, the more grateful I am for a good scribe, and the more
frantic when I end up with a "lemon." Admittedly that rarely happens
in this country any more, but I am aware of situations that made the
judge look like an idiot, when in fact the scribe was incompetent. And I
am sure many of our (for the most part) fabulous American scribes can
easily recall incidents when the judge was not on the ball and the scribe
saved his or her skin.

Avoiding the Hitchcockian Scene

One of the horror scenarios is being partway through a test, especially when judging on a panel, and having the scribe turn to you and say, "It does not say pirouette, it says changes." You try not to take your eyes off the horse while asking the unthinkable question: "Do you have the correct test?" Backtracking is awful when you judge alone because it holds up the whole schedule; doing it while the rest of the jury is waiting is pure torture. A good scribe always checks on the accuracy of the test, since the wrong one can slip in by mistake, and also makes sure that the number the competitor carries is the one printed on the test.

In America we are blessed with show management who realizes that scribes must have a certain amount of experience before you can let them help a judge working the FEI levels. As a matter of fact, some of our new national tests are quite demanding on the scribes, since we now give many more separate scores in rapid succession. Judges are required to give a comment for any movement receiving a "6" or less, and encouraged to comment on higher scores as well. Sometimes competitors deserve to get some good news, or to know why we gave an eight instead of a nine. Since I am guilty of being one of those judges who run off at the mouth, I realize that it is more difficult to keep up with the judges who are more verbal, and that three or four days of nonstop writing and checking is tiresome and rather repetitive. Although nobody, save the judge, is better informed about the action in the ring than the scribe, this person is the one who never gets to see the test. That is certainly a frustrating situation, which was made very clear to me at one of the North America Young Rider Championships, when my scribe would mournfully sigh every time I opened my mouth, as if to say, "Not again!"

After an hour of this lament, I started to feel guilty about not allowing the woman to watch in peace, and had her replaced.

One of my colleagues told me a cute story of a judge who was given a "new" scribe. The judge started the test, gave a six for the entry and halt, a seven for the extended trot, and a five for the shoulder-in. At that point, the scribe threw her pen down in disgust, turned to the judge, and said, "Why don't you make up your mind?"

Our country is, I believe, the only one that offers a group of scribes I would not hesitate to call "professional," although a lot of their work is a labor of love and not particularly well paid. There are such "secretaries" being flown all over to important events, and they are like a club of sages in their field. When you arrive at the show and find that your scribe is a familiar face who knows his or her stuff, it is with a warm fuzzy feeling you crawl into your box. These are the people who will never comment on your scores, whatever their opinion, and never show that they are tired or bored; they will share their blankets when it is cold and their ice when it is hot. They will give you a nudge when a horse enters the ring and you are still busy with the previous sheet, and they will remind you of a transition score when you are slow. They keep track of errors, and even take time to write down the scores as announced. It is a wonderful support to have, and when you also get to keep the same scribe throughout the entire show, life is good!

European "Thrillers"

Let me tell you how it can be even in "perfect Europe," for example, where I have had some of my best "thrillers" in the shape of scribes.

Often it is assumed that just because a person is a judge, it goes with the territory that he or she is also a competent scribe. This could not be farther from the truth. On many occasions, especially in Germany, I have had to insist that the judge-scribe stop viewing the test, start writing down the comments, and refrain from voicing his or her opinion about every score. At this point it is not unusual that the computer operator starts in to protect her buddy, and things can become very intense for a short while, until the rank order is established. Scribing is not a good way for a judge to learn anything but vocabulary and how difficult it can be to be a scribe. To learn more about judging, it is better that the judge "sit in" on the test, observing the performance and listening to the scores. This way the competitor never has to pay for any disturbances in the concentration of the scribe.

Overseas, the tendency is also to replace scribes for every test. At a recent show, I judged six classes with six different scribes, five different computer people, and sometimes a journalist sitting in to listen. This revolving door of personnel does not give any opportunity to establish a rhythm for the work, and I am so glad we do not usually live with that system at our shows.

At one memorable show in Hamburg, Germany, I was introduced to "Mrs. Miller," my scribe, who I was told had been working in that capacity at this particular show for the last thirty years. Great, I thought, she should be able to do this without a judge! We started the class, and I gave a score and the comment. No reaction from Mrs. Miller. I repeated my drill. Nada. I touched her on the arm, whereupon she turned to me, cupped her ear, and said, "What?" Mrs. Miller was extremely hard of hearing, and as I bellowed my scores in her ear, the competitors would go by and throw me a glance that said, "Well, thanks a whole lot!" In the freestyle I roared louder than the music, and ruined many a beautiful and well-edited program.

As a competitor, I do appreciate when the scribe writes legibly—that is, not like the judges, whose writing, if they do their own general impressions, is normally indecipherable. After a while, the competitor learns some of the most common abbreviations, and when we review our sheets we "get in the groove" with the scribes, who try to give us as much information about the performance as they can without getting behind the judge and making mistakes. In that respect there is a unique relationship between the rider and the scribe, because the rider can only receive as much input as the scribe is willing to transfer, even if the judge is generous with comments.

In closing, I would like to give credit to all show managers who check on the capability of each scribe before giving him or her the job, and who know the limits of what is a comfortable level to work with for each individual. In the case of a new scribe, it helps to ask the judges about the performance of their scribe during and after the show. Sometimes judges are hesitant to let show management know when things are not going well, but it is the competitors who suffer when a scribe interferes with the judge's operation. For sure, scribes can get better only if they are being told the truth. And, as I said before, once you have a good team in the box, don't break it up; let the show go on with them united to the end.

2003

– 48 –

a return to tradition at the spanish riding school

In the heart of Vienna, a lovely fragrance lingers like perfume to us lovers of horses. Your nose has not deceived you. Behind the ornate and impressive facade of the Spanish Riding School, seventy-three Lipizzan stallions lead lives similar to those of celebrated artists. Grooms and students make sure every hair is polished and all tack is gleaming before they leave the barn for the morning work session or the afternoon performance, which are both open to the public.

The stallions live in roomy and immaculate box stalls placed along a winding aisle, which gives the impression that they are living in a nice apartment building rather than in a barn. Over each stall watches a white stone carving of a life-size horse head, each with its own personal expression and ear position.

For 436 years, since the school was established, the majestic white stallions have been performing at this same location, one generation following another. Until 2001, the government supported the school, but it's now in the hands of private enterprise, and although the routine of the riding and training hasn't been altered, some innovations have taken place.

Modern Changes

One of them is the installation of a twenty-horse walker, probably one of the largest ever made, which allows the horses to get out for a stroll and a breath of air. Another novelty is that the school now hosts fundraisers and gala events, which are set up in the courtyard between the stables and the grand *manège*, and are at times enhanced by a performance by the stars in residence.

The biggest change of all took place in 2008 though, with a break in tradition when two female apprentices were accepted. This is the first time women have been allowed to apply for the long and extensive training to hopefully one day become riders at the school and take part in the performances.

Two girls, one Austrian and one English, are now part of the four trainees—or *éleves*, as they are called—who joined the school this fall. Perhaps the fact that the business manager in charge, Elisabeth Gurtler, is a woman has helped to open the doors to female participation.

The new éleves are looking forward to years on the longe line and diligent stable duty, which may lead to riding young stallions in the show, and eventually to becoming part of the performance on the more advanced, older horses. After years of proving their worth as assistant riders, the pupils who have what it takes will reach the coveted status of *Bereiter*, and that's as good as it gets. By that time, they do not only master all the movements we are familiar with in competition, but they will also have to perform the "airs above the ground," which is a whole different agenda.

The head of the riding school and leader of the quadrille in the performances is a man we easily recognize: Ernst Bachinger. In the United States we know him as the trainer of Dorothy Morkis,* and he has also trained several other international and Olympic riders. He successfully competed and trained horses for thirty years, but he grew up and started his career in the Spanish Riding School, where his father was a rider.

After seven years, when he earned the coveted title of Bereiter, Ernst developed an interest in competing and followed this urge. Eventually, he found it difficult to maintain a show schedule alongside the demands of the performances at the School, and he left to train and show privately owned horses.

After a satisfying career spanning more than thirty years of developing horses and riders in different parts of the world, Ernst was asked to "come home" and was offered the position as head of the riding school he originated from. He returned to Vienna with a wealth of knowledge and experience to add to his already solid foundation. The effects of his leadership are obvious in the way the horses are worked and in how the new stallions are selected to become performance horses.

A New Model

It had been forever since I was last in Vienna, but I'd seen the Lipizzans perform on their tours, and lately there's an improvement in the quality of the impulsion and regularity of the gaits as well as the correctness, from a judge's point of view, in the movements performed in the quadrille.

---

* *"Dottie" Morkis was a member of the team-bronze-medal-winning dressage team at the 1976 Olympic Games in Montreal.*

The young stallions we were shown were markedly different in type from their older colleagues. Almost all of the dappled gray youngsters could have appeared at a quality dressage show and held their own. They were elastic, free-moving, and traveled well forward over the ground.

This "modern" appearance and way of going, married to the tradition of correct riding, has to produce an even more interesting group of performance horses in the future. What made me wonder, though, is how this taller, more sleek model of horse will be able to deal with the airs above the ground, which is an incredible balancing act perfected by the "older" type of Lipizzan with shorter legs and a more compact body. I guess time will tell.

Competence, Consistency, Compassion

Sixty-three judges from thirty-five nations attended the International Dressage Judges Club General Assembly in Vienna, Austria, hosted by the Spanish Riding School, and we were royally treated to several performances by the stallions. We watched the morning work and the regular performance.

We were also treated to a private exhibition with a guided tour of the movements, and introduced to the new group of young stallions. When observing the work of the young horses, I believe all the judges were considering how nice it must be for a green animal to be introduced to his life as a riding horse by riders who are competent, consistent, and compassionate.

Throughout the session, every stallion remained relaxed, yet alert and eager to strut his stuff. I realize that the pressure of having to prove something in competition is not in the picture, but the older horses performed all of the Grand Prix movements several times and also showed off their levades, courbettes, and caprioles with no signs of tension, except the "good" kind, which you need to fuel the effort. When they finished, they were all dry and calm.

The regular performance included a long-lining exhibition that was a flawless flow of all the Grand Prix movements. The Bereiter was walking so close to the stallion that he touched him with his body, connected to his mouth with only a pair of long lines. The symmetry and communication between these two, both physical and mental, was so strong and yet so subtle that it was almost seductive. That part alone was worth a trip to Vienna.

Although the Spanish Riding School has to support not only itself, but also the stud farm at Piber, it looks to me as if it has experienced a renaissance. Every performance was sold out, new ways of finding revenue appear to be being examined, and the rumor that it would be closed down doesn't seem valid today.

Listening to Mr. Bachinger telling us that they had run out of stalls at the school and were looking into renting a nearby facility to accommodate about twenty new stallions sounded like a nice problem to have. With sixteen full-time riders, four éleves, and a whole staff buzzing around, it looked like the stallions would continue to dance in their glittering ballroom, guard tradition, and thrill the people while sending their "Eau de Cheval" into the Vienna air.

2008

− 49 −

the joy of judging

In the wake of attending a meeting of international judges in Vienna, Austria, I had time on the plane ride home and plenty of reason to contemplate what motivates a person to become a dressage judge, and once you are one, what keeps you going.

I consider myself a trainer and competitor first and a judge second. Yet I have now spent more than thirty years in the judge's box.

Like all of my colleagues, I've endured numerous hours in the cold rain and the hot sun, beaten by wind and eaten by insects. I have traveled thousands of miles and used everything but an ox cart to get to unreachable destinations after canceled flights, slept in horrid motels, and suffered donuts for breakfast and hot dogs for lunch. I have also been treated to luxury accommodations and outstanding courtesy from organizers who went way beyond the call of duty.*

---

* I wax poetic on this topic later in the book—see p. 264.

Meeting (or Not) Expectations

Although the travel has taken me to exciting places I otherwise might not have seen, it sometimes sounds more exotic than it is, because time is tight and one dressage arena looks much like another. Judges meet a lot of new people, and most of them expect a performance from the judge that will please them and fulfill their expectations. Organizers want to accommodate the competitors, the sponsors, and the media, and stay in the black. The riders want to win—although, unfortunately, only one of them can do that per class, and thus the judge will disappoint most riders at every show.

When judging the important European shows, especially those leading to championships and the Olympics, the pressure can be enormous on the judges to produce their final scores in record time for the computers to spit them out before the horse leaves the ring, to be within very close range of each other in percentages, and to have the horses in the same order.

In the past several years, the attitude toward judges in Europe has changed from pleasant and welcoming to critical, demanding, and sometimes even hostile. Competitors complain, trainers threaten, and the media is sometimes downright abusive in their reports.

Before the 2008 Olympics, there were some strong winds blowing about the jury, and although that same jury did a very decent job, the European dressage world is still acting as if they are trying to rid themselves of what they consider the ignorant, annoying, and prejudiced people they no longer care if they please with their ride.

Changes in the Air

As a reaction, the Fédération Equestre Internationale (FEI) has devised an evaluation process for their officials using statistics. It has retroactively, and will in the future, evaluate the performances of all the FEI dressage judges.

The evaluation is based on how close the scores are between all five judges. This process is proposed as a way to prove to the critics that FEI judges are indeed on track and not only know their job but are also fair and even-handed in their judging. Naturally, this can cut both ways, because if judging is all about five people always saying the same thing, why have five and not one judge instead?

And if having exactly the same score for every single ride is all that's important, why, then, do judges get encouraged to "judge their conviction" and "use the whole scale" in every seminar and forum they attend?

There's definitely a catch-22 here. Even though the evaluation system is being proposed by the FEI as a "protection" for the judges, the records will be interpreted and acted upon by the FEI Bureau, and judges who are not up to standard (meaning deviating more than a certain percent from their colleagues on a regular basis) will be warned and possibly removed from the active list of judges. So much for individual thought and the concept that the odd score out could, on occasion, be the only correct one.

Exams every three years are another novelty being proposed, as well as a much more extensive education program for the judges. Education is always welcome, especially since it's not been a strong agenda for the FEI in the past. We used to have to fight to get into the sparse seminars offered, and all judges I know will gladly receive more education.

Exams are fine as well, but not if they are designed to remove you from your status if you fail. Once you have passed your entrance exam to another level of judging, you should keep your position, unless you have broken some Golden Rule. Being "demoted" just because you did not pass an exam is like taking away a doctor's license or disbarring a lawyer for the same reason. Instead, you should be allowed to retake the exam until you pass, or give up.

And, by the way, someone pointed out to me the fact that it takes a minimum of twenty years of practicing and exams to become an FEI "I"-rated judge* but only twelve years to become a doctor. But, of course, that's only brain surgery.

Our Motivations

Both as a competitor and as an official, it's my experience that every judge does his or her best to serve the sport, and most are extremely aware of their responsibility toward the competitors. Weak judges need guidance and training more than threats and pressure, and those who do not improve will eventually not get asked to judge. Thus the system clears them out.

I thought about what motivates us to continue to judge in the face of lack of respect and sometimes unfair criticism. The extremely low daily wage? The dubious "status" of sitting in judgment? Because you want to spend weekends away from home to live in suitcases, sit in airports, and go for long drives? No, it's because the actual challenge of making all those decisions in record time while trying to sort out the excellent from the mediocre becomes a game of passion. Intensely watching the animals we are so fascinated by perform, and living their moments of triumph and tragedy can be an exhilarating experience only another dressage judge can relate to.

In all endeavors, some of the players are more accurate, skilled, and perceptive than others. This is also true about judges. I have several "idols" among dressage judges, whom I look up to because of their special knack of always making sense in their judging, but (as I mention elsewhere in this book) the one I admire the most is long gone. Not only did Dutch dressage judge Jaap Pot have the most incredible memory and clear

---

* *"I"-rated judges are now called 4*.*

assessment of every horse he judged, but he also had the real "feel" for judging, much the same as a rider's feel for a horse. Plus, he was ever enthusiastic and compassionate with helpful comments, whatever your score. He also lived and judged in an era when judges in Europe were appreciated and respected.

I wonder what he would think of the scene there today.

2009

suggestions about judging
the freestyle

*At the end of a horse show, one of our most active
and competent judges, Natalie Lamping, brought
up a subject that is not new, but which may need
to be revisited. She had just finished judging some
Grand Prix freestyle classes. Walking away from
the ring she summed up her impressions, and like
many of us, she felt somewhat inadequate before
the requirements.**

In the freestyles, each judge is, of course, expected to evaluate the technical aspects of the ride. In addition, and at the same time, the judge
has to absorb the following features: the *choreography*, meaning the use
of the entire arena and the symmetry of the ride; *inventiveness*, to avoid
a test-like ride; *degree of difficulty*, which has to work out successfully or

---

** This subject is still in focus today, especially when it comes to "degree of difficulty,"
and the system is again being revised.*

it becomes a detriment; *suitability* of the music to the personality of the horse; and the *interpretation* of the music the rider brings to the ride. With no breaks in this sentence, you are a little out of breath, right?

I remember when Axel Steiner and I conducted the National Judge's Forum* in California and focused on freestyle judging: Some of the judges told me about the pressure they felt to take in and process all the facets of freestyle and get it properly sorted. Some even admitted to a dislike of judging freestyles, not because they did not like the concept, but because the system made them feel at a disadvantage. As Natalie said: "Any judge who proclaims that he or she is able to take in and appraise every nuance of every ride is either a genius or faking it."

"Technos" and "Artistes"

On the score sheet, the last three boxes to fill in on the artistic side carry a lot of weight, since the coefficient on "choreography" and "degree of difficulty" is times four and for "music" times six.† Those scores can make an enormous difference in the final results, and they should, for three reasons:

- As the freestyle is becoming the "showcase" for dressage and audiences become more involved and sophisticated, the composition of the ride and the choice of music takes on increased importance. In the international arena, the technical quality of the rides is ever improving, and as that happens, the artistic side of the score sheet turns into a "tie-breaker" at times.

- The time, effort, and expense involved in creating a truly uplifting program is becoming pretty daunting. No more homemade cassettes with gaps in the editing; quality recordings and designer music are

---

* *See more about my work with Axel Steiner on the National Judge's Forum on p. 207.*

† *Now all artistic marks have the same coefficient.*

becoming the norm. Those programs are not cheap or easy to "ride in," and it behooves us to devote our undivided attention to the efforts put out. And even if the freestyle is a "homemade" product, as they all used to be in the beginning, it needs to be appreciated for all the effort that went into it.

In that vein, Natalie brought up the old subject of splitting the judges into the "technos" and the "artistes." Several years ago, when this subject was tossed about, the idea was to borrow judges from other sports and arts, such as figure skating judges or opera singers, but it was dropped after a few not-so-successful trials. Then we had a period of splitting "real" judges into categories, which died on the vine—why, I don't know. Well, the time may be right for trying that system again. Natalie pro-

posed a panel of five regular dressage judges, with three of them judging just the technical aspects of the ride and two just the artistic. This way each ingredient of the ride could get the full attention of judges who understand what they are looking at and know their job.

Immediately a question arises: since the artistic side of the score sheet actually has five boxes to fill in, which of the judges will be responsible for the top two, which deal with "rhythm, energy, elasticity" (= impulsion) and "harmony between horse and rider" (= submission)? We discussed this for a while and came to the conclusion that the artistic judges could very well take on that responsibility, since they would have every chance to observe the interplay between the horse and rider, and would be even better equipped than the technical judges to get the "whole picture" of the ride.

No Time for Comments

What prompted Natalie to bring up this subject included some experiences shared by judges who worked shows with "open scoring," especially the indoor shows and championships here and in Europe. The trend, vigorously supported by the show managers, is to get final scores up and showing on the screen before the horse leaves the ring, in order to keep the audience involved. And even after this is accomplished, some eager runner rips the sheet out of the judge's hands because the next horse is going around the ring. This leaves absolutely no room for closing comments of any kind, since you have to decide on the final scores on each movement that was repeated and finish the artistic side on the same sheet. It all gets a bit hectic, and although some competitors may not give a fig about your opinion, there are times when I feel a responsibility to tell the rider why I gave a particular score, especially on the artistic side where a low score can become very "expensive." If we had the judges split into categories in the freestyle, each dealing with their own job, they would have time for comments, even in the high-pressure competitions.

Media (Darlings)

While on the subject of scoring the freestyle, there is another issue that needs thinking about. We are all eager, not to say desperate, to gain media coverage for our sport, and we are willing to bend pretty far to get it. There ought to be limits, however, when the media requirements interferes with the fairness to the competitors. Television coverage is usually very expensive and limited to the "cream of the crop" amongst the riders. Therefore, television stations prefer to come in on the end of a class and record only the anticipated winner and runners-up.

In the World Cup Freestyle this system is already fairly well in place, since the starting order is divided into sections with the top four or five combinations from the Grand Prix going last. So far, so good. What is not as easy to accept is that the riders arrive at the World Cup Grand Prix class already sectioned up according to their FEI/BCM World Dressage Ranking. In our quest for transparency and fairness in the sport, it is fairly transparent to me that this is not fair. It is a lot more difficult for non-Europeans who actually live and compete outside of Europe and do not have multiple horses at their disposal to achieve a prominent status in the BCM listing. Yes, of course the judges know how to judge, whatever the order of go. But, thinking and feeling as a competitor, I would certainly dislike arriving "pre-rated" to an event that I had to qualify for and possibly travel many miles to reach. There is time enough to let the judges sort the placings out in the Grand Prix, and a straight draw for that class ought to be a given.*

---

* During my tenure on the FEI Dressage Committee (2010–13), I managed to convince the Committee to have the first straight draw for the World Cup Grand Prix. This was still in effect when my time on the Committee was up in 2013.

In reality, the television crew rarely arrives to record anything before the freestyle anyway, and if they do, it hardly ever makes it to the screen. We want dressage to be media-friendly, but not if it interferes with the basic nature of the sport or favors one competitor over another.

2004

– 51 –

it's "all about" the young horses

As I left balmy Florida to weave my way on planes and trains to Münster, it occurred to me that not even Germans want to be in Germany in January. Sure enough, it was frigid and snowing off and on. Well, at least it did not rain sideways...

The occasion was an FEI seminar covering the training and judging of dressage horses aged four to six. The attending judges had the option to take an exam at the conclusion of the forum, which upon passing, would allow them to judge the Young Horse Classes in FEI-sanctioned competitions.

Numbers and Philosophy

Both the method and concept of judging young horses differs a great deal from the way judges normally operate. Three judges officiate together, and they discuss each horse as it performs. Five scores are given: one for each gait, one for submission, and one for overall impression. After the judges have agreed on the final scores, and before the horse leaves the ring, one judge will give a summary over the microphone to explain to the rider and the spectators how they arrived at the specific numbers. A full set of decimals can be used, which is handy to define exactly where a horse fits in the order of things and helps to refine the system.

The philosophy of judging the young horse differs slightly from our general path as well. There is less emphasis on precision and accuracy. A young horse can be forgiven some tension and shying, and the exact riding from point to point is not as important an issue. Instead more of the focus is on the Training Scale and the proper education of the young horse. What is being judged is the quality of each basic gait, starting with the rhythm. If all is well in that department, and the horse is reasonably relaxed, we assess the elasticity, the contact, the suppleness, and the straightness (or lack thereof). We look for the horse's talent for collection—that is, the tendency to elevate his forehand and shift his weight to the hindquarters while remaining in balance. In the last two marks, the judge also considers the "rideability" of the horse, his responsiveness to the aids, and his willingness to perform what is asked by the rider. Finally, we take a moment to look into the future and evaluate the horse's talent and ability as a dressage prospect. Naturally, the way he is ridden and presented plays a large part in the outcome of the last two scores.

All these points have to be discussed and decided while the horse is performing, since the scores are announced immediately following the ride. As you can imagine, three judges who are used to making up their minds independently of each other do not always agree, and things can get interesting in the judge's box at times. In general, though, all the judges see the same thing, and if not, the compromise usually leads to the correct score.

The system used to judge Young Horse Classes is very popular with audiences. They receive instant feedback on the performances, and whether they agree or not, at least they know what the judges were thinking.

The Experts Weigh In

Eighty participants from sixteen countries, which included a number of trainers and several breeders, were treated to lectures each morning and live demonstrations in the afternoons for two days. In her usual upbeat manner, Angelica Fromming, a prominent German judge and educator of judges, covered the details of the Training Scale—but first she made a whirlwind trip through the centuries of dressage, from Xenophon to Steinbrecht, with short comments on each of the milestones in its history. These glimpses of the past reminded us that our present heated discussions about the frame of the horse* are far from a new occurrence. Through the entire history of riding, these training disputes have flared up with great regularity.

The Training Scale we follow today is based on the principles of the systematic training program as proposed in the German *Reitvorschrift* (Manual of Riding), which first saw the light of day in 1912. It is meant as a means of orientation for the riders and a diagnosis for the judges.

Mariette Withages (Chairman of the FEI Dressage Committee) and dressage judges Christoff Hess and Dr. Dietrich Plewa guided us through the principles of judging in general, and the judging of young horses in particular. One of the points made was that the Young Horse Championships are not to be thought of as an end in themselves, but should serve as a "talent search" and provide guidance for finding the top dressage prospects worldwide. And, of course, it is also a "display window" and opportunity for sales promotion for breeders and trainers.

Our own Dr. Hilary Clayton (veterinarian, researcher, clinician, and author) was responsible for a most fascinating presentation of what actually happens when a horse is in motion. Using effective visuals, she

---

* *See "The Battle of the Frame" in Part IV, p. 184.*

made us aware that what our eye observes is not necessarily what occurs. (So much for "judging what you see"!) It is impossible to review all Dr. Clayton's information here, but I will pick a few of my favorites:

- She showed us how "movement" is created by the horse's hooves pushing against the ground, and how the direction of the movement is in opposition to this force. In the so-called "stance phase," the body rolls over the grounded foot, one leg at a time. Moreover, our obsession with the hind leg may be just a tad exaggerated. Although it is true that the hind legs carry more weight as training progresses, Dr. Clayton showed that the front leg also pushes harder on the ground and literally elevates the forehand. The trained horse has a shorter arch in the stance phase of his front legs, which rest on the ground for a briefer time and touch it in a straighter frame. So, as some of us trainers might have suspected, it is not all about the hind legs!

- Another little gem: We have been carefully taught that in the medium and extended trot, the front foot should land where it is pointing. In reality, the foot contacts the ground in front of (further ahead of) the place where it is pointing—our eyes just cannot "catch" it.

- From judging horses in hand, judges learn that we are not that well equipped to accurately predict how a horse will move when we first view him standing still. Dr. Clayton confirmed some of our suspicions. She showed how the smaller angles of the bones in the hip and hock joints make for better compression and a faster push off the ground. These are things we cannot easily assess from watching a live horse, complete with flesh and muscle to disguise the angles of the joints.

The live demonstrations on the first day took place at the Westphalian Equestrian Association, where we were treated to some wonderful quality horses, such as the five-year-old Champion Damon Hill ridden by Ingrid Klimke. Yes, that was a treat! The second day we were at the

DOKR, the German National Olympic Training Center, to view and discuss another set of youngsters under the leadership of three "O" judges: Mariette Withages of Belgium, Stephen Clarke of Great Britain, and Dr. Dieter Schüle from Germany. The three generously shared their impressions of the horses presented, which were deliberately of varying quality to enable the judges taking the course to use their entire scale.

The initiative by the FEI to create a special showcase for our developing horses has already become a success story, and each year the excitement generated by the championships increases worldwide. Polishing the skills of the judges is just one of the facets of the program, but certainly one of great importance.

2005

– 52 –

new zealand from a dressage point of view

For many years, I've had an urge to visit New Zealand. So when the opportunity arrived to judge and conduct a couple of judges' seminars, I agreed to go, although it fell right in the middle of the Florida show season. The trip from Orlando to my destination "Down Under" took thirty hours door to door, but it proved to be a small effort to make for a trip to paradise.

Back in Time

Christchurch on the South Island was the site of the first show, which was advertised as the National Championships, and for me it was like traveling back in time to the first Palm Beach Derby in Florida at White Fences Equestrian Center. There were a number of rings, including one grass arena for the event horses, a clubhouse, and a large parking lot filled with campers. A clear difference was that the horses were not stabled, but rather lived in tiny paddocks or were tied to trailers, which in New Zealand are called "horse floats."

The competition standard was much like ours about twenty years ago. There were a handful of horses at each level that were capable of pulling a score in the mid to high 60s, but most were struggling with some of the requirements.

The show was run by Fédération Equestre Internationale (FEI) rules, including vet check and foreign judges, but didn't actually qualify as such, probably for financial reasons. Like many of our shows, the whole affair was glued together by the grace of volunteers who had "been there and done that" forever, and they had a really smooth act going. Like ours, the younger judges were in training programs, and I had a judge from Australia "shadow judging" with me and discussing our results afterward.

Since fall sets in around March Down Under, this was the show to attend if you wanted to be part of the selection of the top four- to six-year-olds of the year. After we judged the tests appropriate for the horses' level, a professional rider flew in from Australia to ride the winners of each age group. On the last day, we then selected the "best in show" from all of the youngsters, together with the test rider. It was comforting to find that the horse the judges had deemed the best trained of the lot the day before also proved to be the one picked by the test rider as the one with the superior "rideability."

A Different Wellington

Christchurch is a very "English" town, abundant in trees and flowers, centered by a town square with an imposing cathedral and complete with a "town crier" who amused the college students from atop a ladder with wisdom of the ages and tips from the racetrack.

Throughout the area were the tallest hedges I've ever seen, which were perfectly manicured and very imposing. I was told they shelter the crops from the wind, which sweeps across the islands with sometimes merciless force. There was a bagpipe contest in one of the many parks with at least six bands fighting it out, kilted to the nines. Flower arrangements sailed on the river, artfully arranged on little floats.

The next stop was Wellington, the capital, which is a beautiful harbor city at the bottom of the North Island. It sports the famous Museum of New Zealand Te Papa Tongarewa, and cable cars take you up the steep hillside to the botanical garden and a panoramic view of the inlet to the harbor.

From there, I went by truck on narrow, twisty roads through the mountains where *The Lord of the Rings* movies were filmed. As in the movies, the breathtaking scenery of the green mountains goes on forever. Sue and Brian Hobson hosted one of the judges' seminars: Sue is a well-known and successful competitor, and Brian "builds horse vans for people" (if you know what I mean). They are so well appointed and comfortable you forget they are actually built to transport equines.

An exhilarating five-hour bike ride on the back of Brian's Gold Wing Honda allowed me to view some of the most varying and never-ending gorgeous scenery in the world on the way to Hastings, where the Horse of the Year show was taking place. This was the event of the year for everyone involved in horses in New Zealand, and it included all disciplines: hunters, Western riding, Arabians, ponies, jumpers, and dressage.

With the atmosphere of a carnival, a great trade fair set up around the competition arenas, and fabulous weather, the show could not fail. The dressage competition was a CDI*** and at the same time, there was a National Championship with the determining factor being a freestyle. It was a bit tricky to sort out the champions in many of the freestyles at Second to Fourth Levels without seeing any of the horses in a regular test, but in the end I think we got it right. The CDI was of decent quality, and the Young Riders kept improving from day to day, once the initial tension evaporated. There were many talented horses, several promising riders, and then the ones who had not yet found their way.

Again, I recognized us from years ago.

The Reason for Rugs

I had the opportunity to spend a couple of days on a 650-acre ranch belonging to Carol and Neil Eivers, Hanoverian breeders. They also have several hundred cows and enormous numbers of sheep living on their mountains. Horse husbandry in New Zealand is quite different and sometimes smarter than ours. The lifestyle is much closer to nature as intended for a horse. In the morning I would watch Carol prepare her feed for the breeding stock.

She had chaff (a mixture of oaten and alfalfa, cut up in short pieces) as a basis for the feed. Freshly crushed barley for fiber, and wheat, corn, and molasses were added; the barley and crushed corn were soaked in water overnight. To this Carol added a handful of seaweed meal for minerals and granulated electrolytes and topped it off with a spoonful of copper sulfate.

I'm not convinced her diet is the answer for every horse, but the research and detail that went into planning the best menu for her horses was impressive. The feed and hay was loaded on an ATV and off we went, climbing over just about anything to reach the high pasture. I wondered how she was going to feed a dozen or more horses their grain in the field without causing a war among them. No problem: As we approached the pasture, they lined up in a row and waited politely to have their grain put on the ground in their special spots.

Thinking Outside the Box Stall

Whenever the veterinarian turns to me and ordains "stall rest," I just nod and keep walking the horse, preferably under saddle. Unless he has a broken leg and literally cannot move, there is no way I believe in stall rest for any reason.

Come to think of it, I don't believe in stalls. Keeping horses locked up for the better part of every day the way we tend to do is, I suspect, the reason for a large percentage of their physical and mental problems. This is done for human convenience and is the direct opposite of what nature intended. Horses were meant to roam, to be almost constantly in motion. The human concept of working a horse, sometimes intensively, for less than one hour, and then keeping him in virtual immobility for twenty-three, is bizarre. No wonder we have cribbers, weavers, stall kickers, colic, and mysterious lameness.

Yet we Americans are a lot more tuned in to the need for freedom, even in the trained horse, than some other nationalities. While in Germany for training at a renowned barn which, due to inclement weather, was closed up in October and not reopened until April or May, I observed interesting behavior in some of the horses. In particular one mare caught my attention. She repeatedly tried to climb up toward the window situated high up on the wall in her stall, pawing with her hooves toward the light. Once she tried this project in the indoor arena—with one of the *bereiters* on, no less. That was the end of her stay, and they called her crazy. Having observed her "reaching for windows" for a while, I believe she only tried to signal to us a need to get out in the open.

When it snowed half a meter, my student and I pushed the barn door open and turned our horses out to play. As they were frolicking in the white powder, people came running out of the barn, half frantic. They were incredibly concerned about the safety of our horses, and the fact that the wind had sneaked through the barn without permission.

I realize there is a risk in turning your horse out, and of course it increases if he is not accustomed to being free every day. An FEI-dressage horse is a valuable commodity and a fragile one, and it takes guts to slip off his halter and leave him to his own devices. In the long run, though, it makes for a better mind, a sounder body, and a happier companion. And haven't we all seen how horses determined to get hurt can commit suicide right in their stalls, given the right—or rather wrong—circumstances?

One of Carol's horses had stuck his foot in a fence and ripped off a large part of the bottom of his hoof. It was a nasty wound and still bleeding when we rewrapped it. I made big eyes when she brought out a jar of honey to dress the wound, but it worked like a charm, and already the next day the area around the cut looked dry and clean, with hardly any swelling.

Everywhere I went the horses lived outdoors around the clock, roaming in the hills under a New Zealand rug. If there was a barn on the property, it was usually populated by tractors and farm machinery and used for storage. One stall was kept aside for emergencies when a horse might have to be confined. The usually mild climate and the topography (plus a surplus of available land) allow this kind of healthy lifestyle, which avoids a number of problems such as colic, cribbing, weaving, and injuries from horses being imprisoned in stalls for the better part of their lives.

If I were a horse, I'd want to live in New Zealand. As a matter of fact, if there's a next life, I'd consider signing up for it as a human.

2009

− 53 −

the perfect show through a judge's eyes

The plane lands at its final destination after two delays. It is late; you don't know the area. At this show, you are lucky: There is a real live person there to meet you and you don't have to flounder around in the dark looking for the right limo service or hotel shuttle. Even more pleasant is that you will not have to wait for several colleagues to show up before the ride to the hotel can commence. For total bliss, your luggage arrives on the same plane. Life is good.

Your assignment has been on the calendar for over a year. This show committee was on track and went out early to secure the panel of judges desired. The contract was simple: It spelled out the dates, the place, the fees, the contact person, and the hotel and transportation arrangements. You preferred to arrange for your own transportation, and this met with no resistance as long as you were particular about low cost fares. The hotel is clean and has a telephone in the room; there is a restaurant in the hotel and another one within walking distance. In the room, there is a program waiting, which lists times and class assignments for each judge. The hospitality person who drove you to the hotel tells you when you will be picked up in the morning, and assures you an arrival at the show grounds at least twenty minutes before the start of your class. There is even a little welcome basket on the table with some fruit and nuts, a bottle of wine, and a friendly note. You remembered to pack a corkscrew. Wow.

The following morning there is coffee and tea available, either in the hotel or at the show grounds, and something for breakfast other than donuts. The judge's box is roomy and even has side panels, which will come in handy in the case of inclement weather. An updated program is waiting in the package carried by a scribe who is neatly dressed and appears to have her head on straight. As the day goes on, you grow to love this scribe. She is friendly but not invasive, and competent and alert, noticing riders' numbers, changes, and scratches, remembering to make a note of errors, and even giving you a friendly nudge when you miss a transition score. She does not, however, offer any opinions on the rides or the competitors and their horses, but keeps whatever information she may be privy to under wraps. She always seems to keep up with your scores and comments, and although you tend to babble, she writes legibly and in the right location. Amazingly, this paragon of a scribe is not ripped out of your life at the first lunch break, but stays with you for almost the entire show. A miracle.

The schedule allows enough time between rides for you to make some general comments, which may be helpful or at least amusing to the riders. When nature calls, a PortaJohn is somewhere within reach and there is time set aside for such an eventuality. On one of the evenings, a dinner is scheduled for all the judges and some other officials, which is a nice opportunity to socialize and catch up on the latest "equi-dirt." The other evenings are a free-for-all, which can be a relief if you have a long day and just want to rest, or if you have friends in the area to visit.

The "runners" at the show are friendly and efficient and keep asking you if you need anything, which you really don't because there is plenty to drink available and some snacks provided in (another) basket. At lunchtime, you are marched off to a separate area where you can eat in peace and there are some healthy alternatives to greasy hamburgers available.

While the ring is empty, it is watered and worked. Somebody here knows that not only do the horses and riders suffer from living in a cloud of dust, but judges whose eyes are filled with sand will soon become as blind (as all the jokes indicate they already are).

This show from heaven has seen to it that all the judges, even those working with the national levels, have a bit of variety. Management understands that two entire days of First Level Test Two does strange things to your head. Endless hours of sitting still also adds to the problem as your body goes from stiff to decomposing. No problem; the hotel at this show has an exercise room and a pool where you can hobnob with Major General Burton* at five o'clock every morning. All you have to supply is some discipline.

At the end of a long weekend, the scheduling of the rides on Sunday is set up to accommodate your travel plans without causing white knuckles on the way to the airport. Your check is waiting, expenses included, and you are whisked away, wishing you could linger just a little longer...

The Other Side of the Coin

There are, of course, other scenarios...

...nobody meets you at the airport, and you are relieved you found the hotel at all. There is no information waiting at the desk, or anywhere else.

---

* Major General Burton is an FEI Judge, Technical Delegate, and Chief Steward, and was inducted into the Roemer Foundation/USDF Hall of Fame in 2007.

The next morning there is organized confusion while the judges try to find the show, their box, and their schedule. Your scribe interrupts you in the middle of Intermediaire II to tell you that he or she is writing on the wrong sheet. The wind and rain keep ripping the papers out of your hands and turning the scores and comments into rivers of ink. You are shaking from the cold, looking like a tepee wrapped in hairy horse blankets, and your teeth are chattering so hard you can barely spit the scores out. Lunch is obtained standing in line and swallowed behind the catering truck in keen competition with the flies. The afternoon sun tears through the clouds and bakes your trailer, and while you are moving about trying to avoid its rays, your secretary is huddled in the corner like a passenger on the Titanic. You see the same horses doing the same tests the same way for three days while the insects eat you alive, using the insect spray as gravy and your clothes as a tablecloth. Your classes end so late on the last day that you have hardly a prayer of making it to your plane. The finishing touch is a shockingly fast ride to the airport and a mad gallop to the gate while your luggage gets to take a later flight. You sink into your seat, soaked in sweat, and end up scratching your ankles and wondering what possesses you to spend a weekend in this insane manner.

Yes, there are occasions when a judge has reasons to be less than charming, but those times are blissfully in the minority. Over the years, show management has become increasingly sophisticated, and most of our experiences in judging are positive—not least because dressage judges are passionate about their task. They worry and fuss about making sense with their scores and comments, agreeing on placings when they work on a panel, and giving the competitor a fair shake. Judging is intense and sometimes draining because it is tiresome to make thousands of split-second decisions for days on end. The most rewarding occasions are those when a competitor, especially one who did not win every class, approaches you at the end of the show and thanks you for the educational value of your comments. Ultimately, the goal of every judge is to get the placings right and to be able to help the riders in their efforts to advance up the levels and present their horses advantageously in competition. Judges will, and do, go to work under any circumstances, but it does not hurt to have some comfort and fun available, thanks to good planning and competent management.

1998

– 54 –

we must trust our judges

It was a long time ago, it seems, when people respected dressage judges for their knowledge and the extensive time they'd spent educating themselves. People thought judges had earned the right to evaluate and comment on riders performing a test.

But over the last few years, the grumbling and complaints have grown. The higher the prize money and the more expensive the horses, the more pressure the competitors, the media, and the organizers put on judges to make their judging flawless. Ever since the Fédération Equestre Internationale dismissed the FEI Dressage Committee in 2008, there has been, in effect, an "open season" on judges. The competitors can make degrading comments, the media can write anything they like, and the judges are basically defenseless because their position is a catch-22. Whatever they say to explain their marks sounds defensive and evasive to the non-judge, who generally does not understand how the system works or how the information is processed by the judge.

Changes in the Works
Not that the FEI has been very supportive of their officials in the past. At the International Dressage Officials Club forum in Vienna in the fall

of 2008 (see p. 241), the FEI representative informed judges that their judging was being retroactively researched and evaluated by statistics, that their overall performance was under par, and that there would be a "cleaning up" in the ranks.

This came from an FEI that, up to that point, had shown little interest in holding enough seminars to supply the judges worldwide, had no organized educational system, and had traditionally paid their judges nothing compared to the going rate for any other official duty performed at an international show.

Now the FEI has created a new judges' educational system that has been in place since July 2010. It features a number of requirements for continuing education, exams, and a system for promotion. It will definitely weed out judges who are not active and keep the rest current, as well as point out the path to follow for those looking to advance up the ranks.

In the FEI Dressage Committee, we are encouraging the national federations to look into a reasonable way to fast-track successful competitors to become FEI judges before they are too old to be promoted to five-star status. At all major championships there will be a Judges' Supervisory Committee present to correct obvious mistakes, evaluate the quality of the judging, and report back to the FEI. In addition, a new post has been created for a "Dressage Judge General," who will be the spokesman and leading light for the judges.

At the January 2011 five-star judges' forum in Warendorf, Germany, twenty-four of the twenty-six existing "O" judges were present. Wayne Shannon represented the International Dressage Riders' Club in place of chairman (and dressage Olympian) Kyra Kyrklund. Also in attendance were Frank Kempermann, chair of the FEI Dressage Committee, and sports psychologist Dr. Inga Wolframm, who had previously given her talk at the Global Dressage Forum in 2010.

The Judges Are Aware

Due to lectures by Dr. Wolframm, the ire of the trainers and riders has somewhat changed its focus from pronouncing all judges corrupt imbeciles to saying that the system is useless, and that it's impossible for any human to successfully process the information available and come up with the correct score.

Instead, according to Dr. Wolframm, the judges invent "shortcuts," which exclude some of the details of the movement and focus on specific features.

I think I agree with that assessment, except that in America in our judges' forum, we call these extra ingredients of the movement "modifiers," which we absorb and are aware of, but do not focus on, while we concentrate instead on the essence of each movement. Nothing new there.

Dr. Wolframm suggests that we ought to work with a system of deductions instead of bonus or plus points. I believe just about every judge already does exactly that. As the judge I perhaps respect most in this world, Jaap Pot, always said in his wonderful seminars: Remember that every rider comes in with a "10" in his or her pocket! From there, he advised, you deduct the points from the movements that do not live up to a "10." And be ready to tell the rider why he or she did not gain a full score for effort!

This has been carefully taught to us through the years, and it surely is not a new concept. What was new about Dr. Wolframm's information was that she thinks the complexity of judging aesthetic sports exceeds human capacity. Therefore, to cope, the judges grab on to all kinds of crutches to simplify their decision, such as relying on previous experience of a rider/horse combination, the reputation of said combination, or even the order in which they appear in the starting order.

As mentioned elsewhere in this book (see p. 250), I agree that the starting order in the Grand Prix should never be according to the FEI/BCM

Dressage World Rankings list, because it makes the riders feel "pre-judged" and gives them the impression that their test will be placed in accordance with their starting position.

This system is *not* due to the recommendation of the judges, but rather because the media does not care to be on watch for the entire Grand Prix. The members of the press prefer to show up for the finale when they can concentrate exclusively on the best ranked in the world. It's all about money and time, not about being fair.

However, all experienced judges are intensely aware of these pitfalls, and they fight against any such prejudices with eyes wide open. In reality, I think the judges are way ahead of Dr. Wolframm in most of her discoveries: We have known long before being told by science that our task is overwhelming, and in the face of this challenge we constantly work on improving our skills, our techniques, and our system.

Dressage as Art (When It Can Be)

Perhaps the time has arrived to replace judges with computers. They sure will pick up on all the technical snafus—and nothing else. There will be horses winning with not a speck of elasticity, suppleness, presence, or expression. It will all be very correct, and also devoid of art, charm, impact, or beauty. Only humans can appreciate those qualities and put them into scores, and since the interpretation of art* differs from one human to another, there will always be some margin of difference between scores, which has to be allowed even with the most rigid rules for judging.

---

* *When I began writing a column for* The Chronicle of the Horse *in 1995, I debated that, in fact, dressage is rarely an art (see p. 7). Perhaps I grow more romantic in my conceptions as I grow older.*

When "open scoring"* was proposed to involve the spectators and make the judging more "transparent," many in the sport expected opposition from the judges. They never hiccupped, and the system of showing each judge's score for every movement was introduced. For several years now we have lived with the open scoring, and gradually it has turned into a negative rather than positive influence on the sport. As the criticism of judges has intensified, the game of following every judge's score has turned into a blood sport. Whenever one judge deviates, there is a buzz in the audience and a wave of discontent going through the arena and out from the media. In reality, when huge differences appear, they are often the result of a malfunction of the technology or a human error made by the computer operator in the judge's box. The snafu later gets corrected and doesn't hurt the competitor's score, but this isn't properly communicated to the spectators.

But the most negative thing that has evolved since open scoring arrived is that nobody watches the rides anymore because they are too busy watching the scoreboards. Is that what we want to do to dressage—turn it into bingo? The running score, which shows the comparison between the horse in the ring and the leading combination, is easy to glance at without losing contact with the performance in the ring, and it should be placed out of sight of the judges. With the seven-judge system in the championships, a running score is a much better solution than having a long row of individual scores in front of everyone to distract them from the actual event.

As soon as the competition is over, every score is available to the public and press anyway, and some of it can even be followed on the computers in case anyone prefers the numbers to the horses.

---

* *Read more of my thoughts on "open scoring" on p. 249.*

Judges are not gods. But we must be honest enough to admit that what looks like bias and corruption to us might just be a fallible human being doing his or her job. If we create too many systems to monitor the process, we are really saying that we trust their judgment only when they agree with us. In the end, we must trust the judges to judge, or do away with the institution altogether.

2011

THE FUTURE
OF DRESSAGE:
Well-helmeted kids
on happy ponies doing
Grand Prix in snaffles♡

VI the state and future
of the sport

– 55 –

who's next?

Looking at the top of the heap it appears as if all is well with American dressage. Medals are now attainable in world-class competition.

We are holding at third and looking for an opening to move into second place internationally. Move your eyes down one step, and there is a bustle of activity. Experienced riders fighting for a chance to step into the international arena. Lots of players available, and some very legitimate horses on their way to stardom.

Where Are the Kids?

And below that layer stands an army of youth prepared to take over... Unfortunately not. Encouraging new, young talent and inspiring the kids to try our sport is not an area in which we excel. This weakness will eventually catch up with us. Hours have been spent on discussions in meetings in attempts to design programs that would be attractive and educational for our growing generation of riders. The plans and ideas never seem to get beyond the talking stage, and we still have little to offer the child or teenager interested in dressage. A small number of professionals take a special interest in helping youngsters, but the obstacles are many. Dressage is a long haul: The instant gratification of the equitation division with its myriad of opportunities for quick success, even at the very beginner stage, is not available. Parents, who are not themselves involved, have problems understanding why it must take years to perfect the seat and train the horse to even get to the first show. The long wait for "results" appears unattractive compared to any other discipline of equestrian sports. Even if the parents do have an understanding of the nature of dressage, the cost of a "schoolmaster" for a child is often a problem, especially since this kind of horse is usually an older animal and therefore not a "good investment," except as a learning tool. A young, and therefore green, horse will need to be trained daily, along with the child, and that takes even longer.

Even if there were scores of families willing to spend the time and money required—what is there for the kids to do? Actually, there is precious little available, except for some junior classes in the regular shows with no fanfare attached, and the FEI Young Rider Championships. These Championships are the ultimate goal, but too far in the future to be of interest to the beginner dressage child. You cannot even enter the qualifying classes for the Young Rider Championships until you are sixteen years old.

Can we create more immediate goals? *Dressage equitation*, patterned after the Medal/Maclay classes in the hunt seat equitation division has been suggested.* This would be a group competition, judged on the rider's ability to direct his or her mount while displaying a proper dressage seat. Qualifiers throughout the year would lead to a National Finals at a prestigious, possibly indoor, show at the end of the season. This program has been on the USDF drawing board, but has never gotten off the ground. To become feasible, it needs a strong leader with lots of time to devote to development and organization, as well as cooperation from show man-

---

* *Dressage equitation is now quite a successful national program!*

agers. If put in practice, it could do great things to bring forth riders with beautiful positions and effective aids, much as that of our jumper riders, who are much admired and copied abroad.

*Pony dressage** is another possibility. This division is very popular in Europe, and it has many advantages. No person older than eighteen is allowed to compete on ponies there, and that wipes the adults from the scene. There are local pony classes, pony shows, pony championships, national pony championships, and even European pony championships. The highest level is comparable to our Third Level, and naturally most of the ponies double as jumpers, which is healthy since kids in general love to jump. The ponies with good gaits and minds are sought after, and they usually go on to the next child when the age limit knocks the present one from the saddle. Many ponies bring up several generations of children. Ponies are normally sounder and tougher than horses, they are less demanding to keep and they live and serve a long time. An important aspect of riding, especially for kids, is the socializing. Ponies are easier to kid around with and take for romps in the woods, races in the snow, and swims in the lake. They eat birthday cake and refrain from colicking, they have enough sense not to run into the campfire, and they will find their way back to the barn in the dark. In short: They have some self-preservation. The fun has to be kept in the work, even when dressage is on the agenda, and ponies help with that detail.

Teachers and Sponsors

Between ponies and the Young Rider Championships, there's a gap that needs filling with more vigorous and consistent training programs than are now offered. Clinics featuring European trainers are far between and only available to a chosen few. For more impact, consistency, and rein-

---

* *This has been slow to take off but is starting to gain momentum.*

forcement we need to start a national training program for Juniors and Young Riders. One suggestion has been to draw from our resources at home. We do, after all, have available a number of trainers who have schooled and shown at least one horse to FEI levels and have years of experience training both horses and people. Why not have them take turns working with groups of youngsters and their teachers? Again, such a program requires careful planning and monitoring and, in this case, a lot of trust and cooperation between the various trainers.

Last, but certainly not least: All programs need sponsorship.* In America we do not have the local and national subsidies that so many European agendas enjoy. However, before we can expect to get a sponsor interested in supporting the development and education of our future dressage riders, we must design a system that makes sense. A few years back, I watched a Young Rider's class in Dortmund, Germany. Twenty-five perfect rides, not a foot out of place, not one unsteady seat. I remember feeling grateful I was not in the judge's box for that class. I would have tied them all. This is what the Germans call their *nachwuchs*, loosely translated as the "growth behind us," and it was awesome.

Look behind us, and what do we see? At this time, we see the American constellation of dressage youth displaying a few bright shining stars, and a lot of darkness in between. We need to pay attention to this problem now, before we run out of "old timers" and end up with a void we cannot fill.

1996

---

* *Lendon Gray's Dressage4Kids now has reasonable sponsorship, as does the Robert Dover Horsemastership program.*

– 56 –

a recipe for improvement

Ever since the beginning of serious dressage in this country, which is now going on well over thirty years, we have diligently developed programs to educate the riders, primarily through the efforts of USDF, but also through privately organized clinics with accomplished domestic and foreign trainers.

The word "grassroots" has become almost a "sacred cow" in our midst, but perhaps this would be a good time to revisit and assess this favorite critter of ours. From the grassroots, if they are well tended, it is reasonable to expect grass to grow tall, produce seeds, and develop into even higher, more splendid grass.

Stand back and look at our sport for a moment. Yes, there are indeed tufts of beautiful blades of grass here and there, although some of them are starting to look a bit old and worn. They are still hanging in there and doing well, but where is the new growth? Is there a carpet of new, fresh, strong, and aggressive lawn ready to take over and get ahead? Well, I don't see enough of that to make me want to cheer. Do you?

Perhaps there is a problem with the weeding process? Nature has a system of bringing the fittest to the front, which we humans should perhaps pay attention to instead of fighting it all the time. If we developed a similar system in dressage, maybe we would do better in the long run.

The European Edge

What do the Europeans have that we don't? Right: a qualifying system to move up the levels. I know this concept will make some heads spin, but there is no doubt we need to do something right now to brighten our prospects for the future.

When you want to start your competitive career in most countries in Europe, you don't just saddle up and ride. To enter a show at even the most basic level, you must have the sponsorship of your local riding club, and the clubs take competition seriously. They will not allow anybody to show under their banner, unless they consider the riders capable at the level they wish to compete. "No tickee, no showee," and there is no way around it. As you get beyond the beginner stages, the National Governing Body (NGB) takes over and demands proof of your capability by a qualifying "ladder" of required accomplishments, which not only prevents you from moving up until you earn your way, but also stops you from stagnating at a level. When you have earned certain scores, you have to move up to the next level, to make room for those who are coming on, and to challenge you to greater efforts.

Why do we need a qualifying system? Because we are not seeing the kind of riding nationwide that will make the sport progress. For many years now we have had horseflesh available that is comparable to the best in the world; we have instructors and clinicians who have been there and done it all. Why, then, do the judges not experience an irresistible urge to hand over "8s," "9s," and "10s" to these wonderful horses performing at our shows? Because the riding, which is rarely up to the quality of the horse, prevents it. This situation is frustrating for the judges, riders, and owners, but most of all for the horses. There are all kinds of cruelty. It is not always about the use of spurs and whips, but about being bounced on and pulled in the mouth by a well-meaning but clueless and uncoordinated rider day after day. The fact that you love your horse does not help his tired back and sore mouth. The welfare of the horse is the primary reason we need a qualifying system.

Too Few Good Men (and Women)

A second good reason for establishing a qualifying system is our position in the international arena. We have struggled for years to reach the point when we are sitting third in the world behind the extremely strong German and Dutch teams. Unfortunately, it looks like we are about to lose ground again. Not because our top riders are not up to par, but because we do not have enough of them. One rider can maintain one or perhaps two internationally competitive horses at any given time, and we all know how fragile the very best ones are. When we, as a nation, lose a prospective team horse to lameness or retirement it is a catastrophe, but it should not have to be. There ought to be another ten horses standing by, and twenty riders knocking on the door! Where are they? Well, no horse can perform better than the rider who rides him, and we are obviously not educating our riders in a timely and orderly manner.

As George Morris stated in a recent column about the jumper riders, there has to be a desire to "live" this sport, not just "participate." If you truly want to be a part of dressage, you need to have a perspective of the entire game and a true perception of where you fit in the picture. A qualification system that allows the rider to advance up the levels as he or she earns his or her way through scores and points will give a clear view of each rider's progress. Using the system to assess their own proficiency on horseback, our riders can work on their improvement with much better guidance and goal orientation. It will also put a bit of pressure on the instructors around the country to nail down those basics like position and proper aids until they are installed in their students. Time to bring out and dust off the good old longe line...

The USEF Technical Dressage Committee already has a subcommittee working on the details of creating a qualifying system for our riders to progress from level to level after earning their way.* What they are thinking at this point is that everyone will be allowed to compete without restrictions through First Level. To advance from there, the rider has to earn a minimum of scores, which will convert into points collected, until he or she reaches the amount which allows for entering the next level. This is strictly a rider advancement program, it does not apply to horses or horse/rider combinations. Once a rider has worked his or her way up the ladder, they are "done" for good, and can enter any horse up through the level they have qualified for.

When a fair and easy-to-understand system for rider qualification has been created and is presented to the dressage community, we will hope that our sport has matured to the point that it will be easily accepted by the riders. These days our general philosophy of life is that everyone must be assisted in every way to be able to "feel good about himself or herself." While that tendency can bolster the ego, it can also weaken a person's resolve and prevent him or her from pursuing true accomplishments. Once our riders earn their way to the next level, there will be a real reason for self-congratulation, better-trained and happier horses and, as icing on the cake, eventually a greatly increased number of new international American riders in the wings.

2006

---

* *When a qualifications system was proposed by the USEF Technical Dressage Committee, the negative reaction was so strong the project was abandoned. Unfortunately at the time of writing, it has not been reintroduced.*

– 57 –

our lost generations

Close to forty years ago, dressage was introduced to this country as a "new" concept in riding. Slowly the discipline was accepted, adopted, and embraced by American riders. We have the event riders to thank for the initiative of being the first to bring dressage over here, and once it took hold, its growth in popularity has been rapid and rewarding. That is, for adult participants.

Our giant mistake when dressage first arrived was to make it an "X-rated" sport by promoting it as an exclusively adult activity. Not only were children on ponies not encouraged to participate, in some cases they were actively discouraged, as if we wanted to keep them out. Eventually, and not without resistance, we developed Young Rider and Junior programs for youngsters to compete and participate in FEI events. For seven years, I was very active in the "junior department," and it was sometimes like pulling teeth to get support for the youth to partake and be welcomed to dressage.

"This is not a kiddy sport," was the answer I received from one famous rider when I approached her for help with the juniors, as if this was a well-known and accepted fact. I once had an eleven-year-old student who won the Prix St. Georges Championship at Devon in Pennsylvania. The surprise and upset among the adults was interesting to behold, as if they were thinking, "Who let that child into our playground?"

We have in this country thousands and thousands of gorgeous ponies who all live in the hunter/jumper world and never show up at a dressage clinic or show. Olympian Lendon Gray is one of the few souls who has tirelessly focused on helping the kids who want to ride and compete in our world.

Thankfully, Lendon's annual Dressage4Kids event has become a place for youngsters to pilgrimage to every year, but the sad fact is that there are hardly any other such events available anywhere in this huge country. We sure need more fine souls like Lendon around to copy her, create their own ideas, and focus on the young. And, of course, we need funds to enable us to run programs that support the kids. We desperately need a little league of dressage and people to entertain that notion with their minds and their actions!

A Country to Emulate

When I was in Windsor, England, judging at the FEI European Dressage Championships, I met and talked to Dr. Maarten van der Heijden, director of sports and international affairs in the Netherlands for the Royal Dutch Equestrian Center. He filled me in on some of the successful youth activities in the Netherlands, which are sponsored by Rabobank and supported by all of the best trainers, judges, and organizers.

He also sent me a PowerPoint presentation that outlines the process, and although the program of scouting for talent and educating the young riders is only about ten years old, it's already yielding fabulous results. The sponsor is involved with the activities and constantly checking in and expecting progress. At some of the final events, the audience gets to vote on the winners, which is a great way to win new fans and involve more people.

Here's a whole new and wonderful reason for anyone who has the energy and know-how to raise funds to start his or her own legacy. Once the youth program is a success, whoever supported its beginnings will be not only a pioneer and founder, but also eventually be given credit for the riders who will develop out of the youth program and become our future team riders.

Our second void is the age group twenty-one to twenty-eight, the so-called "Brentina" group. We lose a number of riders when they are no longer eligible for the Young Rider Division. Some of them move on to other things; others cannot advance their horses to the Grand Prix and therefore lose interest.

But many of them are just lost in space and frustrated with no help to continue the training of the horse or guide them. The step from Prix St. Georges to Grand Prix is a big one, almost like working with a whole new sport, and to go it alone for the inexperienced is almost mission impossible.

What the "Brentina age group" needs is a mentor/teacher at home and a national program of education to guide them and provide "checkups" on their training.*

It's Time to Wake Up

To begin with, we need to take inventory of our young talent, then try to find help and advice for them and their instructors.

The US Equestrian Federation will help by inviting them to Developing Rider Clinics, and the US Dressage Federation can help by making avail-

---

* *We now have an educational pipeline headed up by the USEF Developing Dressage Coach Debbie McDonald.*

able their excellent records of shows and championships to assist in finding the riders who deserve to be invited. Our judges can help by alerting the USEF dressage department when they judge or observe an especially talented combination.

Although our Brentina Cup age group experiences growing pains, at least most of them have had the Junior and Young Rider path of competitions as a guideline, while our youngest group, the kids under sixteen, have had basically no encouragement at all to participate. They're offered few opportunities to partake in their own competitions where they are measured against their peers.

Having had no pipeline to produce new riders is the reason we are now scrambling to find viable combinations ready to go down the centerline for major events like WEG and Olympics. Let's not be asleep any longer, but start from the beginning with the toddlers on ponies who will grow up to be experts in their early teens.* Anyone who has been to the Junior and Young Rider shows in Europe comes home awed by the sophisticated riding displayed by the youth over there. They don't have to look for riders and horses to take the place of retired combinations; they have them waiting in line and raring to go.

A true American educational system will need support from every instructor, judge, parent and friend of dressage to take root, flourish, and eventually bring us the American dressage riders of the future. We have to produce our own riders, the way we have started to produce our own horses. If we do not, we'll be again and again looking for up-and-coming riders to fill the ranks and see nothing but another empty space.

2009

---

* *In 2010 we created a Youth Coach position for the under-eighteen group.*

– 58 –

the media and dressage

In 1972, I remember sitting in Sweden in front of the television for two-and-a-half days watching every dressage ride at the Munich Olympics in its entirety. It never occurred to me or anybody else that the dressage would not be aired; it was simply expected.

I realize that the program there was state-owned and run, and that in this country somebody needs to foot the bill, but the difference between our media coverage of horse sports to date and what occurs in Europe is truly discouraging.

Spills, Thrills, and Tragedy

There appears to be only one sure way to get attention in the media for horses, and that is when we have a problem of some kind. When Princess Anne was still eventing and took a spill at the Bromont Olympics, the viewers were introduced to eventing by way of watching the royal equipage turn over again and again until the uninitiated became convinced that the somersault was part of the program and the horses were at peril, as well as the riders. Not a single safe and complete round was shown, and no explanations were offered about the sport of eventing. Ruffian broke her leg on the track and racing got a lot of attention. "Superman" had a horrible accident and horses were suddenly in focus. Prominent horsemen were found to be involved in killing horses for insurance money, and once again we hit the screen, only to be instantly forgotten when the issue became yesterday's news.

As I grew up, I remember watching jumping competitions, which took place all over Europe every weekend. As in many other sports, we had special commentators who made the sport come alive by informing the less initiated, and at the same time kept the experts satisfied with correct information and data. Show jumping was, and is, a household word, and every grandma in Europe knows the "Big Name Riders" and has the scoop on their current mounts.

When I found, while living here, that nothing like it ever was offered on the American screen, although our television overflows with sports programs and reports on baseball, football, and basketball *ad nauseam*, I became curious. Since we had a relative who was heavily involved with NBC sports, I made an appointment to see him at his office in New York. He patiently listened to my laments, and when I was all through complaining, he told me the facts of life.

"You horse people," he said, "are the most vocal of all our critics. We have volumes of letters from all disciplines of horse sports, arguing that you ought to have more air time. We have looked into it, and it is true that except for racing, there is nothing available. Believe me, we would not be opposed to having horses around the clock, but in this country it all revolves around sponsorship. The truth is, there is no interest amongst our customers in supporting horse sports. Find me the sponsor, and you will have horses on TV!"

Although his answer did not surprise me, I found it hard to believe that with all the interest in other sports in this almost fanatically competitive society, there would be no room for horses. Well, many years later, the situation is not much improved. True, we now have special sports channels that actually on occasion when they can find absolutely nothing better to do will cover big dressage finals (usually only the freestyle—see more on this on p. 295) or a particularly prestigious jumping event. The regular channels have yet to cover any horse events, and in the several Olympics I have watched on American television there has been barely a mention of the existence of horses in the Games. It is in the regular coverage of the Olympics that the exposure is so important to all disciplines of our sport, since the true fans will find the special programs hidden on the special channels, but the general public will never bother to look.

Out of the Games?

Some of the reasons given for the threats we repeatedly hear of plans to remove horses from the Olympics are:

- *Riding is not a true team sport.* Neither is gymnastics, boxing, tennis, swimming, ice skating…

- *Riding is an elite sport, unavailable to the common man.* As long as the public does not know enough about the nature of the sport, this will be the perception. Riding lessons are probably one of the least expensive and snobbish recreational activities available. Horses are a lot of work and responsibility and it is a great deal healthier for a kid to hang around the barn than hang out in the mall.

- *Horses are not as big an audience draw as other sports.* Well, which comes first, the chicken or the egg? In Europe the arenas are packed, because people are informed and interested. I firmly believe that dressage could become "discovered" in America if the media coverage, in particular by television, is increased and properly handled. By that

291

I mean presented by knowledgeable and well-spoken commentators. So many times the commentators are chosen for the wrong reasons, and the result is devastating. Why have a jumper rider, never mind how famous, comment on dressage, or vice versa? There is the case of a dressage video from one World Equestrian Games, which has a person speaking who has a lovely Oxford accent but not a clue about the details. At one point he actually says, "Dressage people tell me that this was a good pirouette." The person commenting has to explain and entertain at the same time, and have the expertise, ability, and personality to accomplish both. He or she is incredibly important to the image of the sport, and has the opportunity to popularize dressage or make it seem too complicated to the newcomer, while aggravating the initiated by making incorrect statements.

Dressage has a secret weapon: the freestyle. Remember what it did for ice skating? Well-covered by the media, it could do the same for dressage, and thus open the door for more attention being paid to horses in general.

1996

– 59 –

dressage for dummies

Would you want to know more about the sport that, when it was finally included in television's Olympic sports coverage, was introduced as only slightly more engaging than knitting?

The Basics

To start with, there are three key words that will open the door to this captivating world of arcane activity. The first word is "push." Since you are not giving birth or trying to move your stalled vehicle out of the center lane, it must mean get off and push the horse. But, no, it refers to a motion initiated by your so-called seat, which after years of practice results in the animal moving "forward"—and that happens to be our next magic word. "Forward" will be repeatedly told to you, commanded from you, and on occasion screamed at you until it rings in your ears and tortures your dreams. The third word, "sucker," is often used in place of the proper name of the horse. The three words work well together. As in, "Push that sucker forward!"

The outfits used in competition are certain to impress and confound the uninitiated. In full regalia the rider is decked out in formal black and white somewhat like Mickey Mouse, complete with gleaming gloves. Even the women wear tails and top hats, and they compete with the men on an equal footing. (Well, not really, since there are features such as the flying changes when men are permitted to move about in the saddle, swing their legs and duck their torsos, while women exhibiting the same behavior would lose points.)

The first time you visit a dressage show the funereal atmosphere may surprise you. There is little noise, a few instances of hesitant applause, and if there is music, it is a very discreet murmur in the background. Only the closest of kin and the groom of the horse are present and looking excited when the rider enters. There may also be an instructor with a frozen look on his or her face. On occasion, there's an audience of several scattered people, but don't count on it.

The Levels

Now to the performance. If you are at all familiar with horses, you will realize that at the lower levels the horse displays all three gaits and not much else. What you need to understand is that there are lots of things going on "under the surface," which only the insiders appreciate, such as what the horse is doing with his head. He should wear it like a circus horse just waiting for a plume to sprout up between his ears. Nose in the air may look cute, but is not appreciated; neither is any form of excitement or expression of personality that may liven things up. Judges frown on bucking, rearing, and bolting, all the things that make sports dangerous and worth watching. And there are endless circles. This is one place in life when size *does* matter!

The so-called "upper levels" are to be strongly recommended for your watching pleasure. Now the horses have to skip from one lead to another at the canter like a happy kid, hop around in an imitation of a pirouette (remember *Swan Lake*?) and trot in place like you do Saturdays on the treadmill. All these activities have names that on occasion make sense, but most of the time are totally eclectic, which helps keep the mystery alive. Volumes of books are written on the subject, and some are so complicated that you will need another book to explain what it all meant, much like the commentary after a presidential speech.

The Dance

If you persist beyond the first hour, there is a reward for sticking it out, called the freestyle. Music now takes on a more central part, and the volume and beat put a little life into the picture. When it is done well, it actually looks like the horse is dancing to the music, and you will even see people tapping their feet and cheering their favorite on.

The judging is the ultimate mystery, a fact that becomes evident in heated debates after each championship competition. There are five judges placed separately around the ring in all important events, and although they are watching the same test, this is not always reflected in the results. There are a number of excuses for this, some of them even valid, but that does not do a thing for a disgruntled competitor. When the results of a test confuse you, welcome to the club.

The Pilgrimage

If you get roped into the scene of dressage, the time will come when you simply must go to Europe—in particular, Germany, the "Mecca of dressage." You will become enthralled with everything German and will be overwhelmed by a desire to learn the language. Once you do, you will realize you liked it better before you understood it. Certain things that will be said about your riding are less than complimentary. Soon you will want to import one of their prefab dressage machines. You will be shown some not-very-exciting critters with impressive price tags and, to your surprise, will be told that while they are not very good horses in

Europe, "in America, they will win." This statement worked better in the past, but it is still worth a shot. And, after a bout of fabulous hospitality and irresistible beer and complete exhaustion from flying around on the Autobahn in the rain, you may just say, "I'll take him!" If you are lucky, your timing was perfect, and the horse is a good one who will ensure that you become completely addicted.

The Initiated

Like all secret societies, we have a million rules. There is a "no" for everything, and an army of officials called technical delegates to follow up on them and create more opportunities for developing new rules to augment or slightly change the old rule, until you are clueless.

We are the only people I know who routinely get lost on a quarter of an acre, climb into a dark-colored, wool jacket in 100 degrees to perform, come out of the ring and when asked, "How did you do?" cannot tell until everyone has heard the score.

So, what's the fascination? Well, it was very well put by Ralph Waldo Emerson, who wrote: "Riding a horse is not a gentle hobby, to be picked up and laid down like a game of solitaire. It is a grand passion. It seizes a person whole and, once it has done so, he will have to accept that his life will be radically changed."

That's us: radically changed, for better or worse!

2004

– 60 –

riding schools and ponies: two missing links in our program

Without a way for "normal" people to access horses and training, dressage will remain an elite and relatively unknown sport in the United States.

When it comes to public awareness and appreciation of equestrian sports, it's evident today, more than forty years after dressage started to take hold in this country, that in the big picture of sports in America we haven't even gotten started.

This becomes painfully clear when you travel to Europe during any important jumping, eventing, or dressage competition. The whole thing, soup to nuts, is on primetime television. The horses and their riders over there are as well known as our football players and movie stars. Everyone from children to grandparents talks about them as household names.

In our society it is a microworld for the very initiated. If it were not for Rafalca and the presidential campaign, the word "dressage" would never have been mentioned on any program on the air where it would reach the uninitiated.* There's a long tradition of horse sports and dressage overseas, but that does not explain why in almost fifty years we couldn't have created more excitement at home about a sport that takes up all our attention and so much passion. Why are equestrian sports, and in particular dressage, so sidelined by other sports in the United States? Why do we have such a hard time introducing kids and their parents to the sport?

Access for Everyone

When I look at the structure I grew up with in Sweden, there are two things that stand out as "missing in action" over here. The first is the "local riding school." Almost every village, and certainly every town with self-respect, has a public riding school available by public transportation. This is where the little girls and boys who love horses go to breathe in the "eau de cheval" and worship at the equine altar.

In my hometown there was a sizeable riding school, supported at least in part by city funds. There were at least forty horses and twenty ponies available, and a number of instructors for all levels. The horses had regular personnel who cared for them, but in addition there was a chance for students to sign up to care for a special horse.

This privilege, you understand, wasn't awarded to you without a rigid selection and trial period, and only after you had gone through all the initiation and achieved the approval of the staff, the peers, and the horse could this blessing be bestowed upon you.

Once you were "in" and had your horse assigned, there was no such thing as missing a day, or someone in line would move in and take over. When arriving for your lesson, you were told which horse to ride.

---

* See pp. 290 and 291, where I discuss this in more detail.

As your riding improved, the horses assigned to you became more diffi-cult and complicated to ride, which we saw as a feather in our cap and proof that we were getting better. The day you were assigned a new, green arrival that came snorting off the van and would most likely try to send you into orbit, you knew you had arrived as a rider!

The mostly ex-military riding instructors were gods, and although some of them were real drill sergeants, they were all about making us better riders.

We had club shows every month or so when we competed in jumping against each other. The better riders were selected and allowed to com-pete in regional and eventually even national championships. The trick here is that, for a long while, there was no pressing need to own your own horse, and you eventually learned to ride every horse they assigned you.

Parents became involved at an early stage by paying for lessons (not a horse or maintenance) and coming to watch the club events such as competitions, parties, and the Christmas quadrille. It was social, it was affordable, and it taught us to ride and respect the horses.

The youngsters who stayed in the game past high school usually found a way to keep riding by schooling or exercising other people's horses, and some went on to equestrian schools or apprenticeships to make horses their profession. There are numerous top riders in all disciplines who grew up in Europe not owning a horse for years, but the availability of local or private riding schools gave them their start.

A Way to Dip Your Toes In

For thirty years, my husband and I owned and operated a stable named Knoll Farm on Long Island, New York, with as many as eighty horses on the property. About twenty-five of them were school horses. Some were pretty fancy and successful show horses in both jumping and dressage, but it was the less gifted but incredibly generous ones that safely introduced the kids to riding and got them on their way.

Thousands of children had their first riding lesson at Knoll Farm. We are amazed at how often we hear from our students from the past. Many of them have their own kids now, a number of them are still riding, and quite a few are professional horsemen.

One of our kids from days gone by is now a superstar jockey. His name is Richard Migliori,* and he grew up next to our farm and got his introduction to riding by helping in the barn in exchange for lessons.

This kind of subculture of horses that is second nature in Europe is hard to find here. If there is a barn nearby, it rarely has school horses available to the public. That means parents have to buy a horse or pony for the child to ride, and this fact alone is an enormous stumbling block. Fewer

---

* Richard Migliori's racing career spanned over three decades. Known as "The Mig" (after the Russian fighter jet), he was considered a "thinking man's rider" and since his retirement due to an injury, has become an active ambassador for horses and the sport he loves.

kids get a chance to try the sport, and the growth is stunted. If you cannot afford to play, you cannot learn the game.

This is the crucial point. If kids and young people cannot get in touch with a sport and become involved without a major investment from the family, it becomes an "elite" sport, as riding in this country has been classified.

The solution? Well, the idea of a national riding center or centers has been mentioned from time to time. The problem, as always, is our enormous distances, which makes coordination and contact difficult, plus, of course, the lack of financing for such a network.

If public or private funding could be found, and horses for training were supported by one such school, it could become a model for similar facilities around the country. The concept of creating opportunity for youth to connect with horses could possibly become a popular feature. Perhaps it could eventually get us away from the elite label and move riding into the range of "normal" sports.

Ponies Ponies Ponies

The most confounding subject in US dressage is the fact that we have no "pony culture." I have harped on this subject for years,* but the absence of ponies that are ridden and shown in dressage is still a huge hole in our system. As with the lack of public riding schools, it hurts the very roots of our growth.

Kids and ponies belong together; they foster each other, and every child who likes riding ought to be brought up by a pony. They are very good at putting a kid in his or her place without being as large and potentially dangerous as horses, and the whole family can get involved with the "pony scene" at an early stage.

---

* *As evident in this book! See also pp. 279 and 304 for more on this subject.*

Parents who have "pony kids" are already educated and on board with the equine scene when the time comes for the Junior and Young Rider divisions. When it's time to move to a horse, they aren't stunned at the idea of having an equine in the family; it's just a natural progression. There aren't enough opportunities available for ponies to shine at our shows, and there aren't enough ponies out there competing to fill the classes that do exist.

Many countries outside Europe have the same dilemma, and I've asked for the question to be discussed in regard to global development at the FEI Sports Forum. Perhaps we can brainstorm some ideas about possible solutions. All I know is that when I judged a CDI in France a couple of years ago, and they had more than forty ponies competing at the show, I was green with envy!

2013

– 61 –

a wish list

This is a good place for some contemplation of where we hope to be going. A look back in time confirms that we surely have made considerable progress since dressage first became a known concept in the United States.

More and more US riders are showing and doing well in Europe, but an important difference is that lately many of the horses have been trained *here* since they were started. Nationally, our base is getting stronger all the time, and the USDF, now housed in Kentucky, is the growing ground for our sport.

The educational value of all the programs developed and nurtured by the USDF is huge, since the organization provides the opportunity to learn and develop your skills at each level with a multitude programs. The USEF has a full schedule of governing and also provides a division to promote high performance, which is our window to the world.

So, what else could we wish for? Oh, all kinds of things, both large and small.

Where Are the Ponies?

Beginning with small, why don't we have more ponies showing in the dressage division? We are definitely lacking a strong pony division to get the kids off to an early, fun, and social start,* in spite of being rich in fabulous ponies in our shows, all competing in the hunter/jumper divisions.

Few ponies take the step over the line to dressage. That's sort of crazy and difficult to understand. Perhaps our trainers doubt that young children are capable of focusing on dressage—or is it the parents who think it's too complicated?

Well, go visit Roemer Foundation/USDF Hall of Fame Inductee Lendon Gray's Dressage4Kids in New York and learn otherwise. Or check out the European pony scene, which culminates in a hotly contested championship every year. I've had a couple of experiences myself with seven- to ten-year-old children who were totally fascinated with the sport and capable of grasping the concept and performing up to par.

Where do we start to fix this? Lendon recently wrote on the subject to the other members of the USEF Dressage Committee, and one of her suggestions was an exhibition by pony riders at events such as our Olympic trials and the USEF Pony Hunter Finals in Kentucky to promote little people on small horses. Let's put kids on ponies on top of our wish list.

Half Marks and Full Competence

In 2007 one of the British dressage team members, Wayne Channon, wrote an interesting column on Eurodressage.com entitled, "Is Judging Corrupt or Just Inaccurate?" Although he does some grumbling about

---

Ponies are a theme I return to again and again, with good reason! See more in "Who's Next?" (p. 277) and "Riding Schools and Ponies: Two Missing Links in Our Program" (p. 297).

the former, I was happy to note that in the final analysis he blames the method we use, instead of accusing the judges of deliberately misjudging the rides.

Mr. Channon, who has a career in high-tech and Internet technology, examines our current system of judging and calls it anachronistic. He compares it to the scoring system in gymnastics and ice skating where the competitors regularly score near "excellent," our equivalent of a "10."

He points out that most horses rarely get less than a "6 "for gaits or higher than a "7," and that being the case, it moves up or down from there according to how each movement is performed. This situation "locks" the combination in the 60 to 70 percentage range because the judge has to round up or round down to the whole score. And here comes the part I like: If the judges were allowed to give half marks, not only could they be more accurate and fair, but also the final scores could become considerably higher for the good performances.

After making several mathematical points, Mr. Channon concludes: "Half points would dramatically and considerably improve our sport. It would be more accurate and fairer to the rider, horse, and trainer, make for a better sport, and even allow the judges to appear more reasonable and demonstrate their competence."

I'm not completely certain about the correctness of Mr. Channon's math, and I think most judges already appear both competent and reasonable, but I love the idea of half points being allowed for the regular competitions, just as we now use them on the artistic side in the freestyles.

Every time I have to give a "7" that's actually a "7.5," but not really an "8," I grit my teeth and wish I had the tools to judge it more accurately. There are definitely nuances between movements that deserve to be acknowledged, and we, as judges, cannot express the fact that we know and feel the difference. I would like nothing better than for dressage to adopt the half-point system for all classes and relieve the judges from the handicap of being stuck with whole points.*

A Bit Better

An interesting contradiction in training philosophy is the fact that we are always told that a horse must be started on a snaffle bit and that, ideally, he should remain easy to ride on that bit through his career. Why then, I am often asked, are you not allowed to compete using the snaffle in Fédération Equestre Internationale classes?† I hear myself explaining to my students who ask this question about "refinement" and "tradition," but I realize I'm not making much sense. Why, in fact, are we not encouraged to use the snaffle in, say, Grand Prix? Perhaps we should even get extra points if the ride is good.

I had several FEI horses that never really forgave me for bringing the double bridle into their lives. One of them would willingly grab for the snaffle, eager to get to work. As soon as the double came off the hook, he would clamp his teeth together and twist his head all over to avoid being bridled. In reality, he worked equally well in both bridles, but he was completely insulted about the extra hardware he felt was undeserved.

Once you have tried all the ways you can fit a double bridle to avoid any discomfort and the horse is still unhappy, but immediately brightens up in a snaffle, you have to think there should be an option not to use the double. We will add that one to our list. And while we are on the subject of Grand Prix, which often proved to be the largest class in the show on the Florida circuit this year, would it be too much to ask for

---

* *Half points are now used for all scores and collective marks, and scores must be recorded with a decimal.*

† *The USEF now allows the snaffle bit to be used through FEI levels.*

a special division for the green Grand Prix horses? We now have separate divisions and championships for horses ages four through nine in the Developing Horse Program, special Junior, Young Riders, and under age twenty-eight Grand Prix Riders (the Brentina Cup). However, the horse that is a complete beginner has to dive in with the veteran Grand Prix gang and that can sure be a cold shower. A special Grand Prix class may not be practical to offer at smaller shows, but in the larger productions, a "first year green" Grand Prix class would be a welcome addition.

A Sufficient Helmet Rule

At a recent show, we were judging a horse in the four-year-old division of our Young Horse Program. Suddenly the bay put on the brakes and levitated in the most studied and determined bucks, which made it clear his motives were not pure.

Eventually the rider had to bail out, but she held on to the reins and fell in a position close to the horse's hind feet. One sidekick could have ended in disaster, and it suddenly dawned on me that she was wearing a silk top hat—very stylish and completely useless when a rider's head is in the danger zone. Once it was clear that this time the rider had escaped with nothing but wounded pride, I turned to my co-judge, trainer and longtime FEI and USEF judge Jayne Ayers, and exclaimed, "We need a new rule!"

Jayne stared at me in disbelief, since I'm notorious for opposing any new rules and regularly become comatose during rule discussions in the Dressage Committee. But she agreed that with all our real and imagined safety concerns, it's pretty stupid to allow a top hat in young horse classes. It doesn't matter how skilled and brave a rider may be, green horses do totally unpredictable and bizarre things, which cannot always be prevented. Therefore, I think a safety helmet rule for those classes is a good thing to put on a wish list.*

Wishes Come True

Sometimes it takes a while, but every so often, wishes come true. I've long wanted to make a change in the wording that describes the number "5" in our dressage tests. The original translation was from French, in which *suffisant* does not have the positive ring that our English counterpart has. The English version can be easily interpreted as an approval of a job well done. Well, we finally have voted to replace "sufficient" with "marginal" in our next printing of the dressage tests.

Little wishes can come true if you help them along. While we are at it, let's have a big one: Olympic gold, for example. As they say in the ads for the New York Lottery: "Hey, you never know...!"

2008

---

* See "Tradition Over Safety" for more on the existing rule, p. 50.

– 62 –

are our horses on drugs?

Recently there were a number of emails directed to the USEF president, David O'Connor. The subject matter of all of them was a concern for the use of drugs, which according to the email authors, has become common practice in order to "enhance" the performance of our show horses. Criticism was directed toward our drug-testing programs and the present penalties when someone is found to have broken the rules.

A Strange Way to Ride a Horse

I, however, remember "back when" there was *no* drug testing whatsoever. Shortly after I arrived in the United States over thirty years ago, I went to my first horse show here. This is what I observed: The flat classes, especially the various hunter under saddle divisions, were populated by beautiful Thoroughbreds shuffling along with their noses on the ground like anteaters and an absent look in their eyes. On their backs were hunched-over riders, frozen in position, holding the buckle with the reins in a big loop. The slower and more earthbound the gait and the less energy evident, the greater chance for a ribbon.

To a European, this was a mighty strange way to ride a horse! The animals looked drugged, they moved like they were drugged, and guess what: they were drugged. And it appeared nobody thought anything about it.

Shortly afterward, my husband and I went to look at horses in Virginia. At one of the state-of-the-art sales barns, a groom, much like a nurse, carried around a tray full of injections, which were routinely given to each horse a few minutes before going in the ring. This was done in full view of any observers, and considered a brilliant way to cut down on warm-up time. And it sure was efficient, since no horse went more than twice around the ring in each direction before heading for the first fence. Nobody around us seemed to view this program as strange or unsafe for either horse or rider. On the way home, we discussed the situation, and the concept baffled our minds.

A few brave men and women took a stand against the routine use of performance-enhancing drugs, often at peril to their own safety. Death threats and burnt down barns and houses were some of the things these people had to endure for their convictions. The USEF Drugs and Medications committee started as a result. Today, as a consequence of regulations and testing, are we drug-free? Well, no, but by comparison to the old days, both competitors and their horses are a lot better off.

However, with increased sophistication in both the requirements of the top competition horses in any division, so-called "sports medicine" can sometimes become a gray area. Obviously tranquilizers and stimulants, as well as painkillers, are in direct violation of the principles of the Drugs and Medications Committee rules. But then there are the multitudes of other agents such as hormones, homeopathic remedies, herbs, and feed supplements, which may not enhance performance and are not harmful, or could even be of value to the horse. Some of these are considered "masking agents" in the testing process, and are therefore not allowed.

Sports Medicine or Drug Abuse?

There is a whole science of "dos and don'ts" here, and I marvel at the knowledge and expertise of some of my colleagues, who are very careful not to break any rules but have top-performing horses that are difficult to maintain. The pounding a dressage horse has to withstand when he is headed for the big times is to be compared with a top gymnast preparing for tough competition, and there are many injuries lurking on the way. It becomes necessary for the rider/owner to learn how to best handle every situation to be on the cutting edge. The big question for each individual to ponder then becomes: Where does sports medicine end and drug abuse begin?

We dressage folks have had a habit of congratulating ourselves on being a "clean" discipline. Not because we are better people, but because our sport in general does not lend itself to drug use. Since regularity of the gaits is one of our holy principles, it makes even the slightest disturbance in the gait a disaster. Therefore, it is difficult to mask lameness even with a heavy dose of painkillers. A drugged mind could become a slow reactor in the ring, and consequently it becomes really unpredictable to play with tranquilizers. So, up until now we have been fairly smug about having very few cases of illegal use of drugs in dressage. With the well-publicized international case of Germany's Ulla Salzgeber, and later Isabell Werth, and a couple of high profile national trainers being set down for use of illegal substances, I guess we have to admit we are not lily-white any more.

The letters to our USEF president were full of horror stories from the horse show scene, but also suggestions about how to improve on the program. Today, when a trainer is found guilty, the penalties are a small

Unconventional Wisdom

Out of Breath

Enhancers such as steroids and hormones to "body-build" the horse can be very harmful, as I saw in a recent example of a horse imported from Europe. The animal, a young FEI horse, had an enormous neck, unusual in its exaggerated crest for a gelding. He was a very good mover, and had the whole Grand Prix program "installed." He just could not bend his neck to one side for any length of time without panicking and running wildly to the wall.

After a year of extensive research and experimenting, it appears the large amount of steroids this horse had pumped into him over many years backfired and settled in his lymph glands. The glands on the side of his throat were so enlarged that his wind was cut off when he turned his head.

Obviously he was not interested in anything beyond breathing.

---

fine and a month or two of suspension from shows, plus a tiny notice in the back of the USEF magazine, which is easy to miss.

Among the proposals to improve penalties were, first and foremost, a substantially higher fine for not only the trainer but also the owner of a horse found with a positive drug test. Sums from $15,000 to $25,000 for each were suggested. Secondly, a period of suspension of at least a year, with no possibility to partake in horse shows for either trainer or owner. In addition, many letters advocated the creation of a permanent website where the membership could easily access the list of people currently suspended any time they wished. Most of all, the email writers wished for more testing, such as routinely pulling blood from horses placing in the top three to six, in addition to random testing.

Perhaps some of the proposals were a bit "over the top," but we have to admit that a penalty that really smarts and brings the owner into the picture would create some valuable "checks and balances." Additional testing is, of course, a very expensive proposition, but may not be necessary if the top horses in each class were always the ones selected. Such an agenda is neither unfair nor "politically incorrect" if it is a routine procedure everyone is aware of. It is common practice already at championships and trials, and personally, I think it would work lots better than random testing, which works just about as well as random bag searches do in airports. Now the winners would have to show they are "clean" instead of wasting time and money on testing the amateur-owned, Training-Level horse that gets called up show after show. Poor thing never won anything but has an uncanny knack for attracting the test person when, just like Greta Garbo, his only wish is to "pee alone." This does not do the job of either detecting or deterring the "big fish" from illegal drug use.

Most competitors want a level playing field, and therefore support our USEF drug testing program. There is, however, a fear in the back of every competitor's mind that his or her horse could test positive, even when absolutely no attempt was made to illegally enhance his performance. In the jungle of unaccepted substances or measures thereof, not to mention the "masking agents" that are often in themselves harmless, one has to stay vigilant. Some substances remain in the system for a very long time, and the trainer/rider has to think ahead when medicating a horse, sometimes several weeks before a planned show. Even the most innocuous liniments and fly sprays or oral supplements can become a monster in the test tube.

The worst of all worlds would be to have your horse test positive, knowing you never did anything intentional to beat the system. I still wonder about the Ulla Salzgeber case.* Surely, Ulla knew her horse was likely to end up in the top placings and therefore also subject to drug testing. Since she is neither stupid, nor inexperienced, my feeling is she got caught in the "time warp" between necessary veterinary work and the World Cup. And if that is the case, I bet she went through some tough times we all want to avoid.

2004

---

* At the 2003 World Cup in Gothenburg, Sweden, Ulla Salzgeber's champion mount Rusty tested positive for Testosterone Propionate, which his veterinarian claimed was used to treat an assumed hormonal imbalance that may have caused patchy hair loss.

– 63 –

is the dressage horse an unhappy athlete?

"Training or torture" is the question posed by the editor of the August 2005 issue of St. Georg Magazine *in regard to today's competitive dressage. The German equestrian publication hit the horse world two weeks before the start of the European Dressage Championships, and it caused quite a commotion.*

An article, which is titled "Perverted Dressage," attacks the increasingly common method of riding horses way behind the vertical for long periods of time. In pictures and words, the editorial denounces the so-called "rollkur"* and also points a finger at brutal rein aids; contraptions that tie horses together in a fashion that allows trainers to pull on their legs like a marionette in order to create a spectacular piaffe and passage; draw reins

---

* I called it "rolled up" in its earliest variations—see p. 184.

attached to the double bridle; and even deprivation of water before the competition to keep the lid on hot horses.

"Where there's smoke, there's fire," is probably an appropriate saying here, and I am fairly convinced that the editor of *St. Georg*, Gabrielle Pochhammer, would not have written on this subject if it had no basis in reality. One problem, however, is that although there are German riders named in the article who are believers in the rollkur method, the pictures that accompany the text are all of Dutch team riders. Because of the timing of the publication, right before the European Championships, the Dutch saw this as a German maneuver to weaken the chances for a gold medal for the strong Dutch team. Well, the German team did win, although with a small margin, but Anky van Grunsven took the individual gold.

Anky and her trainer/husband Sjef Janssen felt they had been personally attacked, and they initiated a lawsuit against *St. Georg Magazine*, resulting in a ban being placed on all sales of the August issue. The *St. Georg* issued an explanation stating that it had no intention of suggesting that Anky was involved in all the methods of training named in the article, but it also called in its legal team. And so the battle is on.

Hang the Judges

Not only the top riders in the world of dressage but also the international judges received a lashing in the *St. Georg* article. They are described as a bunch of cowards and ignoramuses who are incapable of telling the difference between a horse that is correctly and humanely trained and one that has been forced to perform with dubious methods. And those judges who might be able to see the light tend to close one eye to please the organizers, place the favorite high, and be invited back to judge.

How are we supposed to react to this? Ignoring the subject is not an option for anybody involved in the sport. Shrugging it off because we are not personally "guilty" of any sort of deliberate cruelty to our horses is not going to make the problem go away. These kinds of allegations tend to put a dark cloud over the entire dressage community, whatever your position within it happens to be. And it is guaranteed to alert the animal activists.

Taking a step back to view dressage objectively is not so easy when you are submerged in the game up to your eyeballs. Still, with some effort, I can see all three sides of this argument, because I wear all the hats at different times.

To be successful as an international competitor you have to be determined, brave, and incredibly focused on those few minutes in the arena that are the culmination of all your work. If you find and can develop a method that works for you and your horses and gets consistently rewarded by the judges, why should you give it up? In every sport, the pressure is tremendous at the top level, and winning is the object. Since our sport involves a silent partner, the horse, the situation is more complicated. Add to this that the kind of animal that takes the honors in today's fierce competition is a very sophisticated and high-powered equine, both physically and mentally. Dealing with some of these equine Ferraris, it has been my experience as a trainer, competitor, and judge, that anything that is forced or unfair in the training does not come out well in the show ring. It is difficult for me to imagine that training that is one long torture session for the horse could lead to something beautiful to watch in the arena.

Nevertheless, I know there are some unavoidable conflicts on the road from green-broke to Grand Prix that need to be worked out. Anyone who thinks that a competitive Grand Prix horse offers every movement it has to learn without occasionally questioning the rider has never trained one. The journey from green horse to Grand Prix is a long, sometimes rocky, but mostly inspiring enterprise. It should be a trip horse and rider take together, and they ought to arrive at their destination both proud of their achievements and eager to strut their stuff. Not all horses are comfortable in the show ring—they may have stage fright, or they may not like being in unfamiliar surroundings—but some really enjoy showing off, and those horses are always fun to watch and to ride!

Being an international judge is a great responsibility and, especially at major events, the pressure can be quite strong to "get it right" according to the riders, the organizers, the audience, and your colleagues. You cannot please all of them, all the time. The decision about each score has to be immediate, correct, and fair, and there are thousands to be made in a weekend. The job description of a judge is limited to what occurs in the arena in front of him or her, and it is impossible for him or her to assess what goes on in the warm-up ring. Naturally, most judges can tell if a horse is tense, unhappy, and appears uncomfortable, and there are ways to express your displeasure about that throughout the score sheet. Remember, however, that there is sometimes a fine line between "tension" and "brilliance," and that a breathtaking performance almost has to include a certain measure of electricity and tension to become exciting. On this issue, judges tend to disagree more than on the technical aspects, and often it is the amount of tension versus brilliance that makes the judges come out differently in the scoring. Diversity in scores is not usually appreciated by competitors, audiences, or organizers, who want to see all their ducks in a row—even the press will sometimes attack a judge who stands out. It is assumed that this judge is incorrect, while it is quite possible that this was the judge who, at that particular competition, was the only one who had a truly sharp eye and the confidence to honestly express what he or she saw.*

---

* *Read more of my thoughts related to this subject on p. 228.*

When it comes to supervising the schooling we have, at least in this country, capable and proactive technical delegates and stewards who are on the ball. For the FEI scene in Europe, our team coach Klaus Balkenhol has suggested for a while now that one judge should be posted in the warm-up, and a score from that judge should be factored into the final results. So far this suggestion has fallen on deaf ears, but who knows?

The observer/journalist is the watchdog of the sport, and although neither competitors nor judges cherish criticism, checks and balances are of importance. If the process of reaching the pinnacle of our sport appears to be harmful to our horses, we need to clean up our act. Unfortunately, "perception is truth" to a great extent, and if our equine athletes appear "unhappy" it does us no good to protest and proclaim how much we love and appreciate them. Instead of indignation and lawsuits, riders and judges have to invite both the press and the public to be part of discussion, dialogue, and participation. For example, two years ago when I judged at the Stuttgart CDIO, we had journalists sit in to listen at the judges' tables. And although anyone can view the schooling at most large events, perhaps the idea of a judge in the warm-up area can at least be tossed about at the next Global Forum.

We need to show the world that we are not involved in dressage to make our equine partners miserable but to build strong and proud athletes, which while they may not be ecstatic all the time, are reasonably pleased with their lot in life as healthy and performing stars.

2005

– 64 –

about past and (perhaps no) future olympic games

Once the dust has settled from Olympic preparations and the Games have concluded, we have a brief period of "R&R" and a year to regroup before the 2010 Alltech FEI World Equestrian Games in Kentucky, which we hope will be a great bonus for all equestrian disciplines in this country.

The Olympic Games seem to me to come upon us more quickly each time. When you've been involved for many years with the committee work that irons out the selection procedures, they sort of blend together. The work we've done on these committees has become increasingly more complicated as each time we create a format that will be totally fair to the athletes trying out and also satisfies the legal departments of the US Equestrian Federation and the US Olympic Committee.

You would think that you could simply use the old formula and keep marching, but things change in the Olympic Games rules for the sport, the venues (except that they're always too hot), and the safety issues.

Veterinary and quarantine requirements vary. So, except for the basic premise, we have to reinvent at least some of the wheel each time. Often we find when the Games are over—and we're equipped with 20/20 hindsight—that there are things we need to improve on. So the work starts all over again.

An Olympic Games Evolution

Looking back with some nostalgia, I remember the first time I was close to the action at the Olympic Games. It was in Montreal in 1976 when we had Colonel Bengt Ljungquist as our US coach. There were three women who had qualified on our team—Hilda Gurney, Dorothy Morkis and Edith Master—and one man, John Winnet. Like this year, only three could ride. At that time, choosing the three riders was up to the coach. I was close with Bengt, and he shared with me the agony of having to make this choice, since John was his friend and the only "guy" candidate. Bengt knew his players, however, and he knew those women were tough competitors with strong nerves who could hold up their end whether they went first or last.

That, in the end, was why Bengt decided to keep the "girls" on and leave John as the alternate.

It wasn't easy for him to tell his friend about the decision, but it proved to be the right one when the United States earned their first dressage bronze medal in modern times. That scenario would never have sold today, when the selections are strictly "by the book" and the coach has limited input in the final selections.

I remember another situation in Canada that's also not likely to ever happen again. We were a group from New York who had rented a camper, and we parked it next door to the horse park. Every day we simply walked over to watch the schooling, and there was little concern about security in the parking area or at the stables.

321

In Montreal, Granat, the Swiss horse ridden by Christine Stückelberger, was the one to watch, and he certainly made it worthwhile. The barn was situated high on a hill, and the training area was below.

Granat came out at least three times a day, and one of those times the giant bay was halfway down the slope when he spied Georg Wahl, the trainer, standing in the ring. Granat did a 180 and bolted back up the hill to the barn with his tiny rider. A few minutes later, two sturdy handlers led him back down to the work area.

Easy, Granat was not, but a forceful mover with endless power and a reach in his half-passes the like of which I have never seen since. And Christine made up in determination what she lacked in size. Their eventual gold medal was well deserved, but there were times in the schooling area when you couldn't be sure Granat would even get in the competition ring.

In the 1984 Los Angeles Olympic Games, Hilda was our anchor on Keen, and Robert Dover was a "rookie" on the team aboard Romantico, doing a creditable job in spite of the horse's somewhat funky gaits. At those Olympic Games, I spent a lot of time with my friends Sue and Terri Williams, owners of the Trakehner Abdullah, who captured team gold and individual silver in the show jumping with Conrad Homfeld. Abdullah* started his career as a dressage and event horse. Before we discovered how much jumping talent he had, I used to teach Sue on him, and I even rode him in the Third Level Regional Championships in Buffalo, New York. It was incredibly exciting to see him and Conrad bring home those medals.

In the dressage competition, there was a horse named Ampere, who was six years old and competing in the Olympic Games, ridden by Jo Rutten. I actually tried this horse on the Santa Anita racetrack after the

---

* *Abdullah was inducted into the US Show Jumping Hall of Fame in 2009.*

competition was over. Since then, the FEI rules have changed, and no horse younger than eight can compete in the Grand Prix. That's a good and horse-friendly rule, and my ride on Ampere convinced me that even with the most willing horse, facing Olympic competition at six was a bit too much, too soon.

I'd hoped the 1996 Atlanta Olympic Games would be my turn, since I had two promising Grand Prix horses to try out on. As the time neared, however, I developed a medical issue that led to the sale of my stallion Leonardo II, and after much denial and indecisiveness, I also leased Metallic to Jane Forbes Clark, Robert Dover's sponsor. Dressage was only one of the FEI disciplines Jane supported; she had her jumpers going in another ring and also fielded a four-in-hand driving team on the side.

Consequently, in Atlanta I found myself an owner, which was way more stressful than riding, because of the imposed passiveness and the nervous waiting around.* At any important competition, there's bound to be a certain tension in the air, but Olympic fever is beyond that. While the previous year we'd enjoyed great team spirit at the Pan American Games in Argentina, I was somewhat disappointed in the lack of cooperation and cohesiveness among the team members in Atlanta.

We Can Make a Statement

The Olympic Games are considered the pinnacle of all achievements in sports, and yet they're riddled with politics and a great deal of commercialism. It's become so important to the athletes to build their career on Olympic Games that the sportsmanship and spirit of fair competition have suffered in some areas, and hence we have drug testing.

In principle, it's absolutely essential that any cheating is prevented, or the Games cannot continue. However, it's becoming difficult for peo-

---

* *I regale you with my experiences in an owner's shoes in Part IV, p. 164.*

ple who would never go near performance-enhancing drugs themselves, or consider giving them to their horse, to avoid every kind of masking agent and common topical product that may interfere with the testing or show up as a problem.

In an interview by the British magazine *Horse & Hound*, Princess Haya, FEI president and member of the International Olympic Committee, warned about the very real possibility that all equestrian events will be removed from the Olympic Games. And here's what she had to say about dressage in particular: "The popularity of dressage is abnormally low, and there are complaints about judging and the makeup of judging panels and committees. Anyone who thinks equestrian sports are secure for London is mistaken."

She then shows her fighting spirit by pointing out some of the high points of the eventing and show jumping, and also by encouraging the English to show enthusiasm for all three disciplines and work to keep equestrian sports in the Games. I well understand the excitement and fascination of Olympic Games, and yet I'm not married to them myself. I have had more fun at every World Equestrian Games (WEG) I've attended, because it's all about horses. Like everyone, I realize the value of being considered an "Olympic Sport" and the funding and prestige that goes with it. For those reasons, I do hope the FEI can convince the IOC to keep equestrian sports in the fold.

Should we lose our spot in the Olympic Games, there is, however, a chance we could make a stronger statement in the media and at the venue without having to compete with other sports for the attention. And maybe, by making the WEG our most prestigious event, we can concentrate on informing and advertising for one major effort and build a stronger fan base that way. There just might be life after the Olympic Games!

2008

– 65 –

looking beyond the olympics

It's time to look for ways to make the next Olympic Dressage Team even stronger. Here are a few things that come to mind.

Recruiting Relationships

Americans are horse poor and ring rusty compared to our European counterparts. By that I mean that each accomplished rider here usually is limited to one FEI competition horse.

Although we aren't to blame for the huge distances we have to travel to compete in this country, the situation is at least partially our own fault. We have a number of viable professionals and past US team riders who didn't try out for the Olympics this year and are not even competing at the FEI levels. These riders aren't retired from competition; they're busy training and teaching. So busy, in fact, that for years they appear to have had no time or interest in producing new horses coming up the ranks. It looks like some successful riders are simply waiting for a sponsor to insert a ready-made Grand Prix horse under their seats, while they are too occupied or unmotivated to school their own.

Riders have learned from the past that they can get on our team on prefab horses, mostly imported from Europe. Sometimes they could even get a medal. But that was yesterday, and a new age is dawning where to play at the very top you need a close, ongoing relationship with your horse. What made the magic disappear for quite a while when the outstanding Dutch Warmblood Totilas was sold? The stallion looked, moved, and performed all his exercises basically the same as before, but the chemistry that existed between horse and rider when he was piloted by Dutch champion Edward Gal had evaporated.* And why weren't we surprised? Wasn't the reason we became involved with dressage, which means *training*, the fact that there is training involved?

Admittedly it takes time, money, tears, disappointments and lots of sacrifice in other areas to produce just one Grand Prix horse from "scratch." I know the drill since I'm on my sixteenth green Grand Prix horse. For sure, all my past horses were not stars, but one, Metallic, was on two US medal teams.

Although in the end, you may not have a Uthopia (ridden by Carl Hester of Great Britain) or a Totilas, you could be out there competing on the international circuit, gaining experience and giving us much needed visibility overseas.

On the 2011 Pan American gold-medal team, we had four US-trained horses, and two of them were US-bred. Paragon was *born* under the watchful eye of his rider-owner Heather Blitz, and there is no mistaking that they have a very close relationship. Hopefully it will also serve our present Olympic team well that all our riders have been longtime partners with their mounts.

---

* *Edward Gal and Totilas were the first rider-and-horse combination to sweep the gold medals in dressage at a single FEI World Equestrian Games.*

Keep the Pipelines Flowing

We desperately need many more horse/rider combinations like that to create depth, but immediately the question of who or what will finance this program comes to mind. It's easy to point to German Olympic rider Isabell Werth and praise her proficiency in bringing horses along when she has a fabulous backer like Madeleine Winter-Schulze! It's not all about solid sponsorship, however. Some capable and educated riders who have financial backing haven't necessarily produced new horses, while people who had to tough it out themselves have.

Any rider who is serious about staying in the game has to be busy creating a pipeline of horses to keep him or her in the ring and available for Games to come. The best way is to attempt to acquire affordable young horses, since there are very few even partially trained horses out there worth the enormous prices they command. And there is always the option of bartering training for the ride on a great prospect, which benefits all parties. We have many accomplished and experienced riders without a horse who would welcome a partnership with an owner or breeder!

Now, when we have an educational system of national coaches in place, we need to have the horses to train and the riders willing to do the work.

It appears dressage isn't the only equestrian discipline lacking a solid base. George Morris* has often expressed his frustration with the situation in show jumping, and when I spoke with him recently, he had some choice words for what he called the "complacency of the riders." Mr. Morris could just as well be talking about dressage when he was quoted in the *Chronicle of the Horse*, saying: "People are comfortable at home, and when you are comfortable in a competition situation, you get a bit

---

* *George Morris, one of the most influential riders and trainers in equestrian sport, was chef d'equipe of the US Show Jumping Team from 2005 through 2012.*

deluded about how things go. We have to have a very strong base on our soil, and then the people who are ready should go to Europe to compete as a finishing school."

It looks like we're in the same boat, but at least in jumping things are less predictable than in dressage. A miracle round could happen on the jumper course to upset all the predictions, while this is indeed a rare event in the dressage arena.

On to London

The competition in London this summer will be incredibly intense. Anyone who has followed the results over the last year is aware of how fast things are changing in the ranks and how the scores are soaring as the Games get closer. The spotlight moves from one sensational new horse to another, and they all seem to offer endless possibilities. Whenever a new star arrives on the scene, that horse gives its team a boost, and the rapid changes in team status are fascinating to follow, especially since this is very much a new phenomenon on the world dressage scene.

A few weeks ago, the US dressage team was selected at the US Equestrian Team Foundation headquarters in Gladstone, New Jersey. It was an extremely well organized and smoothly run event. The grounds have never looked more beautiful, the judging was spot on, and the quality of the competition high. Horses I have followed over the entire show season stepped up their performances to a whole new level, and there was no room for error. One mistake was a disaster, two would cost you the placing. It started to look like a "fault and out" division by the second weekend, and until the end of the last Grand Prix Special, we weren't sure who our three team members and one individual would be.

The riding overall was sophisticated, and the atmosphere in the barns and during training, warm-up, and competition was focused, yet positive and friendly. Naturally, some of the riders had more horse under the hood than others, but we can be proud of how well each horse was presented. In the end we're blessed with a great team of experienced horses and riders: Steffen Peters on Ravel, Tina Konyot on Calecto, Jan Ebeling on Rafalca. Riding as an individual, we have Adrienne Lyle on Wizard making her debut as a USEF team member on the highest international level.

As a bonus, we had Stephen Colbert giving us a huge leg up by finally admitting dressage to primetime television on Comedy Central's *The Colbert Report*. We thank the Romney presidential campaign for the opportunity and embrace the foam fingers and the jokes. They even picked clips of Rafalca* at her best and spelled dressage correctly. Life is good!

During the trials, the USEF had an in-person meeting for the Active Athletes Committee, and we invited all the riders in the competition to attend. The result was a most productive exchange of ideas for improving our sport countrywide. Although we conduct riders' meetings at all the major CDIs, I never before had the feeling that the athletes had this kind of an inspired exchange while thinking of themselves as a part of a *nation*, rather than a region.

Americans are great visionaries. We now need to envision a plan for the next four years and beyond by pooling our resources in training ability and by starting and producing new horses at home, to make sure there is an even better life for American dressage after these Olympics!

2012

---

* *Rafalca is an Oldenburg mare owned by Ann Romney, wife of 2012 presidential hopeful Mitt Romney, with Amy Ebeling (wife of rider Jan Ebeling) and Beth Meyer, a longtime friend of the Romneys.*

– 66 –

2012 olympic games: in perspective

London was in focus like never before, and what a fantastic show the Olympics were! The British people have every right to burst with pride, not only because they hosted probably the best Games ever, but also because their athletes excelled in every sport, including equestrian. They gave us all an unforgettable experience and an accomplishment to look up to in every way.

A Need for Depth

I like my job, but since the day I accepted the US Equestrian Federation position as Technical Advisor for the Dressage Team almost three years ago, I wasn't looking forward to the Olympic Games. Our lack of depth in the big tour loomed large, and short of manufacturing new combinations out of thin air, the prospects weren't looking good. We were especially hard hit by the accident which robbed us of our valuable team rider Courtney King Dye and the loss of sponsorship for Guenter Seidel.

The trials correctly selected the best we had, and our riders did as well as they could with horses that couldn't quite measure up to what Europe has produced lately. I was particularly impressed with how well Jan Ebeling presented Rafalca, keeping his focus in spite of all the hoopla around her and the presidential election.* Ravel did us one last of many favors and kept the team in a respectable sixth position. That was his final gift to US dressage, and not until it was all about him did he lose his concentration and miss a couple of Steffen's cues. He will now be retired, and I can assure you, we will have occasion to lament the loss of the combination of Steffen and Ravel.

Great Support

Once you become a member of the American dressage team, the USEF has a great support system in place. In 2011, the staff went to the test event at Greenwich, and we also traveled to several locations outside of London to find a stable where we could have our training camp. We settled for the lovely "yard" offered by Jack and Linda Keenan, who are expatriate Americans and the most wonderful, supportive and generous people on earth!

The two-and-a-half weeks spent there were great for polishing final details, test riding and team building. The charming village of Hadleigh was welcoming and peaceful. The horses arrived in excellent condition, and our team veterinarian, Dr. Rick Mitchell, not only flew with the horses, but also was present for the entire time we were in England. And the team riders had the staff, their trainers, the team coach, the veterinarian, and a sports psychologist available via phone.

With an impressive setup like that, there was only one thing missing for the last three years: Plenty of horses ready to compete at Grand Prix of

---

* *You can read a bit more about the "hoopla" in "Looking Beyond the Olympics," p. 329.*

the quality that is needed for success on today's international scene. We have the riders, but with Ravel gone* and very few in the wings, we have to be more critical of ourselves before sending another team out to fight windmills.

When you go to compete at the Olympics, the philosophy is that winning is not the essence; it's how you play the game. We played well, and our riders were good ambassadors for our country, but because we had no chance at a medal it was at times frustrating and difficult to subdue the "go get it" instinct that lives within every true competitor and make do with "participating." You can do your job and hope for a miracle, but you still live with reality.

Where Are Our Next Grand Prix Horses?

The root of our problem is in our lack of depth and how we go about promoting the horse-and-rider combinations we would like to field on our team. I bet anyone who is well informed about American dressage would have a hard time giving me even four names of combinations they expect will represent us and possibly medal in Normandy (France) at the 2014 Alltech FEI World Equestrian Games.

Ideally, we should be able to name ten right off the top of our heads. That's never happened here yet, but we've been stronger in the past. Locating horses and riders coming up is the first obstacle facing us. If and when we find a precious few contenders, we don't have much of a structure to offer them except clinics and a few limited USEF grants to support their education and competition.

What they really need is a controlled program that sends them overseas to stay long enough to compete against the Europeans. They need to

---

* *Ravel, a modern-day legend in American sport, won many medals and championships under rider Steffen Peters before being retired after the London Olympics.*

compete in foreign arenas, in front of judges who can compare them with the horses that we must try to measure up to and hopefully surpass. Frequent showing on European terms until our riders become as seasoned in the ring as those of the nations we're up against is of the essence. Our horses have to be seen repeatedly until the judges are familiar with them and know what to expect.

In short, our best combinations have to "live and play" overseas because our sandbox is not where the action is.

"Money makes medals," said Prime Minister David Cameron in a television interview, when he reviewed the success of the British athletes and the effect of the lottery money, which supported them with a total of 164 million pounds over the last four years (almost 30 million went to equestrian). This was used to scout out talent and support it, as long as it produced results. The chosen riders could spend their time training instead of stressing about teaching, traveling to give clinics, trading horses, worrying about maintaining support of the horse, or having to sell it. What a concept!

There must be some way to finance American equestrian athletes that will add to the private sponsorship, which has carried the burden alone for as long as I've been involved in dressage. These true and patient supporters of the sport have provided us with team members over and over again, but as we lose some of them, we aren't gaining new ones.

And why should the same people be expected to repeatedly supply us with team horses without any additional support coming from neutral funds that could help riders without private sponsors? Even if one or two team members are fully sponsored, they need additional combinations to ride with them, and we have to find a way to financially support the riders who own their horses but have no sponsor.

Without money, it's impossible to make any long-term plan that makes sense, and without a plan that starts right now, we cannot expect to be ready for Brazil in four years!

2012

– 67 –

forward bound after
a last look back

USEF president David O'Connor put it to me in clear language when I asked for his advice before signing the contract to serve as USEF Technical Advisor for the Dressage Team three years ago. In the job as coach, he said, you're a combination of teacher, disciplinarian, and cheerleader.

Right on. As time went by, I could add a few items to the list such as psychologist, planner, listener, and very frequent flyer.

Coming to the end of my time as Technical Advisor and looking back, I've learned a great deal about people and organizations, some of it the hard way. However, I've truly enjoyed working with our elite riders because I understand and share their passion for riding, training, and showing. I understand the pressure of competition, the thrill when things go well, and the desolate feeling that comes with defeat. The team dynamics that exist before international games are a subject that could fill a book, and it's been fascinating to follow three different team constellations through the World Equestrian Games, Pan American Games, and Olympic Games. I feel privileged to have been connected with some of our greatest horses and their riders.

An American System

My true motivation for taking on this task, however, had little to do with winning medals. Back in 2008, I stated in a letter to the USEF that we needed to set up a system for training our own riders and horses in the United States. I wanted to promote the creation of an American system of training.

In the past three years, we have indeed established and filled the positions of Developing and Youth Coach. Scott Hassler was already working as Young Horse Coach* before I came on board. We now have in place a national teaching staff. They are available to guide, advise, and help our riders at all levels. This is, of course, all in its infancy and should be expanded to include more coaches as we go.

What I would like to see added as soon as possible is a Pony Coach, since the lack of pony activity in American dressage is one of our greatest weaknesses. The people in the positions will change over time, but as long as the system stays in place, we have a foundation. I will try to continue to watch over this program in whatever capacity I can.

When I asked the Dutch and, recently, the English leaders of the sport how long it takes for a new educational system to really show results, they both answered: approximately ten years. Not surprisingly, 2011, which was the tenth anniversary of our Young Horse Program, exhibited a great upswing in both the quality and the training of our next generation of horses.

---

* See "It's 'All About' the Young Horses," in Part V, p. 252.

The focus on medals is naturally strong leading up to and during any international games, but it shouldn't be allowed to overshadow the long-term goal of building our sport, slowly and persistently, until we have enough depth that we don't have to worry where our next team horses are going to come from.

Good things take time, and it will take some time before we see results coming from the new system. But at least there is now a pipeline available to work through, people to contact, and help available in this country.

Realistic Expectations

While spending a lot of my last three-plus years on the road working in clinics, observing our elite athletes and their trainers at shows, having meetings with them, communicating on the phone and via emails and watching videos, I got a very good feeling for our inventory of viable combinations. Being an international judge for many years certainly helped me assess the quality and evaluate how competitive a horse would be in the international arena. But when you are working with your team leading up to games such as the London Olympics, this kind of insight can be a double-edged sword. You just know too much, and it could temper some of your "happy puppy" enthusiasm and make you more focused on trying to beat the odds.

Coming into the Alltech FEI World Equestrian Games in Kentucky, I felt we had a viable team and a chance with Ravel and Steffen for an individual medal. Well, they won two, and we very narrowly lost the team bronze with three "rookie" riders on the crew. We qualified for the Olympics and had a good showing overall.

Moving on to the Pan American Games in Mexico, we appeared with the right horses ready for the proper task, and the United States swept the team and all three individual medals. Obviously, our system works when we bring combinations that fit the bill.

In England, we arrived with two team horses that had a Grand Prix show record hovering around 69 to 72 percent for several years. Yet they were correctly chosen by our panel of judges at the trials as our best available to join Ravel, who has always been an established top world-class horse. We left no stones unturned to polish their performances, but you don't raise a horse's average percentage by 10 points in a couple of weeks.

At the Olympic Games, all our horses put their best hoof forward and did their job. Nobody, and certainly not me, is blaming the horses for not having the genes and ability of some of the "super equines" ridden by our competition. Our horses did not disappoint us. They stepped up to the plate, but others were superior. Rafalca, a horse I have followed closely for many years, had her absolute best two tests ever with Jan Ebeling in London, and yet her score was according to her past record. All our horses stayed over 70 percent, which is a first for us in the Olympics. No excuses, no blame. Sixth place by a very small margin is not the end of the world!

What really tickled me personally was to have our individual rider, Adrienne Lyle, show her great riding ability and super composure under pressure. That is a young lady with a future who needs a couple of really good horses to bring along, as do several of our very capable riders of all ages. We have, at the present, more good riders available than we have horses, but only a few of these riders are busy bringing any horses along up the levels.

Made in America

Quality costs a lot today, even for horses of a very young age, and the trained ones that could win for us are either prohibitively expensive or usually not for sale. So we are back to what we used to do in the old days: find one—or even better, *several*—good quality youngsters and start training! Those were the horses that used to bring us to the podium:

the Keens, the Gifteds, the Flim Flams, the Brentinas, and Graf Georges. Bought young, made here.

It would not surprise me if dedicated owners and sponsors continue to provide us with ready-made team horses. We become grateful and excited, because it perks up our prospects for medals. But there are two pitfalls: The new rider has to gel with the horse, and even with a Grand Prix horse, that can take a while and become complicated. We learned from the saga of Totilas that the magic doesn't always work.*

As a nation, we also tend to sit back, relax, and use these instant combinations as temporary Band-Aids to cover up for the fact that we haven't produced new growth of our own. In the best of all worlds, this won't be the case in the future, and instead we will see a number of new stars of all stages entering the arena starting next season.

It was my great pleasure to work with Debbie McDonald, trainer of Adrienne Lyle, and Christine Traurig, who advises Jan Ebeling as well as the Saudi Arabian jumping team. Both these trainers are educated, dedicated, and confident in their ability. This makes it easy to share the work and ideas with them, which can lead to improvements. Nobody can reach his or her utmost goals as a competitor without a capable and loyal trainer at his or her side, and the triangle of rider/trainer/horse that works is a powerful thing!†

The USEF leadership is now going over the records in all the disciplines and having meetings with the US Olympic Committee as well as the

---

* *Following his astounding success with Dutch rider Edward Gal, Totilas—"the most successful dressage horse in history"—was sold to German sport horse breeder Paul Schockemöhle and under his new rider Matthias Rath, has yet to achieve the level of performance displayed under Gal.*

† *See "The Magic Triangle" in Part II, p. 65.*

---

various committees to look into new ways of approach in reference to coming games. I'll be working on a newly formed committee called the "Blue Ribbon Panel," which spans all our disciplines. Hopefully something truly useful will come of our efforts.

Once all the information is gathered and the input from athletes and the discipline coaches sorted out, a plan for the next four years will be created.

In the long run, I think the London Olympic experience will be viewed as the great wake-up call that inspired us all to move onward and upward. As the saying goes: What doesn't kill you makes you stronger.

2012

– 68 –

what makes dressage grow, and could we do more?

A while ago I was interviewed by a journalist who wanted to know why dressage is increasing in popularity. I gave her some quick answers off the top of my head, but later I thought about it in more depth, and here are some of the reasons, as I see it.

Paradise to Parking Lot

One sad, but true, fact that has "helped dressage along" is the disappearance of virgin land. In most horse pursuits, an open landscape is part of the requirements, but we are closing in on ourselves and slowly but surely eliminating the wilderness in favor of roads, "McMansions," and strip malls. Paradise is becoming a parking lot. Fortunately, the pursuit of dressage can fit into a quarter of an acre without any tightening of the belt whatsoever.

Fossil Appeal

An expanding population of people who live and stay active longer is certainly a contributing factor to the increased interest in dressage. The riders who used to event or ride hunters and jumpers may decide (or have other family members decide for them) that it is time to stop jarring those bones and taking unnecessary chances. However, riding becomes part of your blood, and gravitating to dressage becomes a natural transition for those who want to ride with a goal in mind and perhaps continue to show after switching disciplines. This way the fossils over fences can look forward to a bright future as aging "dressage queens." It's good to be queen!

At first the riders who leave jumping behind may miss the excitement and element of danger that stirs the adrenaline as you go over the course, but they may well find a different kind of challenge as they pry deeper into the secrets of dressage. The difference is in the more proactive use of the aids, which tends to surprise the convert from the jumping game. New dressage enthusiasts often look at me and say, "I never realized how much physical fitness and coordination it requires to keep the horse on the aids and in front of the leg." They find that, although they are well balanced and comfortable in the saddle, they have to use a number of new muscles and techniques to influence the dressage horse.

The intellectual challenge of trying to fulfill the requirements of the training scale adds to the mystery, and before you know it we have discussions about Pluvinel and Baucher and we have to go home and read up on the ideas of the old boys. I think a lot of people grow into dressage as they continue to ride, like you may progress from playing blackjack to bridge and end up moving on to chess. I freely admit, however, that those of us who used to ride jumpers, or evented or fox hunted, will always miss it, because nothing compares to sitting on a horse that loves to run and jump.

Follow the Music

The elevation of the freestyle to the Olympic level is our best move to promote dressage so far. Ever since the freestyle became part of equestrian championship events, dressage is sold out before any other discipline, and we are not complaining. What baffles me, however, is the fact that we cannot get it to run on the regular television channels so it can develop into a household word like figure skating or ballroom dancing. I realize it takes advertising money to get this ball rolling, but why we cannot get off the sports channels at two o'clock in the morning and move to primetime remains a mystery.*

"Horse Time"

Some riders find that dressage relieves the stress of the fast-moving pace of today's workplace, changing technology, and never-ending intrusion of cascading information. The horse is an archaic animal. He has not changed much for thousands of years, and although breeders of today fall all over themselves to produce the perfect jumper or dressage machine, those horses still need the same training. Good things take time, and a horse requires that you take the time to make him ready, warm him up, go through the daily drill, and cool him out. Shortcuts catch up with you, and there is no machine to fill in for the human touch or speed up the process. We just have to go with "horse time," and to many people that is both comforting and therapeutic. Dressage can absorb your thoughts and energy to the point that the world disappears when you mount your horse. He walks forward, and for a while the world steps aside, while you and your horse are focused on the same kind of journey that has fascinated riders for thousands of years.

---

* A relation at NBC broke this issue down for me in very clear terms—see "The Media and Dressage," p. 289.

One thing that appeals to some people, not just those involved with dressage, is that as riders and trainers we all have a level playing field. Perhaps one of us could afford a fancier horse than the next person, but a horse does not care what he cost, or what status the person who rides him has in the world of human beings. Rich or poor, educated or not, doctor or janitor, if you can ride, the horse will accept your guidance. If you cannot, all your credentials will get you nowhere. This in itself is a draw and challenge to people who normally can buy or bully their way to what they want. When you are out there alone on the horse, you are playing with a whole different set of rules, and you are basically at the mercy of an animal who can get rid of you in a flash if he really wants to. You can't sue him and he is not likely to offer an apology.

Selling Our Sport

Although dressage seems to be on a roll, we could do even more to promote it. Let's take a look at how we market our sport locally, starting with our dressage shows. Obviously, it will be difficult to inspire the uninitiated by starting them off with a dose of Training Level, so let's take the prospective dressage enthusiast to the FEI ring. Several judges and scribes are sitting in their boxes, staring into space. Discreet music is playing, and nothing is happening in the empty arena. "There has been a scratch," you explain. Eventually a horse and rider appear, and you walk the neophyte through the test, explaining what the horse is supposed to do. Just as you pick up momentum and spot a glimpse of interest in the eyes of your guest, there is another twenty-minute break. Well, perhaps we can go and watch the schooling. Not really, since there is nowhere to sit, and no shelter from rain and sun. Well, there is always the trade show—or is there? A decent place to eat or have a beer? Not likely.

Even the freestyle, by far our best promotional tool, often suffers from the "scratch syndrome." Thus, the sport loses spectators along the way, which we may never regain. The seats may be full when the class starts, but after a couple of unscheduled breaks the ranks thin out. Perhaps the time has come for organizers and riders to unite and try to close up the gaps, at least at the FEI levels. Any show that can accommodate and expects a crowd should have the option to give the riders provisionary times with an established "order of go" to be confirmed an hour before the class. Thus the class can be condensed to keep the flow of the performances and the spectators in their seats.

Keeping up the momentum is incredibly important to all spectator sports, and shows like Dressage at Devon and the Palm Beach Derby acknowledge this by inviting exhibitions and different kinds of entertainment to fill out the dead spots. Anything from longtime dressage announcer Brian O'Connor's entertaining and informative dressage demo with his rubber pony to dog tricks and acrobatics is welcome, and will keep the family and friends who are not "into" dressage (yet) on the premises. Trade shows to tractor pulls, whatever it takes, plus a variety of foods and drinks, and we will be on the way. People need to be introduced to dressage and then encouraged to stay until they are hooked.

Who knows—this might bring better media coverage, and perhaps some of the people in the audience will become so inspired that they select a rider they would like to sponsor. A good deal for the entire sport.

2007

– 69 –

new concepts and stimulating prospects for american dressage

The most exciting new thing that happened in our sport in 2013 was last on the agenda at the end of the year: the US Dressage Finals in Lexington, Kentucky.

Ever since the Insilco US Dressage Championships back in the 1980s, we've been struggling with the concept of a national championship. We needed a venue for the riders who have no interest or ability to play the international game but are aflame with the desire to show how they are developing dressage at home.

I rode in the Insilco Championships with my students. In spite of a valiant effort from everyone involved, it didn't have the "horsey" feeling. The venue lacked charm, being situated in the middle of the Kansas City meat-packing district, and many of the horses arrived sore from long van drives, due to the fact that, at the time, the riders and owners weren't very well versed in how best to ship a horse long distances. The whole enterprise proved to be too costly, and I guess the sponsors gave up, because if you think we have sparse audiences now, you can imagine things were not glorious back then!

The Timing Was Right

I cannot tell you how many times the proposal for another national championships has come up and been tabled in our USDF committees for the last twenty years, and the big stumbling block, as always, has been financing. But there was also the fear that there wouldn't be enough interest from the competitors in traveling to a central location in this huge country. Well, it appears that if the location is right, "central" is not all that important, since Kentucky is not exactly in the middle of the country. When they gave the party there, all of them came! I was amazed at the enthusiasm among my colleagues and students for the championships this year. It proved to me early on that we were, indeed, finally ready to roll.

It took a huge leap of faith for the USDF and USEF to join in this venture, but the timing was right, and as we all know, timing is everything! Our competitors rose to the challenge with fervor, and the applications poured in. Not only did the riders apply, but they also fought to qualify in their regional finals, and when they did, they got on the road. From every state they came, and no doubt that is the most important proof that we have matured on a national basis. As my favorite ice skater, Peggy Fleming, said in an interview when asked about the secret of success: "The first thing you have to do is show up!"

Well, they did, from all over the country, and although I wasn't there, I've spoken to competitors, judges, and spectators and read the reports. Some of our top amateur riders and many of the professionals went to Kentucky and made the inaugural national championships in this century a super-quality event.

The fact that Lexington is horse country and headquarters for the USDF and USEF is definitely one reason for the success. Experienced managers, competent judges and a top venue run by people with horse "savvy" contributed to the success. From now on, I think we're going to look to the national championships not only as a triumph in itself, but as a proving ground for international success as well.

Raising Certification Standards

In 2013, the USDF built another milestone into their educational system: the addition of an FEI licensing program for the Instructor Certification Program. A lot of preparatory work has been done in committees to arrive at this step, and I believe the program will fit in smoothly and become a finishing touch for the certification program.

There has also been a process of grandfathering past US prominent and productive instructors into the teaching program. This is intended to involve our most successful trainers in the development and certification of future teachers of our dressage riders and horses.

The ultimate goal is to have a mandatory certification for all instructors before they're allowed to teach, just as any other serious profession requires proof of capability. Most countries in Europe have very strict requirements before you become a certified or approved teacher, and our time has come to work toward raising our own standards.

Prudent Moves in Europe

In spite of not having many players to send out to bat, the USEF High Performance Committee decided to field an American team for Aachen (Germany) and Hickstead (England) in 2013. This was a prudent move, since we were aware that the top European combinations would likely be too preoccupied with preparing for the ECCO FEI European Championships to compete in these events with their top combinations.

Get in the Mix

The next time you say to yourself, or somebody else, "How on earth could the (insert governing body or organization at fault) make a decision like that—do they have their heads put on backward?" consider coming to the next meeting of said governing body or organization. Find out how they go about messing things up and come prepared to help fix it.

The best way to get over your feeling of being a victim of "those committees" is to become active in the decision-making yourself. As soon as you have been involved in the first couple of meetings, you will marvel at the newfound wisdom of your organization, and you will also realize that it is not all that easy to find a quick solution to every problem. Learning about the detail of each case puts a whole new light on the subject, and you might find that riding several opinionated horses in a row is preferable to working on revising the dressage tests in hours upon hours of committee work.

We need for our riders, judges, and show officials to become more involved in the inner workings of the sport. The best kind of committee, I have learned, is one consisting of the "old faithfuls" who have a good grip on past history and can prevent enthusiastic newcomers from trying to re-invent the wheel; the "in-the-know" crowd who are active out there in one capacity or another and can make field reports; the rule enthusiasts who can give everyone a half-halt when they overstep their boundaries; and the "new blood" who prevent everyone from becoming complacent by not exploring new avenues. We actually have some of those combinations working for our sport right now, and if you want to be part of the process, step right up. Be prepared to give a lot of your time and effort and to travel plenty with no expectations of reimbursement or reward. When a decision is not popular, you will take the heat as a committee member, and people will be sure to let you know what they think. If something works out just right (fat chance), you probably will never hear from anybody. But then, just as you are ready to bag the whole thing and only concern yourself with your own little world, a card arrives from a Junior Rider thanking your committee for making her medal moment possible, or a dressage team goes to Europe on training grants agonized over by your committee, and they win the Nation's Cup!

With new wind in your sails, you will be off to your next meeting...

When the new USEF Dressage Chef d'Equipe/Technical Advisor, Robert Dover, took his position in March, he moved ahead according to plan. It proved a good course of action, since our team placed third in Aachen and second at Hickstead, thus regaining some momentum after the 2012 Olympics.

Quality Better Than Quantity

By the time we came to our USEF Dressage Festival of Champions in October, we had a class of only eight Grand Prix entries. This was partially due to the fact that some of our riders were still training and showing in Europe. The overall quality in the Grand Prix was good, and quality is better than quantity.

Legolas and Steffen Peters reigned over the field, although the pilot had a bout of amnesia in the Grand Prix Special when I was the judge at C and had to ring him back on track. Steffen told me later he learned this trick while watching at the Blue Hors FEI European Dressage Championships in Denmark, where the top three contenders all went off course, one right after the other.

Watching that happening in Denmark was almost surreal but also comforting, since every competitor I know (except Hilda Gurney) has gone off course some time or another. The devastation you feel for letting your horse down is palpable, and at the same time it is so easy to lose your concentration for a split second when the horse does something that catches you unaware. Although the test you are riding is imprinted on your brain, it can evaporate for a moment, and in an instant you are lost on a quarter of an acre! The fact that the best riders in the world are not safe from the "off-course syndrome" is a consolation to all of us who have it happen more often than we like to admit.

The European Dressage Championships again raised the bar for all dressage competition, and the top contenders were extremely close. Suffice it to say that the quality of the top twenty or so horses was fabulous, and the best twelve were almost surreal in their power, presence, and accuracy. The mature presentation by some of the young British and German riders, such as Charlotte Dujardin and Helen Langehanenberg, is almost scary, but it's great to see more youth at the highest level. The quality of the horses they ride is constantly on the rise, and one wonders when it will no longer be possible to produce a more perfect equine dressage machine.

More Olympic Horses

2013 ended my four-year term as a member of the FEI Dressage Committee, and the new non-European member is Maribel Alonso from Mexico. It's been an honor and a stimulating experience to work with the intelligent and committed members of this group, although some of the issues presented to the committee are not so easy to deal with.

Last year, I was most pleased that we brought back the format of four horses per team in the Olympic Games, starting with Brazil in 2016. We also managed to get ten more dressage horses on the start list than we had in London.

The qualifying procedures for Brazil are not as favorable for Americans as we'd hoped, since we now have only one opportunity for a team qualification at the Pan American Games, and only three teams will go forward from the World Equestrian Games. I'm not in agreement with this program, although I believe the United States can live with it, while Canada and the South American countries are more at a disadvantage. One of the reasons given for the adoption of the new qualification system was that it leaves room for more individuals to qualify and thus adds more "flags" to the Games.

The FEI Dressage Committee added two tests called Intermediaire A and B. These tests are designed as a stepping stone between the small and big tour to introduce the green Grand Prix horse to the piaffe and passage with less emphasis on transitions by calling for half steps in and out of trot in one of the tests and allowing the horse to move two meters forward in the piaffe. There aren't as many sequence tempi changes, and the lines in the lateral work are less steep.

The two tests will make up their own "division" and are intended to encourage riders to bring their young horses along to the CDIs and get their feet wet without having to compete against the "big guns." It's hoped that this division will also encourage riders in the developing countries to move their horses up to Grand Prix.

Reason for Excitement

As far as the United States is concerned, things are looking up. During 2012 and early 2013, we had little depth of internationally competitive horses, but luckily, some exciting horses have emerged in our developing programs. In talking to Robert Dover, who had just finished his first observation tour on both coasts when I saw him, I found him more than enthusiastic about the horses he'd seen and worked with.

I was most encouraged after listening to Robert because it seems the lean times are over—with our competent riders and an expanded number of horses, plus a little bit of luck, we could do very well in the years ahead!

2014

afterword

It is my sincere hope that you enjoyed the "essays" in this book as much I liked writing them over the years. My dressage columns in *The Chronicle of the Horse* led to contact with many people around the country, and their feedback became an additional source of inspiration: Communicating with them has given me access to other points of view beyond those reigning at the apex of the sport. Reader comments can be most sobering for those of us who are highly involved with this country's dressage competitions and committees, and the professional end of the horse business. Often readers provide a necessary reminder to "see the wide screen" and take into consideration the views of many rather than only a select few. They can also force you to focus on the details that make up the whole.

In my writing, I have tried to cover both ends of the spectrum over the years. I have sometimes been sharp in opinions or criticism but hopefully never unfair or hurtful. Honesty has been important to me because I do not believe in "singing with the choir" to be popular or stay in the game. In the end, whether you agree with my take on the various topics in this book or not, the fact that you are paying it any attention at all tells me that you are passionate about dressage—and I hope, at the very least, you got a laugh or two out of reading it!

My personal journey through dressage and its evolution in the United States has been a wonderful adventure. I have been blessed with the opportunity to ride alongside and work with the very best riders in our country. I have shown at, judged, and coached at almost every top show and championship in the world. Looking back, I do not regret a single minute, and I love seeing new wind in our dressage sails going toward the 2014 World Equestrian Games and beyond. The highly decorated dressage rider and former Olympian Robert Dover, who was appointed as Technical Advisor to the US Team after I resigned, is full of enthusiasm at the helm of these efforts. The educational pipeline I created during my time as Technical Advisor is alive and well, and it is now starting to produce results by offering some structure to up-and-coming horse-and-rider combinations. More horses are available to us now than even a year ago, and a few of them are even trained by Americans!

This has been my mantra forever: *We absolutely must produce our own top horses.* We can talk about gold medals until the cows come home, but so far the only ones we have produced, or even come close to, are in the Pan-American Games where, lo and behold, the majority of our horses are American-trained. In 2011, when we swept all the medals in Mexico, every horse on the team was "made" here!

By continuing to buy ready-made Grand Prix horses, perhaps riders can make it onto the US Dressage Team, but we will never get to the top of the international podium on European hand-me-downs. I have said this for many years, and I know most people who are "initiated" agree with me. This is why I was both surprised and disappointed by the lack of initiative and grit amongst our top athletes in the years leading up to the 2012 London Olympics. Many of our very best riders did not even have *one* young horse "coming up the ladder," and their complacency about creating new horses was difficult to understand. It was thanks to Jan Ebeling, Tina Konyot, and Steffen Peters, who all had long-term relationships with their horses, that we had a 2012 Olympic Team at all, but the depth was lacking.

In the dawning days of dressage in this country, the attitude amongst US Team hopefuls was just the opposite: Back in the 1970s and 80s it never occurred to any of us to sit and wait for a sponsor to put a trained horse under our behinds. It was this "do-it-yourself" mentality that led to horses like Keen (Hilda Gurney), Gifted (Carol Lavell), and Graf George (Michael Poulin) coming on the scene, and they gained a lot more attention and caused far more excitement in Europe than any of our "borrowed feathers" ever will.

Granted, today we need even better quality horses—the bar is raised in every way, with higher demands in terms of performance and brilliance. But I remain certain that when the horses are "Trained in the USA" and the quality of our mounts is up to the European standard, our riders will make the impact they are capable of making. I have all the confidence in the world in American dressage, but our riders need to train their own horses—as they used to!

index

Abdullah, 322
Age issues, 31–34, 107–11, 117, 342
Agnelli FRH, 132
AHSA, 174
Ajax, 33
Alonso, Maribel, 351
Amateurs, 39–43, 79–83, 281–84
Amazonas, 75–76, 116, 120, 138–39
Ampere, 322
Art, dressage as, 4–5, 7–8, 272–74
Attire, 50–52, 293–94
Attitude, 5–6, 15–19, 102–6, 108, 152–53,
   222–26
Ayers, Jayne, 307

Bachinger, Ernst, 238
Balkenhol, Klaus, 47, 129, 132, 201, 202–6,
   319
Billy Joe Freckles, 110
Blitz, Heather, 326
Body control, 12, 44–47, 189
Boldt, Harry, 12, 39, 200
Bonaparte, 183
Bonfire, 122
Breed considerations, 33, 99, 123
Brentina Cup, 287, 288
Briar, 119
Brooks, Jackie, 51–52
Brown, Dick and Jane, 140, 165
Burton, Jonathan, 266
Buying horses
   expectations in, 17, 18, 82
   process of, 41–42, 95–101, 112–16, 172,
      295–96

Calecto, 329
Calumet, 136–38
Cameron, David, 333

Canter, 99, 127, 198
Capellmann, Nadine, 132
Cavalry, legacy of, 207–8
Channon, Wayne, 304–5
Children. See Young riders
Clark, Jane. See Forbes Clark, Jane
Clarke, Stephen, 256
Clayton, Hilary, 254–55
Clinics, 72, 205
Collected work, 125–27, 130–32, 182–83,
   188–192, 205, 253
Color, of horses, 99
Communication, 11, 14, 71, 73, 76–77
Community, 5–6, 15–19
Competition. See also International
   competition; Young Horse classes
   experience of, described, 15–19,
      151–53, 174–78
   horse/rider exposure to, 56, 206
   outsider's view of, 293–96
   purpose of, 158
   rider focus on, 9–10, 157–59
   warm-up at, 197–201, 318–19
Conant, Abbie, 216
Concentration, 13–14
Conformation, evaluating, 99, 122–25
Connection, 44–47
Consistency, 11–13
Contact, 44–47, 182, 253
Corlandus, 131
Cummins, Denise, 70–71
Cyrus, 131

Damon Hill, 255
Davidson, Bruce, 6
De Némethy, Bert, 34
Deep and round, 184–85
Developing and Youth Coaches, 336

Developing Rider Clinics, 287
Disposition. *See* Personality, of horses
Dogs, 20–25
Donnerhall, 78
Double bridles, 306–7
Dover, Robert, 36, 164–68, 322–23, 350, 352–53, 358
Dressage Equitation program, 278–79
Dressage4Kids, 280, 286, 304
Drug use, 309–14, 323–24
Dujardin, Charlotte, 351

Eastwood, 135–36
Ebeling, Amy, 329
Ebeling, Jan, 329, 331, 338, 339, 358
Economic considerations, 82–83, 218–19, 298–300, 333–34, 347
Eden, Lesley, 65–68
Eivers, Carol and Neil, 260
Elasticity, 253
Emerson, Denny, 17–19
Emerson, Ralph Waldo, 296
Emotional aspects, of dressage, 148–49, 161
Equestrian sports, support for, 297–300, 324, 333
Equitation, 13, 44–47, 189, 278–79
Escorial, 130–31
Europe
    competition opportunities, 29, 332–33, 348, 350
    equestrian sport audience in, 132–33, 295–96, 297–98
    horses from, 303, 358–59
    jury system in, 242–44
    rider programs, 280, 282–83, 286–87, 295
Eventing, 152, 157
"Excuse horses," 104–5, 142
Exhibitionism, 152–53
Extended gaits, 179–183, 205, 255

Fashion/fads, 120, 122–27, 136. *See also* Attire

Feeding/nutrition, 114, 136, 310–11, 314
Feel
    in horse-rider relationships, 14, 47, 77
    for judging, 215–16, 245
FEI
    Dressage Committee, 269–270
    helmet rules, 49–50, 308
    instructor certification, 348
    judging evaluation, 242–44
    ranking system, 250–51, 271–72
    test design, 126–27, 129–130, 204–5, 352
Ferrell, Craig, 50
Finances. *See* Economic considerations
Fitness issues, 35–38, 199
Floriano, 119
Fly fishing, 88–91
Focus, 13–14
Forbes Clark, Jane, 119, 164, 166, 323
Fore, Lilo, 177
Frame, of horse, 184–87, 203–4, 254, 255, 315–19
Freestyles
    history of, 207
    horse size and, 120
    judging of, 210, 246–251
    popularity of, 292, 295, 343, 344–45
Fromming, Angelica, 254

Gaits, 125–27, 129–130, 179–183, 205, 255
Gal, Edward, 326
Gender stereotypes, 216, 237
Genius, 120
Gestion Idool, 132
Gifted, 75, 122, 359
Giltner, Lisa, 66, 137–38
Giving, of hands, 46–47, 194–96
Gracioso, 132
Graf George, 140–41, 359
Granat, 120, 122–27, 200, 322
Grand Prix
    challenges of, 132–33, 306–7, 317–18
    green horses in, 147–150, 322–23
    movements in, 125–27, 179–183

starting order in, 250–51, 271–72
training time for, 107–8, 117–19
Grant, Chuck, 110
Grassroots. *See* Amateurs
Gratitude, 74, 86
Gray, Lendon, 280, 286, 304
Grethe Jensen, Anne, 122
Grunsven, Anky van, 122, 132, 185, 200, 316
Gurney, Hilda, 3–4, 321, 322, 351, 359
Gurtler, Elisabeth, 237

Hakansson, Ulla, 33
Half marks, 304–6
Half-halts, 46–47, 189–190, 193–96
Harmony, 5, 7–8
Hassler, Scott, 169, 336
Head injuries, 48–52, 307–8
Head position. *See* Frame, of horse
Health/welfare, of horses, 10–11, 134–39, 261–62, 283
Heijden, Maarten van der, 286
Helmets/helmet use, 48–52, 307–8
Hess, Christoff, 254
Hester, Carl, 326
Heuschmann, Gerd, 203–6
Hinneman, Johann, 129
Hobson, Sue and Brian, 259
Homfeld, Conrad, 322
Hormones, supplemental, 312, 314
Horsemanship, 17–19, 28–29, 202–6, 280
Horse-rider relationships, 9–14, 134–39, 326, 339
Horses
motivation of, 8
as team member, 66–69
from US, 303, 325–28, 338–39, 358–59
Humility, 5–6

Idocus, 119
Ignorance, danger of, 10
Impulsion, 182, 249
Insilco US Dressage Championships, 346–47

Instincts
in horse behavior, 104
judges' reliance on, 215–16
Instructors. *See also* Trainers
availability of, 298–300
certification of, 348
professional relationships, 42, 66–69, 70–74, 84–87, 95–101, 176–78, 283–84
responsibilities of, 73
value of, 26–30, 279–280
Insurance issues, 51, 111, 117
International competition, 55–57, 283, 325–28, 332, 335–340, 348–352. *See also* Olympic Games

Jack Russell terriers, 20–25
Judging
credentials for, 217–221, 222–26
demands of, 16, 213–16, 245, 318
experience of, described, 214–16, 241–42, 264–67, 272
of freestyles, 210, 246–251
jury system of, 227–230, 242–44, 273
motivation for, 244–45, 267–68
quality of, 154–55, 242, 270–74, 295, 316, 318
scribing and, 233–34
trust and, 269–274
of warm-up, 201, 318–19
Jumping, 152, 290, 327–28, 342

Keen, 4, 322, 359
Keenan, Jack and Linda, 331
Kemmer, Heike, 183
Kempermann, Frank, 270
Kennedy, 119
Kids. *See* Young riders
Kimmel, Tom, 156
King Dye, Courtney, 48–49, 330
Klimke, Ingrid, 255
Knoll Farm, 300
Knowledge, 10–11, 71
Konyot, Tina, 329, 358

Kristall, 199
Kyrklund, Kyra, 33, 56, 270

Lahunta, Alexander de, 139
Lamping, Natalie, 246–49
Langehanenberg, Helen, 351
Lavell, Carol, 75, 122, 359
Leg movement, in horses, 125, 182, 255
Legal considerations, 162, 171, 220
Legolas, 350
Leitch, Midge, 167
Leonardo II, 199, 323
Lette, Eric, 125–27
Licensing, of judges, 217–221, 222–26
Life, dressage resemblance to, 13
Lipari, Lisa, 32
Ljungquist, Bengt, 27, 183, 321
Long and low, 185–87
Longe lessons, 13, 45, 90, 178
Love, 10
Lucky Lord, 100
Ludwig, Marianne, 221
Lundholm, Elisabeth, 9–14
Lyle, Adrienne, 329, 338, 339

"Magic triangle," 65–69
Malone, Janine, 80
Marzog, 122
Master, Edith, 321
McClellan, Paul, 140
McDonald, Debbie, 287, 339
Media coverage, 250–51, 272, 289–292, 297–98, 319, 344–45
Medium trot, 181, 255
Metallic, 164–68, 323
Meyer (professor/author), 184
Meyer, Beth, 329
Migliori, Richard, 300
Miller, Jordan and Michael, 148
Mistakes, 27, 350–51
Mitchell, Rick, 331
Moore, Frank, 88–90
Morkis, Dorothy, 238, 321
Morris, George, 17–19, 283, 327

Motivation, 8, 53–57, 159, 244–45, 267–68
Movements, generally, 127–28, 130–32, 255, 294–95

National championships, 346–47
Navicular syndrome, 115–16, 138, 142
New Zealand dressage, 257–263
911 terror attacks, 58–61

O'Connor, David, 43, 309, 345
Off-course errors, 350–51
Oliveira, Nuno, 7–8
Oliver, Linda, 109
Olympic Games
    equestrian sports in, 324
    media coverage of, 291–92
    past performance in, 167–68, 320–24, 328–29, 330–34, 338–340
    upcoming, in Brazil, 351–52
"On the aids," 186
Open scoring, 273
Otto-Crépin, Margit, 131
Owners. *See also* Sponsorship
    author's experience as, 164–68
    expectations of, 17, 18, 299–301, 339
    professional relationships, 39–43, 169–171
    trainers as, 173

Pan American Games, 337, 352
Paragon, 326
Parental influence, 18, 278, 299, 300–302
Passage, emphasis on, 125–27
Passion, 29, 53–57
Pasturing, of horses, 260–63
Patience, 29, 107–8
Pepel, 122–27
Performance-enhancing drugs, 309–14
Persistence, 29, 134–39, 147–150
Personality, of horses, 11, 102–6, 124, 143–44
Peters, Steffen, 51, 119, 329, 337, 350, 358
Petushkova, Elena, 122
Piaff, 126

Piaffe, emphasis on, 125–27
Picasso, 66–68
Plewa, Dietrich, 254
Pochhammer, Gabrielle, 316
Ponies, 279, 286, 301–2, 336
Pot, Jaap, 215, 244–45, 271
Poulin, Gwen, 65
Poulin, Michael, 140, 359
Pre-purchase exams, 17, 112–16, 141, 144
Professionals, 39–43, 79–80
Public image/popularity, of dressage, 292–96, 341–45. *See also* Media coverage

Quadrilles, 209, 238
Qualifying systems, for riders, 281–84

Rafalca, 297, 329, 331, 338
Raiser, Courtney, 65
Ranking systems, 250–51, 270–71
Rath, Matthias, 339
Ravel, 329, 331, 332, 337, 338
Rehbein, Herbert, 75–78, 89, 186
Rehbein, Karin, 78
Rein aids, 44–47, 194–96
Rembrandt, 122, 126, 185
Retirement, of horses, 31–32, 108–9
Rhythm, 181, 253, 311
Ride times, 154, 250–51, 271–72
Rideability, 253, 258
Riders. *See also* Students; Young riders
    education of, 176–78
    qualifying system for, 281–84
    responsibilities of, 66–69, 70–74, 84–87, 169–171, 176–78
Riding schools, 298–300
Risk aversion, 5, 18–19, 144, 171
Rohlf, Karen, 188–192
Rollkur. *See* Frame, of horse
Romantico, 322
Romney, Ann, 329
Royal Charger, 143
"Runners," at shows, 266
Rusty, 131, 183, 314
Rutten, Jo, 322

Saddle fitting, 204
Safety issues, 48–52, 97, 154, 307–8
Salzgeber, Ulla, 131, 183, 200, 311
Savoie, Jane, 135–36
Schaudt, Martin, 183
Schockemöhle, Paul, 339
School horses/schoolmasters, 18–19, 31–32, 96, 299–301
Schüle, Dieter, 256
Scoring, 126–27, 271, 273, 304–6, 308. *See also* Judging
Scribes, 16, 231–35, 265
Seat. *See* Equitation
Seidel, Guenter, 51, 140, 330
Selling horses, 161, 326, 339
Shannon, Wayne, 270
Show management, 153–55, 219, 232, 235, 249, 264–68. *See also* Competition
Size, of horses, 98–99, 119–121. *See also* Ponies
Smith, Linda, 131
Snaffle bits, 306–7
Soundness, 112–16, 119, 121, 140–44
Spanish Riding School, 236–240
Sponsorship
    for media coverage, 290
    of riders, 16, 160–63, 279–280, 327, 333, 339
Sport, dressage as, 7–8, 18, 35–38, 79
Sports medicine, 136, 310–11
Stalls/stabling, 154, 261–62
Starting order, 250–51, 271–72
Steiner, Axel, 207, 247
Steiner, Betsy, 35–36
Steinkraus, William and Helen, 4
Steroid use, 312
Stewards, 319
Stockholm, 39
Straightness, 182, 189, 253
Stückelberger, Christine, 100, 120, 122, 322
Students, 13–14, 18–19, 26–30, 73, 171, 298–300. *See also* Riders
Submissiveness, 182, 249

Supplements, 114, 136, 310–11, 314
Suppleness, 181, 253
Swedish Warmbloods, 33

Talent, 29, 53–57, 283
Tappan Zee, 99, 143, 148
Technical Delegates, 201, 296, 319
Television. *See* Media coverage
Tempo, 194, 205
Tension, 5, 181, 205, 318
Thoroughbreds, 99
Totilas, 326, 339
Trainers, 39–43, 169–171, 173, 311–12, 339.
  See also Instructors
Training
    of dogs, 23–24
    of horses, 11–13, 19, 134, 171, 336, 343
      (*see also* Young horses)
    of judges, 217–221
    rider motivation and, 159
Training Scale, 181–82, 253, 254
Transitions, 180, 181, 191, 198
Traurig, Christine, 339
Trenzado, 108–9
Trot, 99, 126–27, 179–183, 205, 255
Turnout, 260–63

Uphoff, Nicole, 29, 122, 185
US Dressage Finals, 346–47
USA Equestrian, 174
USDF, 218–221, 278–79, 303, 347, 348
USEF
    dressage championships, 347, 350
    drug rules, 310–13
    founding of, 174
    rider development initiatives, 284, 287,
      331
    Technical Advisor position, 335–340
USET, 174
Uthopia, 326

Vet exams. *See* Pre-purchase exams
Volunteering, 349–351

Wahl, Georg, 200, 322
Walk, 99, 126, 205
Warm-up, 197–201, 318–19
Weather, as competitions, 199–200
WEG, 324, 337, 352
Weight issues, 38, 199
Weltall, 183
Werth, Isabell, 132, 185, 200, 311, 327
Wilcox, Lisa, 29
Williams, Jimmy, 30
Williams, Sue and Terri, 322
Winnet, John, 321
Winning, 157–59
Winter-Schulze, Madeline, 327
Withages, Mariette, 254, 256
Wizard, 329
Wolframm, Inga, 270–72
Working students, 28–29

Xenophon, 207
X-rays, 113, 142

Young Horse classes, 129–130, 204–5,
  252–56, 258, 307–8, 336
Young horses
    gaits, 127
    inexperienced riders and, 96
    training of, 40–41, 118–19, 169–173,
      203–6, 322–23
Young riders, 81, 277, 278, 285–88, 298–302

Zander, 32
Zapatero, 135